The Short Oxford History of Europe

Europe since 1945

The Short Oxford History of Europe

General Editor: T. C. W. Blanning

NOW AVAILABLE

The Seventeenth Century
edited by Joseph Bergin

The Eighteenth Century
edited by T. C. W. Blanning

The Nineteenth Century
edited by T. C. W. Blanning

IN PREPARATION, VOLUMES COVERING

Classical Greece
The Romans
The Early Middle Ages
The High Middle Ages
The Late Middle Ages
The Sixteenth Century
The Early Twentieth Century

The Short Oxford History of Europe

General Editor: T. C. W. Blanning

Europe since 1945

Edited by Mary Fulbrook

OXFORD
UNIVERSITY PRESS

OXFORD
UNIVERSITY PRESS

Great Clarendon Street, Oxford OX2 6DP

Oxford University Press is a department of the University of Oxford.
It furthers the University's objective of excellence in research, scholarship,
and education by publishing worldwide in

Oxford New York

Athens Auckland Bangkok Bogotá Buenos Aires Calcutta
Cape Town Chennai Dar es Salaam Delhi Florence Hong Kong Istanbul
Karachi Kuala Lumpur Madrid Melbourne Mexico City Mumbai
Nairobi Paris São Paulo Shanghai Singapore Taipei Tokyo Toronto Warsaw

with associated companies in Berlin Ibadan

Oxford is a registered trade mark of Oxford University Press
in the UK and in certain other countries

Published in the United States
by Oxford University Press Inc., New York

British Library Cataloguing in Publication Data
Data available

Library of Congress Cataloging in Publication Data
Data available
ISBN 0–19–873179–5 (hbk)
ISBN 0–19–873178–7 (pbk)

10 9 8 7 6 5 4 3 2 1

Typeset in Minion
by RefineCatch Limited, Bungay, Suffolk
Printed in Great Britain by
T.J. International Ltd, Padstow, Cornwall

General Editor's Preface

The problems of writing a satisfactory general history of Europe are many, but the most intractable is clearly the reconciliation of depth with breadth. The historian who can write with equal authority about every part of the continent in all its various aspects has not yet been born. Two main solutions have been tried in the past: either a single scholar has attempted to go it alone, presenting an unashamedly personal view of a period, or teams of specialists have been enlisted to write what are in effect anthologies. The first offers a coherent perspective but unequal coverage, the second sacrifices unity for the sake of expertise. This new series is underpinned by the belief that it is this second way that has the fewest disadvantages and that even those can be diminished if not neutralized by close cooperation between the individual contributors under the directing supervision of the volume editor. All the contributors to every volume in this series have read each other's chapters, have met to discuss problems of overlap and omission, and have then redrafted as part of a truly collective exercise. To strengthen coherence further, the editor has written an introduction and conclusion, weaving the separate strands together to form a single cord. In this exercise, the brevity promised by the adjective 'short' in the series' title has been an asset. The need to be concise has concentrated everyone's minds on what really mattered in the period. No attempt has been made to cover every angle of every topic in every country. What this volume does provide is a short but sharp and deep entry into the history of Europe in the period in all its most important aspects.

T. C. W. Blanning

Sidney Sussex College
Cambridge

Contents

List of contributors

J. DAVID ARMSTRONG was appointed Professor of International Relations at the University of Exeter in 1999, having previously held the Chair of Politics at Durham University. A Fellow of the Royal Historical Society, he has published several books on subjects ranging from Chinese foreign policy to the history of international organization. He is currently researching the evolution and spread of international legal norms.

BARRY EICHENGREEN is George C. Pardee and Helen N. Pardee Professor of Economics and Political Science at the University of California at Berkeley, Research Associate of the National Bureau of Economic Research, and Research Fellow of the Centre for Economic Policy Research. His books include *Globalizing Capital* (1996) and *Forging an Integrated Europe* (1999, co-edited with Jeffry Frieden).

MARY FULBROOK is Professor of German History at University College London. Educated at Cambridge and Harvard, she has also held a lady Margaret Research Fellowship at Cambridge. She was founding Joint Editor of *German History* and has served as Chair of the German History Society. Her books include the best-selling and widely translated *Concise History of Germany* (1990), as well as *Piety and Politics: Religion and Rise of Absolutism* (1983), *The Divided Nation: Germany 1918–1990* (1991), *Anatomy of a Dictatorship: Inside the GDR* (1995) , *German National Identity after the Holocaust* (1999), and *Interpretations of the Two Germanies* (2000). Edited volumes include *National Histories and European History* (1993), *Citizenship, Nationality and Migration in Europe* (1996, with David Cesarani), and *Representing the German Nation* (2000, with Martin Swales). She is currently completing a book on *Historical Theory: Ways of Imagining the Past* (2001) and working on a *Social History of the GDR*.

ERIK GOLDSTEIN is Professor of International Relations and Chairman of the Department of International Relations at Boston University. He was previously Professor of International History at the University of Birmingham and is the founder-editor of *Diplomacy & Statecraft*. He is the author of *Winning the Peace: British Diplomatic*

Strategy, Peace Planning, and the Paris Peace Conference, 1916–1920
(1991), *Wars and Peace Treaties* (1992), and co-editor of *The End of the
Cold War* (1990), *The Washington Conference, 1921–22: Naval Rivalry,
East Asian Stability, and the Road to Pearl Harbor* (1993), and *The
Munich Crisis: New Interpretations and the Road to World War II*
(1999). He is a Fellow of the Royal Historical Society.

HARTMUT KAELBLE is Professor of Social History at Humboldt
University, Berlin. His recent books include *A Social History of
Western Europe, 1880–1980* (1990), *Income Distribution in Historical
Perspective* (1991, edited with Y.S. Brenner and Mark Thomas),
*Nachbarn am Rhein. Entfremdung und Annäherung der französischen
und deutschen Gesellschaft seit 1880* (1991), *Der historische Vergleich.
Eine Einführung zum 19. und 20. Jahrhundert* (1999), and *Europäer
über Europa. Das europäische Selbstverständnis im 19. und 20.
Jahrhundert* (2000).

AXEL KÖRNER is Lecturer in Modern European History at University
College London. He studied Musicology and History in Bonn
and Berlin, obtained his MA in Lyon and a PhD at the European
University Institute in Florence. He is author of *Urbane Eliten und
kultureller Wandel* (1996, with C. Gerbel et.al.), *Das Lied von einer
anderen Welt* (1997), and *1848—A European Revolution?* (2000). He is
currently working on a cultural history of Bologna.

KLAUS LARRES is Reader in Politics and Contemporary History at
the Queen's University of Belfast. He holds a Jean Monnet Chair in
European Foreign and Security Policy. He was educated at Cologne
University in Germany and the LSE in Britain. He has published
widely on the Cold War and post-1945 European and international
history as well as on Anglo-American, German-American, and
German-British relations. His publications include *Politics of Illusions: Churchill, Eisenhower and the German Question, 1945–55* (1995,
in German), *The Federal Republic of Germany since 1949: Politics,
Society and Economy before and after Unification* (1996, edited with P.
Panayi), and *Germany and the USA in the Twentieth Century: A Political History* (1997, in German, edited with T. Oppelland). He is the
editor of *Uneasy Allies: British-German Relations and European Integration since 1945* (2000), and *Germany since Unification: The Development of the Berlin Republic* (2nd edn., 2000).

DONALD SASSOON was born in Cairo and educated in Paris, Milan, London, and the USA. He is Professor of Comparative European History at Queen Mary and Westfield College, University of London and a Leverhulme Major Research Fellow. His works include the prize-winning *One Hundred Years of Socialism* (1997) with five translations so far. His book on the popularity of the *Mona Lisa* is due in 2001. He is writing a history of cultural markets since 1800.

List of abbreviations

APEC	Asia–Pacific Economic Cooperation
ASEAN	Association of South East Asian Nations
BTO	Brussels Treaty Organization
CAP	common agricultural policy
CD	Christian Democratic Party (Italy)
CDU	Christian Democratic Union (Germany)
CFSP	common foreign and security policy
CIA	(US) Central Intelligence Agency
CIS	Commonwealth of Independent States
COCOM	Coordinating Committee for Multinational Export Controls
Comecon	Council for Mutual Economic Assistance
CPSU	Communist Party of the Soviet Union
CSCE	conference on security and cooperation in Europe
CSSR	Socialist Republic of Czechoslovakia
CSU	Christian Social Union (Germany)
EBRD	European Bank for Reconstruction and Development
EC	European Community
ECSC	European Coal and Steel Community
EDC	European Defence Community
EEC	European Economic Community
EFTA	European Free Trade Area
EMS	European monetary system
EMU	European monetary union
EPC	European political cooperation
EPU	European Payments Union
EU	European Union
Euratom	Eurpean Atomic Energy Community
FDP	(liberal) Free Democratic Party (Germany)
FRG	Federal Republic of Germany
G7	Group of Seven
GATT	General Agreement on Tariffs and Trade
GDP	gross domestic product
GDR	German Democratic Republic
GNP	gross national product
ICOR	Incremental Capital Output Ratio
IMF	International Monetary Fund
KGP	Smallholder Party (Hungary)
MLF	multilateral nuclear force

NATO	North Atlantic Treaty Organization
OECD	Organization for Economic Development and Cooperation
OEEC	Organization for European Economic Cooperation
OPEC	Organization of Petroleum Exporting Countries
OSA	Overseas Sterling Area
ÖVP	People's Party of Austria
PASOK	Panhellenic Socialist Movement
PCI	Communist Party of Italy
PPS	Socialist Party of Poland
PSI	Socialist Party of Italy
R & D	research and development
SALT	Strategic Arms Limitation Treaty (or Talks)
SEA	Single European Act
SPD	Social Democratic Party (Germany)
SPÖ	Socialist Party of Austria
UN	United Nations
WEU	Western European Union
WTO	World Trade Organization

Introduction: Europe since 1945

Mary Fulbrook

In the early summer of 1945 the centre of Berlin was in ruins. Around Bahnhof Friedrichstrasse, one of the overground S-Bahn stations close to Berlin's central avenue Unter den Linden, women worked in human chains, handing rubble from one to the next to clear the bombed-out buildings. Like others all across the city, clearing the ruins and trying to reconstruct a semblance of normal life, these women and their children also spent much of their time bartering on the black market to sustain some form of physical existence. Many had to sleep in cellars and ruins, and, although no longer woken nightly by bombing raids, often lay awake with worry about the return of maimed and wounded menfolk from prisoner-of-war camps, or agonized about the possible fate of those from whom they had had no word. Filled with a combination of self-pity and exhaustion in the struggle for survival, the majority of them gave little, if any, thought to the fates of the millions who had been murdered by the Nazi policies of expansion, conquest, and genocide.

If we jump forward to around the middle of our period—let us say, to the summer of 1973, shortly after East Germany had officially been recognized by the West as a separate state—we find that the Friedrichstrasse S-Bahn station had taken on a rather different political significance. Bahnhof Friedrichstrasse was by now not merely a station like any other, but one of the few highly controlled crossing points between worlds: between dramatically different parts of a divided city, a divided country, and a divided Europe. All S-Bahn trains had to halt here for thorough searches before entering the hermetically sealed airlock between East and West, Capitalism and Communism, Democracy and Dictatorship. Although those with the right papers could travel from West to East (and back again), it was virtually impossible to pass in the opposite direction. Those 'rubble women' of 1945 who had landed up in the West were by now, for the most part, affluent beneficiaries of the Western economic miracle: they might choose to ignore or forget the difficult past and divided present; or they might cross at Friedrichstrasse to visit friends and relatives who had remained in the East, bringing small luxuries and gifts with a combination of condescension towards and incomprehension of the very different circumstances in which their former compatriots now lived. A crossing of a few metres: a crossing of political light-years.

The dark, drab corridors of the Friedrichstrasse station, the small windowless offices in which travellers had to show their papers to men in uniform, the back cells into which they might be taken for further interrogation—and possible detention if the papers were not in order—together constituted a place filled with an atmosphere of oppression and foreboding. For all but the ideologically converted, the passage from West to East in Bahnhof Friedrichstrasse was one marked by bureaucratic unpredictability, visible displays of unfathomable power, accompanied by a frisson of fear. Passage from the East to the West was, apart from those Westerners with return visas, only for the very few: politically reliable and privileged 'travel cadres'; old-age pensioners or others able to obtain special visas for particular purposes; or the tiny handful of those who, like the small child hidden sleeping in a shopping-bag trolley whose inadvertent dreaming snuffles were rapidly muffled by the sudden complicitous coughing fits of other passengers, managed in some way to accomplish a highly dangerous illicit one-way trip to the West without discovery.

Jump ahead again to the end of the century: the summer of 1999. Bahnhof Friedrichstrasse was again a station, not only like any other, but almost better than any other: more like a wing of the departures area in any international airport. Brand new glass-fronted shops; not only fashion and baggage chains, but a computer outlet with the latest in PCs and a range of multicoloured iMacs boasting instant Internet connection; mobile phone outlets so that, through a quick purchase, any new arrival could immediately be linked by telephone to virtually anywhere in the world; fast-food chains, offering anything from American-style burgers and fries through Turkish kebabs to more Germanic Pretzels, *Brötchen*, and Frankfurters; newspaper stalls with the world's press. For anyone who had passed through here barely more than a decade before, when armed East German soldiers, border guards, and secret police had patrolled the enclosed corridors of fear, the place was simply unrecognizable. It took an almost impossible leap of the imagination to accept that this might, indeed, be the same physical spot of ground.

Bahnhof Friedrichstrasse, in a small, specific, and symbolic way, might serve to assist in visualizing the extraordinary waves of transformation which washed across Europe in the second half of the twentieth century. The geographical location was the same: the people, the politics, the parameters had all been fundamentally altered. The purpose of this book is both to sketch the major trends and patterns of change, and try to tease out in detail some of the themes and variations in different areas.

Key developments and trends

The cold war, decolonization, and European integration together radically altered the nature of Europe in the latter half of the twentieth century. And a number of highly significant general trends, often conveniently summarized in terms of globalization and internationalization, fundamentally transformed the wider context. These developments, taken together, had major implications for the functions and character of individual European states.

First, the cold war, which divided Europe—and much of the world—into wholly opposed ideological, political, and economic systems, dramatically affected the character and development of West and East European states under their respective spheres of American and Soviet influence. No history of any single European state post-1945, whether Western or Eastern, can avoid the question of the economic and political—and hence also social and cultural—influence of one or other of the two new superpowers, the Soviet Union or the USA. Whether by acceptance or rejection, unwilling adaptation or ambivalent internalization, all East and West European states were intimately affected by the processes of economic aid or exploitation, political alignment or subjugation, offered to their willing or less willing allies by the Americans and Russians. In a myriad of ways, the patterns of political structure, economic growth, and social and cultural development of East and West European states were intrinsically affected by the cold war, such that the two sides of Europe divided by the Iron Curtain became more different from one another, and the constituent elements within each part became more alike. Then, with the collapse of the cold war, came a degree of convergence of former communist systems towards Western political and economic models, in principle if not entirely in practice. At the end of the twentieth century, notwithstanding local variations and some qualifications in terms of detail, the Western model of liberal democracy and a socially regulated form of market capitalism had become the model for virtually the whole of Europe, East as well as West.

Secondly, in the decades following the Second World War, the former imperial powers in Europe withdrew from major roles on the world stage, with all the consequences of decolonization both at home and abroad. With renunciation, to a greater or lesser extent accompanied by strife and bloodshed, of influence across the globe came a reconsideration of their own identities and roles. Countries such as Britain and France had to come to terms not only with a changed status in the world and in Europe, but also with new immigrant communities and new constructions of national identity at home. What it meant to be English or British, for example, began to change in significance.

Thirdly, and intimately related to these developments, a process of European integration began in a handful of core states within Western Europe, subsequently spreading through widening circles in the West and, after the collapse of the Iron Curtain, beckoning even towards some of the rapidly reconstructed post-communist states in the East. This process of integration was multifaceted and never uncontested: the impulses behind it ranged from, on the one hand, a purely functional, pragmatic belief in the importance of a common market for goods and labour, to the quite different and more visionary ideals embodying commitment to closer political as well as economic union in what was held out as the promise of a post-nationalist era. Such fundamental differences over ultimate purposes and goals were further cross-cut by specific debates over topics such as social rights, monetary union, or the extent of integration in terms of deepening and widening. Yet even as these debates took place, real changes on the ground—movements of peoples, migration for both economic and political reasons, cross-cultural contacts, and international developments—served to transform the nature of what it was that was being argued over.

There were also a number of highly significant general trends across our period. On a worldwide stage, supranational and international organizations were developed to seek solutions to military, political, and environmental problems. Long-term trends continued: industrialization, urbanization, the expansion of the service sector, scientific research and development, the growth and spread of multinational corporations. A series of communications revolutions—from ever faster mass transport of people and goods by air, motorway, rail, to the almost instantaneous communication of information and culture by fax, email, the Internet, satellite and cable television—radically transformed the living and working conditions of Europeans.

The age of nationalism, a force which had dominated the previous era and ignited two world wars, thus appeared to have been superseded by an age, if not of uncontested European integration, then at least of remarkable convergence of the socio-economic, cultural, and political profiles of individual European states. Do the developments of the later twentieth century add up to the creation of a Europe which is internally more homogeneous, externally more clearly defined and delimited, than ever before? And what do these developments mean about the changing role of the European nation state?

From fragmentation to convergence?

Internally, European countries began to become more like one another during this period, for a variety of reasons. There were certain common experiences, and common imperatives, to which states responded or by which they were affected in similar ways; to paraphrase John Donne, no state is an island, complete of itself; each (even Britain!) is part of the main.

At the same time, although to varying extents in different areas, increasing similarity of political, social, and economic structures within states was accompanied by a degree of increasing integration or at least mutual influence and coordination in certain policy areas across states. While concepts of national sovereignty and national interest were fiercely defended by individual governments (particularly in areas such as foreign policy), by the end of the twentieth century European states had become a great deal less different from one another, and more subject to common supranational institutions and organizations, than they were in 1945.

It should perhaps first be said that increasing internal similarity— or, to put it slightly differently, strikingly similar patterns of change in response to common challenges and experiences—is not an entirely new phenomenon in European history. Although the eastern boundaries of Europe, in particular, have been defined differently at different times over the last two millennia or so, 'Europe' is not and has not been simply a geographical land mass stretching over a particular area of the world.[1] From the Roman Empire through the spread of an internally divided, proselytizing Christianity, to the European Enlightenment and the modern explosions of science and technology; through the ages of discovery, expansion, and imperialism; through the periods of industrial revolution and the spread of capitalism; whichever area one looks at, there have been common socio-economic and cultural trends and patterns across Europe, refracted differently in different areas, but always within an interrelated system where changes in any part affect others. Even the emergence of distinctive states within Europe (from the diffuse sovereignty of medieval feudalism right through to the often bitterly nationalist struggles between modern forms of autocracy, democracy, and dictatorship) was a product of interrelations within the whole; it should not be forgotten that the development of state bureaucracies for the collection of taxes and recruitment of armies clearly pre-dated the spread of articulate conceptions of modern nationalism (as opposed to dynastic loyalty).

What was new, therefore, about the latter half of the twentieth century was perhaps not so much the fact of a series of transitions in some sort of tandem, but rather the specific character of these transitions and the changing place of Europe within the wider world. In particular, the starting-point of 1945 was perhaps peculiarly a

[1] See previous volumes in this series.

moment of national fragmentation: the end, in a moment of exhaustion, of a cataclysmic era of warfare engulfing the whole of Europe and indeed the world. This starting-point, in a wide variety of ways—mental and emotional, as well political and economic—set the scene for developments in Europe over the latter half of the century.

Military expansions, conquest, and warfare had always been major factors in European history. But the wars of the first half of the twentieth century were on a qualitatively new scale, and their impact was rather different as far as the roles of European nation states were concerned. The Second World War had massive effects, both in the short term and over the longer term, on all of Europe in a variety of ways.

There were, first of all, the immediate, visible effects: the loss of millions of lives, and the mass movement of peoples in the aftermath; the destruction of cities, transport networks, and productive capacity; the presence of the armies of the Western and Soviet Allies. Of major importance was the redrawing of the political boundaries of Central Europe in the post-war settlement, and the involvement of the superpowers in European affairs. There were also long-term economic effects: the injection of American Marshall aid to the West, fuelling the sustained economic growth of the 'long 1950s', and more broadly but no less importantly altering the character and mentality of West European industrial and class relations, on the one hand; and the concomitant radical reorientation of East European economic systems under Soviet influence, on the other. Far more difficult to define and quantify, but of equally fundamental importance, were the diverse memories of war, both private and public, both institutionalized and subterranean, which stamped their mark as much on official policy formation as on popular attitudes and mutual perceptions among the peoples of Europe. The reactions of many leading European politicians (not least, Britain's then prime minister, Mrs Thatcher) to the unexpected fall of the Berlin Wall in November 1989 dramatically illustrated the extraordinary heritage of collective memories of war.

There were not only common European experiences and memories—however divided on lines of erstwhile aggressor, collaborator, opponent, or victim—but also certain common imperatives, certain common questions (to which there might be different answers) which had to be faced in a changing world. All European states, whether ultimately choosing to join or remain outside particular new frameworks (the EEC, NATO, and so on), had to confront the issue of the increasing internationalization of economic, political, and military affairs in the latter half of the twentieth century. To choose to remain neutral, to remain outside a particular supranational organizational framework, was not and could not be a decision for retaining the status quo of a rapidly disappearing era in a changing world environment.

Certain pressures were quite general and affected all of Europe, though with differential impact in different areas at different times: the economic power of multinationals, such as fast-food chains which first colonized Western Europe and in the 1990s made the leap to the East (Erich Honecker would be turning in his grave at the sight of chains of McDonald's across eastern Germany); the powers of international television advertising and an increasingly global popular culture in music and fashion; the need to reach certain international standards of accommodation and provision in seeking to attract the tourist industry, as much in the older ski resorts of the Alpine and Nordic regions of Europe as in the newly opened regions of a rediscovered Central and Eastern Europe.

More specifically, within the EU at least, there were particular pressures for standardization or harmonization, and edicts on matters as diverse as the quality of wine, beer, and chocolate, on the one hand, or human rights and the corporal punishment of schoolchildren on the other (the highly desirable standardization of electric sockets still awaits the attention of an assiduous Eurocrat). There were also conscious policies to reshape the nature of Europe and Europeans, from regional development funds to schemes for assisting the mobility of people within Europe. Even quite mundane matters such as the European passport and blue Euro-starred car bumper stickers might have a subliminal effect.

Although, as Axel Körner points out in his chapter on culture (Chapter 5), there remained quite distinctive local styles in culture, the simple fact of increased exposure to other influences led to an inescapable dialogue among, if not increasing similarity of, international styles and art forms; mutual cultural influence can take many forms, including not only adoption or incorporation of elements of other styles but also adverse reactions and explicit rejection. Nor should it be forgotten that the premium on originality in the sphere of culture is itself a cultural constant common across Europe.

Harder to explain are some examples of political convergence, as analysed in the chapter on politics by Donald Sassoon (Chapter 2): most notably, within the first half of our period, the ending of fascist regimes in Southern Europe and their replacement by liberal democracies; and, quite dramatically, the collapse of communist states within a couple of years of one another in 1989–91, and their replacement by (often still tenuous) democratic regimes; more generally (and with far greater variability), the odd way in which many major West European governments appeared to switch colours—from conservative to socialist or social democratic, from socialist or social democratic to conservative—almost in tandem, or at least in visible waves. Even where the governing parties were of quite different political colours, there often seemed to be a degree of marching in tandem with respect to certain areas of policy—as in the well-nigh universal post-war development of the welfare state, although with specific national variants of particular social and health care schemes (see particularly Chapter 3, by Hartmut Kaelble). A distinctively European form of national politics of the centre ground appeared to be emerging, if in shuffling and not always well-coordinated gait. To some extent these areas of convergence related to broader secular trends: economic cycles of growth and recession; increasing longevity, an ever larger population of the elderly, and a shrinking proportion of adults in employment; and very broadly shared assumptions about communal responsibility and state intervention in social engineering (sustained even under governments of the right who proclaimed there was no such thing as society).

Yet, for all that has been said about convergence, it is worth underlining the degree to which different governments fiercely retained conceptions of national sovereignty, and defended the right to be independent and different. There was still choice; Europe at the end of our period was still a Europe of distinct regions and states. Even more strikingly, subjective patterns of identification and emotional attachment had run in a very different direction during this period. For all the homogenization or convergence in social, economic, and political structures, for all the upwards integration in terms of policy formation, there had not been a corresponding movement at the level of perceptions of identity. If anything, movement was in the other direction: downwards or backwards, towards identities rooted in local areas, or historical (ethnic, cultural) roots. Although Europeans were becoming more alike in many respects, there were no particular reasons (such as threats from a common enemy) to promote articulation of a widely shared European identity.

Towards a European identity?

The idea of Europe and of what constitutes European identity has taken many different forms over the ages. Taking a rather long view of the question, one might hazard the generalization that Europeans have perhaps been most aware of their common characteristics when confronted (particularly in a hostile situation) by the culturally or ethnically constructed Other: in face of the Barbarian, the Infidel, the Savage, or, more recently, immigrant populations of non-European origin (or at least non-white appearance). When discussing the question of European identity, we have to take care to distinguish among different groups and different contexts of identity construction.

In the twentieth century, and particularly in the period since 1945, several major conceptions of European identity may be distinguished. There are of course quite different versions propagated by particular elites: the visionary notions of the 'European ideal', often yearning towards some sort of peace and harmony among Europeans, to be embodied in a United States of Europe, must be sharply distinguished from the more pragmatic, functionalist views which saw a European common market as a means of enhancing economic growth and the mobility of goods and labour between what were to remain quite separate sovereign states. And these rather specific political and economic conceptions, tied to particular programmes for association or integration, are different again from the vaguer, general vision, rooted in part in rather unexamined notions of a common cultural heritage and values, in part in common wider interests in peace and the environment, associated with Mikhail Gorbachev's evocative notion of a 'common European home'. Nor, in this context, should it be forgotten that many elites were quite opposed to any idea of Europe beyond that of the wider arena for the pursuit of what were deemed to be national interests.

As far as popular conceptions are concerned, the position is far less clear. The European passport, and the dropping of internal border controls, were launched well ahead of popular perceptions of identification, which largely remained stubbornly national rather than European. There was little development at grass-roots level in many areas of Europe of anything which might be called a real sense of European identity. Professions of belief in such an identity were most apparent in states where there were problems with national identity and low national pride—most notably, West Germany after the Holocaust.

Somewhat paradoxically, a sense of European identity became more evident, perhaps for more pragmatic reasons, in regions of Europe which had a strong sense of local identity and felt that local or regional interests were not always best served by the institutions of the nation state (particularly when seen as being in reality a state constituted by several nations, of which one was dominant). Within the United Kingdom, Scotland and Wales particularly come to mind in this respect. In a rather different manner, the Republic of Ireland—with a strong positive sense of Irish national identity—also developed strong commitment to a sense of European identity (possibly reflected, for example, in its strong explicit commitment to the teaching of European languages). On the other hand, the European ideal might also be found appealing by members of subordinate groups who were driven by circumstances to migrate for economic or political reasons.

Yet at the same time there are strong tendencies towards an emphasis on cultural diversity and on identities based either in specific local regions, or in longer historical roots. In cosmopolitan areas or regions with large multicultural populations we have groups appealing to the recovery of ethnic or cultural–religious roots, such as Afro-Caribbean, Turkish, Islamic; not to mention the revival of bloody ethnic conflicts in the Balkans, with which the twentieth century seems to have both begun and ended. We have the resurrection or invention and celebration of historical identities, even, paradoxically, in the 'musealization' (*Musealisierung*) of their passing—as in the mushrooming of the heritage industry right across Europe. We have an emphasis on local and regional identities which have long been a feature of federal states; also in those which were relative latecomers as nation states, welding together remarkable linguistic and cultural diversity, such as Italy; and even in areas of long-centralized states such as the Basque region of Spain. We have the articulation of identities rooted in particular social and economic, as well as cultural, experiences (as in the emergence of a distinctive East German identity after the collapse of the GDR). There are overtly politicized parallels in the case of the renewed appeal of nationalist movements in Eastern Europe after the removal of the communist straitjacket, and the break-up of former multinational states, most notably, of course, the former Soviet Union, as well as Yugoslavia and Czechoslovakia.

What is particularly interesting about the current situation with respect to 'Europe' is that processes of integration—in terms of overcoming linguistic diversity and fostering the mobility of people and the broadening of horizons—appears to be simultaneous with an attempted resurrection (or downright creation) of local, ethnic, or other forms of identity. So we have simultaneous trends running in divergent directions: towards greater interaction, integration, and intercommunication, on the one hand; and towards stronger support for, or appeals for the renewal of, specific local, cultural, or ethnic identities on the other. 'European identity' has become more like a mosaic floor, made up of many different stones within larger patterns, rather than a woven carpet with large splashes of colour.

Identity is not only a matter of answering the question of what features a population considers itself to have in common, whether in terms of past heritage or current attributes; it is also about the expression and common celebration of shared values and ideals, which are often only articulated in face of a common enemy; and about notions of a common future. While Europeans might in many respects share similar features and attributes (and those citizens of the EU even a common passport, though not necessarily the same political rights across different European states), notions of shared values and ideals, common enemies, and a common future are strikingly absent. There are no shared dreams, however illusory (the Land of the Free, the Open Frontier, the Melting-Pot, the Great Society). Nor—despite common military engagements in the Gulf War or Kosovo in the 1990s—shared views on the use of military force. Without any emergent European 'dual identities' (no notions of being a Latvian European, Black/Asian European, Dutch European, along the lines of 'Hispanic American', 'Polish American', and so on), or any sense of common values and common cause outside the highly mobile circles of certain economic, professional, and political groups, Europeans by and large remain without an overarching sense of common identity.

Each of the thematic chapters which follow analyses in some detail the key processes and patterns of change in politics, society, the economy, culture, and relations within Europe and between Europe and the rest of the world. Taken together, these analyses present a complex picture in which general trends are seen to be refracted differently in different institutional and historical conditions. Within Europe at the end of the twentieth century there remained significant diversity between individual states and between different areas of Europe—not only between Eastern and Western Europe (both pre- and post-1989), but also between inner core and peripheries, southern and northern fringes, and across different cultural and other divides. Yet, for all the complexities, certain broad patterns of convergence still emerge; there are common processes and trends which have rendered Europe an internally more homogeneous region of the world, even in all its still characteristic variety and diversity.

Some Europeans will deplore, others will rejoice in, the fact that a common, widely shared sense of European identity does not appear to have accompanied increasing internal convergence or homogenization. It is worth remembering that, historically, notions of Europeanness appear to have been at their strongest and most explicit when articulated by groups possessed of a distinct sense of superiority in face of what they saw as inferior peoples, savages in the jungle. Postcolonialism, and a demoted place in world affairs, have indeed been accompanied by a more tightly guarded set of European barriers of one sort or another (particularly with respect to immigration and rights to citizenship). It is arguably no bad thing that this has remained dissociated from subjective bonds of emotional attachment and identification, or a sense of collective European purpose against a clearly defined Other. Perhaps we should remind ourselves of the response of Mahatma Gandhi when asked, on arrival on a trip to London, what he thought of the idea of European civilization: his reply was that he would be very much in favour of it.

2

Politics

Donald Sassoon

Successful settlement of wars usually involves eliminating the causes of the conflict. Forcibly or willingly, the defeated party—if it survives—is integrated into the system of values of the victors, thus precluding a return match. The great European civil war of 1914–45 was no exception: German militarism, whether in its Nazi form or in any of its previous incarnations, was obliterated along with all its ideological allies, whether in Rome, Budapest, or Helsinki. Subsequently no manifestly pro-Nazi party was able to become a significant political force anywhere in Europe. Across the ideological dividing line which partitioned Europe after 1947 there was a near-universal consensus on at least one aspect of the recent past: Nazism was regarded as a barbaric force and an absolute evil. This held true also where surviving regimes had features which resembled those of the demolished fascist dictatorships: Spain and Portugal. Even there, pro-Hitler or pro-Mussolini sympathies expressed during the war were conveniently tempered and rapidly forgotten. In any case, these conservative authoritarian regimes had taken no part in the war, made no political or territorial claim, and had neither the means nor the design to dominate others. Similarly, the military junta which ruled Greece between 1967 and 1974 disclaimed any connection with the legacy of fascism and Nazism and constantly reiterated its loyalty to the West.

Thus the revanchism which was one of the chief political features of the 1920s found no sizeable supporters in post-1945 Europe. Between 1947—when the inevitable post-war adjustments had taken place—and the collapse of the communist system in 1989–91 there were no fundamental changes in borders or in the territorial integrity of the European states, or any substantial alteration in the internal regimes of any of the European countries except in Spain, Portugal, and Greece in the mid-1970s. Until the break-up of Yugoslavia in the 1990s a state of peace prevailed among all European states. In comparison to the pre-1950 decades, there was no substantial civil strife. The use of mass terror by the state (purges, large-scale deportations) was circumscribed to the USSR, where it did not outlast Stalin's death in 1953. The quasi-official terror gangs of the 1920s—the Freikorps in Germany, blackshirts in Italy, and Black and Tans in Ireland—did not reappear. Militarized police force was used by the authorities to quell strikes and demonstrations in East Germany, Poland, Italy, Spain, France, Greece, Yugoslavia (especially in Kosovo in the 1950s), and elsewhere at different times and for different causes. Such use of force was relatively limited, but the repression of the demonstrations in Berlin by Soviet forces on 17 June 1953 brought about the deaths of at least fifty-one people.[1] In the democratic countries of the West the peak of state violence was probably reached in 1961, when over 200 Algerian demonstrators were killed by the Parisian police under the orders of Maurice Papon and dumped in the Seine. Elsewhere in Eastern and Central Europe the numbers of those killed were much higher but never reached the scale of the massacres of the past.

The intervention of Soviet-backed troops in Hungary (1956) and Czechoslovakia (1968) did not lead to prolonged fighting and, by the tragic standards of the preceding decades of European history, did not bring about a massive loss of life: in Hungary 3,000 were killed by the Soviet troops, 350 by Hungarian anti-Soviet revolutionaries; in Czechoslovakia 229 people were subsequently executed, while a further ninety people died as a consequence of the Soviet-backed intervention.[2] The wave of terrorism that plagued some European countries in the 1970s and 1980s (mainly Spain, Italy, Northern Ireland, and West Germany) led to no significant political changes. Until the collapse of communism post-war Europe exhibited an impressive stability. When change occurred, it was almost invariably in the direction of parliamentary democracy (Southern Europe in the 1970s, Eastern and Central Europe in the 1990s) and, usually, peacefully or with minimal violence—with the significant exception of the

---

[1] Karel Bartosek, 'Europe centrale et du Sud-Est', in Stéphane Courtois (ed.), *Le Livre noir du communisme* (Paris: Robert Laffont, 1977), 477.

[2] Ibid. 478–81.

former Yugoslavia, where bloodshed escalated throughout the 1990s and led to the first military action by the forces of the Atlantic Alliance.

The Second World War, far from being followed by anything approaching political unity, had led to a division of the continent wider than ever before. Yet the unusually prolonged period of European peace was underpinned by a lengthy process of political and economic convergence that was equally unprecedented. As the century reached its end, the nation states of Europe were closer to each other than at any time in their entire history. One of the many paradoxes of this convergence was that it was accompanied by a pronounced increase in the number of states: the twenty-seven states that were extant in 1945 (including the two Germanies, which became distinct states in 1949) had become thirty-seven some fifty years later. Assuming Turkey and Cyprus to be outside Europe, and not counting Malta and statelets such as Liechtenstein and the Republic of San Marino, the following states constituted Europe until the collapse of communism: Albania, Austria, Belgium, Bulgaria, Czechoslovakia, Denmark, Finland, France, the Federal Republic of Germany, the German Democratic Republic, Great Britain, Greece, Hungary, Iceland, Ireland, Italy, Luxembourg, the Netherlands, Norway, Poland, Portugal, Romania, Spain, Sweden, Switzerland, the USSR, and Yugoslavia. After the collapse of communism, the reunification of Germany, and the subsequent break-up of the USSR, Yugoslavia, and Czechoslovakia, the number rose to thirty-seven by including (along with Russia) Lithuania, Estonia, Latvia, the Czech Republic, Slovakia, Ukraine, Moldavia, Belarus, Slovenia, Croatia, Bosnia, Serbia-Montenegro (still known as Yugoslavia), and Macedonia. Further fragmentation cannot be ruled out.

The most vivid feature of the post-war fracturing of Europe was the divide created by the cold war between a system of states dominated by communist parties in its eastern and central land mass and a 'Western' sector where capitalism prevailed. The latter was in turn further fragmented along political lines. Democracy prevailed in most countries, but pre-war authoritarian regimes persisted in Portugal and Spain, while Greece, recovering from civil war (1946–9), was far from being a consolidated democracy. The pivotal state of continental Europe, Germany, originally divided into four zones, developed into two distinct states. Some Western democracies—

notably Ireland, Sweden, Finland, Austria, and Switzerland—opted for neutrality, while the majority aligned themselves to the Atlantic Alliance along with Turkey, Portugal, and Greece, while Spain enjoyed a close relationship with the United States.

Disharmony appeared to deepen with the formation of distinct Western trading associations—the European Economic Community and the European Free Trade Area (EFTA). Eastern Europe looked more monolithic, but it was never an undifferentiated communist bloc: soon Yugoslavia and later Albania abandoned the Soviet fold, espousing different roads to socialism. Romania eventually adopted an independent foreign policy. Poland maintained a large private sector in agriculture. By 1980 Hungary had acquired a thriving, if undeveloped, market economy.

The process of European integration under the aegis of the EEC (later the European Union) was enhanced in the 1970s with the entry in 1973 of Great Britain, Ireland, and Denmark, thus undermining the survival of the EFTA bloc. The expansion of the Community continued after the collapse of the authoritarian regimes of Portugal, Greece, and Spain in 1974–5 and their successful bid to join the EEC. By 1985, when Mikhail Gorbachev began the reforms that would precipitate the end of the USSR, all market economies of Europe had a similar liberal-democratic parliamentary system. The end of communism brought about the unification of Germany, the break-up of Czechoslovakia, and the return to full sovereignty of the three Baltic states. Nearly all former communist states adopted the economic and political system of Western Europe. Their party alignment—a group of centre-left parties facing one of centre-right parties—was an almost exact replica of those of the West. The exceptions are far from insignificant: the Russian Federation, the Ukraine, Belarus, and Moldavia remain politically and economically unstable. The break-up of Yugoslavia brought about the formation of relatively stable nation states, such as Slovenia, Croatia, and, possibly, Macedonia. Serbia's borders, however, remained far from assured, while Bosnia became a battle zone with no secure central authority—the first instance of extended warfare in Europe since 1945.

At this stage it is impossible to prognosticate whether these issues will be satisfactorily settled over the next years and decades or whether they will lead to a new era of discord and disintegration. The history of Europe has long ceased to be under the exclusive control of

Europeans—as it had been since the end of the fifteenth century. Its future looks as uncertain as that of the rest of the planet.

The historical verdict on the second half of the twentieth century can only record that those European nation states that emerged out of the great conflicts of the first half with a democratic system of government, a market economy, and a welfare state faced on internal or external threats, survived all crises, and became the model to which other European states eventually conformed. This great success was not unique. In the rest of the world, democratic countries with market economies, such as Australia and New Zealand, Canada, the United States, and Japan, also seemed to offer apparently less fortunate nations a vision of stability, democracy, and wealth. The triumphalism which heralded the end of communism and which led some to proclaim, somewhat ahistorically, the 'end of history' thus had a basis in reality.

Reshaping Europe after 1945

The political systems of those countries that had stayed out of the war remained unaffected. In Sweden, Switzerland, Ireland, Iceland, and Portugal politics proceeded following the same rules and under the same conditions as before the war. The same can be said for Spain, where Franco had taken advantage of the period of warfare to consolidate his 1939 victory in the civil war by the wholesale slaughter of his opponents: thousands of supporters of the defeated Republic were killed; many more were imprisoned.[3] By 1945 he was firmly entrenched, although some guerrilla activity continued until 1951.[4] Some of the West European states also exhibited remarkable continuity: Great Britain, Norway, Denmark, Belgium, Luxembourg, and the Netherlands. They had all been constitutional monarchies before the war, and remained so afterwards.

France too returned to the pre-war political system. There was an attempt to disguise this as the beginning of a novel era by drafting a new constitution for the Fourth Republic. In reality, the differences

---

[3] See Gabriel Jackson, *The Spanish Republic and the Civil War, 1931–1939* (Princeton: Princeton University Press, 1965), app.

[4] Paul Preston, *The Triumph of Democracy in Spain* (London: Methuen, 1986), 4.

between the Fourth and the Third Republics were insignificant. Both were based on a weak executive, a figurehead president, and a powerful parliament dominated by fractious political parties. The same instability that had characterized the Third Republic plagued the governments of the Fourth. Charles de Gaulle, who had led the anti-fascist forces during the war, failed to secure the strong presidential system he desired and left politics, albeit temporarily.

Elsewhere in Western Europe changes were more significant. Italy had experienced fascist rule for the whole of the inter-war period, had been Germany's closest ally in 1940, and had turned against it in 1943. A referendum in 1946 established a republic. A new constitution was drafted resulting in a political system relatively similar to that which preceded fascism and analogous to that of the French Fourth Republic.

Austria's debatable claim that it had been forced into an alliance with Germany worked to its advantage: permanent partition was avoided and the country returned to the parliamentary system it had had in the 1920s. The USSR withdrew its troops and Austria complied with the main condition exacted—permanent neutrality—a situation accepted by all main parties and welcomed by public opinion. Finland, which had also been occupied by Soviet troops, followed a similar course.

Even in Germany there was a return to a previous political system—at least in that section that had been partitioned among Western powers. Though the differences between Weimar Germany (1919–33) and the FRG should not be underestimated, the constitutional similarities are remarkable, bearing in mind that in the hiatus between the two were twelve years of Nazism, including six years of total war, and that the outcome was the division of the country.

There was some degree of continuity even in Greece. After the defeat of the communists in the civil war (1949) repression and a rigged electoral system kept the communists and their allies at the margins of political life. Though there was no reversion to the dictatorship of the Metaxas era, there was a return to the old political cleavage between traditional monarchists and liberal modernizers. It was only after the return of full democracy in 1974 that a modern socialist party emerged.

The political institutions that prevailed in Western Europe shortly after the end of the war had thus been tried before it. Nevertheless, beneath the relative continuity of institutional politics and constitutional arrangements there were significant developments. The first was that political democracy was finally consolidated: true universal suffrage became the norm; members of the legislature were now elected by the entire population; women finally obtained the right to vote on the same terms as men in France (1944), Belgium (1948), Italy (1946), and Greece (1952). Switzerland remained the bizarre exception to universal suffrage until 1971.

The second major development was the considerable advance of the parties of the left, as evidenced by their massive gains in the first post-war elections. Previous major political divisions, such as centralizers versus decentralizers or anticlericalism versus clericalism, became secondary. The primary ideological cleavage—within an overarching consensus—was that of left versus right, that is between parties inspired by socialism and those committed to a capitalism tempered by traditional values. The Republic of Ireland, where the national question dominated politics, was the only significant exception to the primacy of the left–right split in democratic Europe.

In Britain in 1945 the Labour Party, for the first time in its history, won an absolute majority of seats in the House of Commons and 48.3 per cent of the vote. In Sweden, Norway, and Austria socialist parties gained over 40 per cent. Where these fared less well—as in Finland, France, and Italy, where they gained 20–25 per cent—the communist parties gained at least 20 per cent or more. The positive electoral performance of the parties of the left was one aspect of the wave of anti-capitalist feelings that pervaded Europe after the war. In most instances the right or centre-right, far from being dominated by overtly pro-capitalist parties, was led by Christian parties committed to the containment of market forces and the defence of traditional values against unconstrained individualism. Such development was particularly evident in Germany, Austria, Italy, Belgium, and Holland.

This explains the wide political consensus that permeated Western Europe. It enabled post-war reconstruction to be initiated by a coalition of parties representing the left, the centre, and even the centre-right. The two important exceptions to this were Great Britain, where Labour ruled alone until 1951, and the FRG, where the first general elections occurred only in 1949—when the left tide had already subsided—resulting in the victory of the conservative Christian Democratic Union (CDU) within a coalition government.

By this stage most of the countries of Western Europe had laid the foundations of their welfare systems. The parties of the left were the main proponents of this development, regarding welfare reforms as a form of socialism or as an advance towards a socialist society. The evolution, however, was not seriously disputed by their conservative opponents, who could legitimately claim that the historical forerunners of welfare reforms had been 'social' liberals like Lloyd George, authoritarian conservatives like Bismarck, or social Christians. Indeed, the agenda for a post-war welfare system had been drafted during the war by a British Liberal, William Beveridge. This consensus across the political spectrum explains not only why the welfare states were established in the first place, but also why they outlasted the initial electoral successes of the left. Nevertheless, it was in the one country where the left had overall control of parliament, Britain, that the most comprehensive free national health service was established and where a complex system of social protection, from pensions to unemployment benefits, was set up. The more prosperous nations, above all the Scandinavian countries, pursued the same path. Fear of old age, illness, and unemployment would no longer trouble the citizens of Europe—or so it was hoped.

The enlargement of the sphere of the state into welfare—replacing, in many instances, the provisions of charitable bodies, usually religious—was accompanied by its extension into the economy. In some instances, notably in Austria, Italy, Britain, and France, this was achieved directly through the nationalization or municipalization of some or all of the utilities (such as gas, water, telephones, and electricity), and some of the manufacturing and extracting industries. Radio and later television remained totally or in part in the hands of the state, even in market economies. Only in the 1980s was there a systematic expansion of private capital in broadcasting throughout Europe. In all cases the state, through monetary and fiscal policies, took upon itself the task of overseeing the general performance of the economy at the macroeconomic level. The aim was to ensure that the capitalist economic cycle would never again be out of control, plunging the European economies into a devastating depression of 1930s proportions.

The state had thus become much stronger throughout Western Europe, even in those states, such as the FRG, Austria, and

Switzerland, that had opted for a far less centralist structure than, say, Britain, Sweden, France, and Italy.

West European capitalism emerged from this reconstruction both weakened and strengthened. It was weakened in the sense that entire areas of economic life—for instance, health, transport, gas, electricity, water supply, central banking, and a whole host of public services, from street cleaning to mail delivery—were removed from or kept out of the market. It was strengthened because the rationalization of industries through nationalization led to reduced costs, and because the socialization of public services (health, education, pensions, insurance) amounted to a socialization of expenditure that would otherwise have had to be borne by individuals. This, in turn, contained the pressure for higher wages. More generally, the provision of welfare made capitalism more acceptable by reducing the possibility of market failures in the delivery of critical services.

The political fate of the countries of Eastern and Central Europe sharply contrasted with that of their Western counterparts. This was not surprising. Before the war they had all, with the exception of Czechoslovakia, been under some form of authoritarian regime. All had been occupied by Germany. All (except Czechoslovakia) had a large agricultural sector. All had suffered massive losses and devastation—well in excess of all other Western countries except Germany. Post-war adjustments were made more complex by widespread 'ethnic cleansing' (the practice had preceded the coinage of the expression), especially in Czechoslovakia, Hungary, and Poland, from where millions of ethnic Germans were expelled. By 1950 there were 8 million so-called *Heimatvertriebene* ('people expelled from their homeland') in the FRG. The Czechoslovak–Hungarian Treaty of 1946 led to the exchange of some 50,000–60,000 Slovaks and Hungarians (though over 350,000 remained in Czechoslovakia). Sporadic fighting amounting to near civil war persisted in Poland until 1947.

All the countries of Eastern Europe had been liberated from Nazi rule by the Red Army, except Albania and Yugoslavia. As a result, communist takeover in these two countries departed from what became the established pattern. The Yugoslav communist leader, Tito (Josip Broz), rejected calls from London and Moscow for a national coalition government with the monarchists, and declared a republic in 1943. As the war was approaching its end, he turned against those opposing him with methods that included the destruction of villages deemed to have supported Serbian and Croatian nationalists. When Soviet troops entered Yugoslavia, it was with the understanding that Tito's partisans would remain in power. In Albania the communist party established full control rapidly. Its leader, Enver Hoxha, declared a republic in 1945 with the backing of the Allies, while Stalin's diplomatic support enabled him to resist Tito's attempts to incorporate the country into Yugoslavia. Thus a link was forged between Albanian 'national' communism and Stalinism that outlasted the Soviet condemnation of Stalin's crimes.

Elsewhere in the East the reorganization of democratic political life occurred under the aegis of Soviet power. The consequence was that the communist parties enjoyed considerable advantages. In any case, immediately after the war the communists had gained in popularity because of their role in resisting Nazism and the prestige of the USSR. Even among those not ideologically inclined towards communism there were some who were so disenchanted with the past that they regarded the communists as representing modernity and a better future. It was believed that they would get rid of corruption and backwardness. It is impossible to gauge accurately the magnitude of this initial popularity, though the results of the first elections (relatively free of interference) indicate that the size of their electorate was comparable to that of the stronger communist parties of Western Europe. Their real influence was, of course, wider than their electoral support. The authoritarian right had been wiped out, its leaders purged. The political parties that re-emerged were reluctant to take a strong anti-communist line, for this might have tarred them with the brush of fascism. The presence of the Red Army and the weight of the USSR was a substantial obstacle to the free expression of anti-communist views. Political opportunists swelled the ranks of the left as they had previously swelled those of the right. Communist parties that had been tiny organizations before the war grew exponentially in numbers—a phenomenon that also occurred in Italy, where the Italian Communist Party, the PCI, grew from 6,000 in 1943 to 2 million in 1948. The communists pushed everywhere for the formation and/ or continuation of governments of national unity. While these broad coalition governments emerged throughout most of continental Europe, in the East the communists always had the upper hand because they benefited from financial, logistic, and organizational help from the Soviet Union. This is the situation that prevailed between 1945 and 1947–8.

The coalition strategy adopted by all communist parties assumed that governments of national unity would oversee the entire period of post-war reconstruction. In the East, where they had a position of strength, they used it to maximize their hold on political power. Initially, however, there was no blueprint for a generalized takeover. Soviet policy, in so far as it had clearly defined aims, was directed towards ensuring that all neighbouring states would have governments friendly to that of the USSR. The communists were cautious and prudent, pursued compromise, and avoided an excessively radical agenda, concentrating instead on demanding agrarian reform and a limited expansion of the public sector.

This explains why in Romania the communists, led by the independent-minded Gheorghe Gheorgiu-Dej, allowed the monarchy to survive the war until 1947, supported a 'friendly' non-communist, Petru Groza, as prime minister, included representatives of the liberals and of the National Peasant Party in the government (1946), and promulgated a moderate agrarian reform that left Church lands untouched. But in 1947 the National Peasant Party was banned, the social democrats were pressured into merging with the communists, and King Michael was forced to abdicate. The landslide victory of the new People's Democratic Front—in effect the communist party—in the rigged elections of March 1948 ensured the final takeover.

In Bulgaria the coalition strategy was equally short-term. Widespread purges ensured the elimination of all possible anti-communist forces, the rest being forcibly compelled to join the communist-dominated Fatherland Front, this process being completed only in 1948 with the forcible absorption of the social democrats.

In Hungary the communists had obtained only 17 per cent of the vote in 1945, their socialist rivals a little more, while the Smallholder Party, or KGP (itself a coalition of disparate groups), gained an absolute majority; their leader, Ferenc Nágy, became prime minister in a coalition government that included the communists. By 1947 the purges of former fascists and collaborators had weakened further the anti-communist forces. In spite of irregularities during the 1947 election campaign, the Hungarian communists obtained only 22 per cent, though, with their allies, which now included the rapidly disintegrating KGP, they constituted a bloc of some 60 per cent. By 1949, when new elections were held, this bloc had turned itself into the communist-controlled Hungarian Workers' Party, which no other group dared to oppose. The establishment of a single-party system was complete.

A similar pattern occurred in Czechoslovakia: first the constitution of a national unity government, followed by a merger between communists and socialists, and then the expulsion of the right from the coalition leading to the communist takeover of 1948.

In Poland the Nazi genocide of the Jews, the shifting of the boundaries some 150 miles to the west, and the ethnic cleansing of Germans had made the country more ethnically and religiously homogeneous than ever before. The first initiatives of the government of national unity—nationalization and a three-year plan—were devised by the socialist PPS. The creation of a new party—the Polish United Workers' Party—was as much, if not more, the work of socialists ensuring their own future than that of the communists themselves.[5] Other parties were allowed to survive, while in the rural sector the strength of the peasants' associations and the need to ensure farmers' support to feed the country prevented any significant collectivization.

In Germany, on one view, the Soviet leaders had asked for a demilitarized Germany rather than the establishment of a distinct state in the East. It was only when they realized that the West would not accede to this request and after the Federal Republic was created that they authorized the formation of the GDR.[6] This was ruled, until 1990, by the SED, the *de facto* communist party—the result of a merger with the social democrats with the cooperation of their leader, Otto Grotewohl.

Thus was completed what is generally known as the communist takeover of Eastern and Central Europe. The expression is technically valid in the sense that communist rule was never electorally sanctioned or put to the test. It is nevertheless misleading if it is taken to signify that there was some grand plan hatched somewhere in the Kremlin instead of the far more likely, if less exciting, explanation: all

[5] Norman Davies, 'Poland', in Martin McCauley (ed.), *Communist Power in Europe 1944–1949* (Basingstoke: Macmillan, 1977), 48–50.

[6] See Wilfried Loth, *Stalin's Unwanted Child: The Soviet Union, the German Question and the Founding of the GDR* (Basingstoke: Macmillan, 1998), for the controversial view that Stalin did not wish to have a separate German socialist state.

parties reacted to events by maximizing their power and undermining their opponents by all available means. The idea of a grand plan
became widespread after the takeover by both sides in the cold war,
either to confirm the myth of the far-reaching political intelligence of
communists as the holders of the keys of History, able to mould
events at will, or to stigmatize them as unusually devilish conspirators
against whom it was necessary to be permanently vigilant.

These events should not obscure the fact that, initially, the main
economic and social policies advanced by the communist-dominated
coalition governments in Eastern and Central Europe prior to 1947
were not significantly different from those advocated in the West by
democratic socialist forces: agrarian reform and the extension of the
public sector through nationalizations. Later the process of elimination of private property proceeded rapidly, if unevenly, in the East,
while it was contained in the West.

Thus, by 1947–8 communist rule was in place throughout Eastern
and Central Europe. In Western Europe political 'anomalies' such as
the presence of communists in the coalition governments of Italy and
France (1947) were removed by anti-communist majorities. The new
European cold war order was born. The responsibility for this state of
affairs has at times been attributed to the conferences at Yalta and
Potsdam in 1945 or to the Churchill–Stalin 'percentage' agreement of
October 1944. As the boundaries of the so-called Iron Curtain
coincided almost exactly with the territories liberated by the Red
Army, it seems reasonable to conclude that no international conference before or after 1945 was likely to modify significantly the results
achieved on the battlefield. In fact, those communist countries which
the Red Army *did not* liberate—Yugoslavia and Albania—had freed
themselves from Soviet control by 1950 and 1960, respectively, while
remaining communist.

The single most important cause behind the communist takeover
of Eastern and Central Europe was the deteriorating international
situation. The proclamation of the Truman Doctrine in 1947 and the
subsequent announcement of the Marshall Plan was seen by the
USSR—not unreasonably—as the clearest indication that the United
States intended to undermine Soviet power in Eastern and Central
Europe.

Initially this view was not shared by some communist leaders,
notably in Poland and Czechoslovakia, who contemplated accepting

the US offer—not a surprising move if one considers that anti-Americanism had not yet become a major feature of communist politics, and that the destitution still prevailing in most of Central and Eastern Europe made the prospect of foreign aid somewhat enticing. This initial communist response shows how seriously they had taken the idea that 'people's democracies' were an intermediate form between Soviet-style communism and Western capitalism. But this was no longer regarded as a feasible option by the USSR. The Soviet grip was intensified. Dissident communists were purged, imprisoned, or executed, sometimes after show trials, a reminder to those left behind that their room for manoeuvre had been reduced. This had become manifest when the USSR re-established a coordinating body—a less centralized successor to the Comintern—known as the Cominform (or Communist Information Bureau) in 1947, with a membership restricted to all the ruling communist parties as well as those of France and Italy.

The division of Europe had been achieved rapidly, but previous to this, political developments in the two halves of most of continental Europe had not been markedly divergent. On both sides there had been broad coalitions where left and right coexisted uneasily. On both sides there was widespread agreement that laissez-faire capitalism had no future, that major social reforms had to be implemented, and that remnants of the past, such as large landholdings, where these still existed, had to be broken up through agrarian reform. Nevertheless, if one can be so boldly counter-factual, it can be surmised that, without the existence of the USSR and the control it exercised, most of the countries of Eastern and Central Europe (Yugoslavia and Albania are the most likely exceptions) would have been ruled not by the communists, but either by a radical government of the left operating within a market economy or, more probably, by a traditional conservative regime. In the West, however, even if the United States had reverted to isolationism and had washed their hands of the destiny of Europe, there would still not have been a successful takeover by communists—even where they were relatively strong, such as in France, Italy, or Greece.

Stability and control: the boring 1950s

By 1950 the political systems of the European states had stabilized. They remained essentially unaltered until 1990 except for Greece, Portugal, and Spain. In Eastern and Central Europe the communist regimes were sufficiently entrenched to fend off any threats either by resorting to internal force, as in the GDR in 1953 and Poland in 1956, or through the decisive intervention of the Soviet military, as in Hungary in 1956 and Czechoslovakia in 1968. In Western Europe the war-generated wave of radicalism subsided very quickly. The British Labour Party lost the election in 1951, paving the way for thirteen years of Conservative rule. In Italy the PCI and the socialist party, the PSI, continued to cooperate (uniquely in Western Europe), but lost the 1948 elections and found themselves in opposition. In Federal Germany the social democrats remained, likewise, in opposition until 1966. In Austria the socialists were in a virtually permanent coalition with the Christian conservative Austrian People's Party (ÖVP). By 1960 the left was still in power only in Norway and Sweden.

The one common feature which united the two blocs in Europe in these years was an exceptional and historically unprecedented economic growth that was particularly rapid in the late 1950s and early 1960s.[7]

The most important social transformation of these years was the remarkable decrease in the size of the rural population. The process developed, unevenly, throughout European societies, regardless of their political system. Such rapid urbanization was achieved relatively painlessly. It did not lead to massive unrest, lasting resentment, or uncontrollable social problems. It did not bring about any significant political change; not even the collapse of major political parties or the advent of new ones. The outcome of this process was the establishment of a thriving consumer society in the West and the industrialization of the more backward parts of the East. The overall improvement in social conditions was one of the principal pillars of the consensus underpinning the regimes on both sides of the ideological divide. However, this improvement was also, as we shall see, a major cause of political change.

[7] See tables and comments in Ch. 4 in this volume.

In the West this impressive growth provided both an ideal fiscal foundation for the expansion of the welfare system and the real underpinning of the consumer society and hence of support for capitalism. Growth rates were, of course, far more striking in countries that had to catch up, such as Italy and Germany and, to some extent, France, than in Britain, where full employment had already been reached well before Germany or Italy. Inflation rates, though low, were not the same throughout Europe. Nevertheless, the expectation that things would always get better was enhanced by an economic system that provided jobs and the purchasing power necessary to equip households with an ever expanding array of consumer goods. That this development occurred under the aegis of the United States, the leading consumer society in the world, only strengthened the political, ideological, and military connection between Western Europe and the USA. In the East there was no such correspondence. The USSR was the politically hegemonic country, able to impose its own model of society. However, even though it had started the construction of socialism well before all the others, it was not in the vanguard by its own criteria of economic progress, namely industrial growth and social conditions: the citizens of the GDR, Czechoslovakia, and Hungary were better off than their Soviet counterparts—as they had been before communism had been imposed upon them.

In the West the products of American culture (music, films, best-selling books) were sought after and increasingly regarded by all, except the intelligentsia, as more exciting than most locally produced popular culture. In the East Soviet culture had no such popular basis and was usually seen as an imposition. In the West periodic elections forced the political elites to compete and be in constant touch with their electorates. In the East this was not so, and political power—far more concentrated than in the West—was blamed for any distress.

The lack of widespread popular support (as distinct from generalized acquiescence) was compounded by the debilitating purges that most of the ruling communist parties undertook after establishing their rule. Show trials, often leading to executions, had eliminated those leaders who had taken seriously the conception of a national road to socialism that prevailed in 1945–7. Tito alone was able to resist and break away from the influence of Moscow. To intervene in Yugoslavia's internal affairs Stalin required some local support, at least within the communist party. What he had was insufficient, and he was forced to desist. Elsewhere the communists accepted unquestioningly his bidding, and tied their countries to the USSR militarily through the Warsaw Pact and economically through the Comecon. In the USSR itself the war, far from leading to a more liberal approach to economic and social problems, had brought about an ever greater internal tightening of controls, renewed party purges, deportations, and forced labour. In all likelihood the enormous wreckage and devastation caused by the war would have led to greater centralization even without the astonishing growth of an unparalleled cult of personality. This reached its peak with the celebration of Stalin's seventieth birthday in December 1949: for nine months three-quarters of the space in *Pravda*, the party daily, was dedicated to birthday greetings from all corners of the world.[8] By 1950 the industrial structure of the USSR had more than recovered. The peasants paid a heavy price: they were only able to subsist thanks to their private plots.[9]

When Stalin died in 1953, he left behind an institutional system characterized by the complete identification of state and party. Subsequently nearly all major reforms within the USSR or any of the other socialist states occurred through the communist party, with the main exception of Poland in the 1970s and 1980s. At times the initiative came from below, but encountered violent repression whenever it challenged the foundation of communist power. The first outbreak of popular protest after Stalin's death occurred in East Germany. It took the form of a workers' uprising on 17 June 1953 and led to the further transformation of the SED into a party of loyal communists.

When Nikita Khrushchev denounced Stalin and his crimes at the Twentieth Congress of the Soviet Communist Party in 1956, there were demands for radical change from within the Polish Communist Party. These led to widespread workers' demonstration. Frightened, the party recalled Wałdysław Gomułka, a victim of the previous internecine conflicts, who assured Moscow that its primacy would continue unchallenged as long as Poland remained free of direct Soviet interference. This satisfied Polish national pride—a major factor— and the crisis was contained.

---

[8] Seweryn Bialer, *Stalin's Successors* (Cambridge: Cambridge University Press, 1982), 30.

[9] Alec Nove, *An Economic History of the USSR* (Harmondsworth: Penguin, 1978), 293, 300.

In Hungary a far more serious situation developed, though initially it followed the Polish pattern. Following riots in Budapest on 23 October, Imre Nágy, who had been expelled from the party in 1955, was recalled to lead a new government. He included in it several non-communists, restored a multi-party system, demanded the removal of Soviet troops, and announced Hungary's withdrawal from the Warsaw Pact. This move proved disastrous. The West—caught in the midst of the Suez crisis—was in no position to help, and Nágy lost the support of Tito, who was as frightened of multipartism as Moscow. Soviet troops intervened militarily to restore communist order. Nágy was arrested and executed. The lesson learned was that reforms were permissible and even encouraged, but they had to be pursued within rigid limits patrolled by Moscow: loyalty to the USSR and strict compliance to the doctrine of one-party rule had to remain unquestioned. The leader of the Hungarian communists, János Kádár, understood this perfectly well and proceeded to reform Hungarian society at a snail's pace with greater success than anywhere else in Eastern Europe.

In spite of internal differences, Eastern and Central Europe appeared to many external observers as a monolithic bloc. The West was more diversified. Within the framework of parliamentary democracy and a mixed economy there were diverse policy options. Each country could choose the proper mix of state and market, its institutional arrangements, and whether to join NATO or the EEC.

In Sweden negotiations between the social-democratic government, the employers' associations, and the trade unions led, towards the end of the 1950s, to the adoption of a highly centralized system of wage determination and a labour market sustained by well-funded state-sponsored training programmes. In France a series of indicative plans attempted, rather successfully, to modernize what was widely regarded as an archaic capitalist system. In Germany the dominant Christian Democrats established what was called a 'social market economy'—one of many labels since given to the European model of 'managed' capitalism. The particular German contribution to this was the development—in key industries such as coal and steel—of limited workers' participation in management, the so-called *Mitbestimmung*, or co-determination. A partnership between employers and trade unions (later known as corporatism) prevailed in most of

Northern Europe as well as in Austria, though not in the United Kingdom.

The cold war enabled West Germany to achieve rapid rehabilitation. It was, after all, the West's most important outpost facing communism. While Weimar Germany had been burdened by war reparations, Federal Germany was the recipient of generous financial aid. Loyalty to the West was the only price to pay, and this was not exacting. The German chancellor, Konrad Adenauer, had his political base in the Catholic Rhineland while his allies, the Christian Social Union (CSU), controlled Catholic Bavaria. He looked to the West, away from Protestant Prussia, and was in no hurry to reunify Germany. Memories of the war made German nationalism distasteful to all except a few extremists: this reassured everyone, especially the French. Rebuilding the FRG and becoming wealthy became the main preoccupation of the German people and their political elites.

In Italy the coalition led by the Christian Democrats (CD) had similar concerns. The country's entry into the European Community as one of its founding members bolstered the ruling parties of the centre because it reassured a population obsessed with the idea of falling behind and not being in Europe. The CD used its expanded public sector to mop up unemployment, erected a complex system of patronage and clienteles, and promulgated agrarian reform in the underdeveloped south. Thanks to these policies it managed to steer a careful balance between upholding traditional Catholic values and modernizing the country.

The weakness of West European countries in a world dominated by nuclear superpowers was so manifest that foreign policy was neither important nor particularly divisive. Only two significant issues had to be debated: whether or not to be in NATO and whether or not to be in the EEC. Once NATO membership had been accepted by those few parties of the left that had originally opposed it—the SPD in 1960 and the Italian socialists in 1963—it ceased to have much relevance. The EEC was far more controversial. Usually, however, once a country was inside it, the issue of withdrawing was never seriously entertained by the party in power, and this has been true even of Great Britain.

Only two West European countries, France and Britain, still dreamed of exercising world influence. This led them to send troops to Egypt in 1956 to prevent the nationalization of the Suez Canal and reassert their influence in the Middle East. The ensuing debacle compelled them to rethink their role. After resolving, at great cost, the decolonization of Algeria, France turned decisively towards Europe by entrenching its special relationship with West Germany in a peace treaty, the Franco-German Treaty of Friendship (1963). The ensuing Paris–Bonn entente has dominated the European Community ever since, withstanding all subsequent changes including the expansion of the Community, the collapse of communism, and the unification of Germany. British foreign policy, by contrast, remained in a state of permanent indecision, wavering between a 'special relationship' with the United States (which appeared to bring no clear advantage) and establishing a constructive presence within the European Community.

In general West European countries in possession of large empires were able to withdraw from their colonies without excessive internal commotion. Some *ex post facto* interpretations attributed this to the far-sightedness of their leaders and the good sense of their citizens. In reality the weakness of European countries was so manifest that most colonies were lost with minimal resistance. The political and economic costs of keeping colonies had become unnecessary, since many of the gains could continue without direct control. In some areas, such as Indonesia and Indo-China, decolonization was turned into a cold war issue because the independence movement was pro-communist.

Only two regime changes can be directly attributed to the loss of colonies. One was the collapse of the Portuguese dictatorship in 1974; the other was the end of the French Fourth Republic. This occurred in 1958, half-way through the Algerian War (1954–62), after a revolt by right-wing extremists in Algeria. De Gaulle was called back to power and a government of national unity was formed (without the communists). It took a further four years to reach a peace agreement with the Algerian liberation movement. The crisis led to a reshaping of the French political system towards presidentialism: the Fifth Republic.

This relatively minor change was the only political innovation of note in a Western democracy since the start of the cold war. In the East stability was enforced by a mixture of repression and concessions.

The radical 1960s

It is tempting to counterpoise the radical 1960s to the conservative 1950s. The evidence, at least in so far as Western Europe is concerned, is impressive. From Helsinki to Rome, from London to Bonn, the forces of the left, which had been excluded from power during the 1950s, staged a comeback. The end of ideology, announced in the late 1950s, turned out not to have arrived, or not yet, as Marx, Lenin, Trotsky, Mao, and other revolutionaries were rediscovered by new generations of young intellectuals. The embourgeoisement of the working class, object of many well-funded studies, did not prevent workers from staging militant strikes in 1960–3 and, more widely, in the late 1960s.

In Great Britain, after thirteen years of Conservative rule, a Labour government was returned in 1964, was re-elected with a greatly increased majority in 1966, and remained in power until 1970. In Italy in 1960 there was popular resistance to a half-hearted attempt by the right wing of the DC to seek neo-fascist parliamentary support. This accelerated the constitution in 1963 of a centre-left coalition between the DC and the PSI. In the FRG the Social Democratic Party (SPD) finally acceded to power. This occurred in two stages: a *grosse Koalition* with the CDU in 1966, followed by an SPD-led coalition with the Liberal Party in 1969, which lasted until 1982. In Sweden the hegemony of the social democrats was further confirmed: they were in power uninterruptedly until 1976.

In Austria, Denmark, and Norway the record was more mixed; nevertheless, the left was usually the dominant force throughout the 1960s. It is true that the Socialist Party of Austria (SPÖ) was a junior coalition partner until it was forced into opposition in 1966, but it regained power in 1970 and ruled on its own between 1971 and 1983, in coalition with the Freedom Party until 1987 (when this party was taken over by the far right), and after 1987 and until 1999 with the People's Party (ÖVP, the Catholic party). The Danish left was in government until 1968, when it lost power, but was back in office in 1971. In Norway the Labour Party was out of power between 1965 and 1971. In Finland socialists and communists were in government together between 1966 and 1971. In Belgium the socialists were the junior partners in most coalition governments between 1960 and 1973.

Elsewhere during the 1960s the left was less successful. In the Netherlands it was almost uninterruptedly out of office. In France socialists and communists were out of power throughout the 1960s and 1970s. It was this anomalous situation that compelled the French left to sink their differences and form a common front against the ruling Gaullists.

Thus, with the exception of France and the Netherlands, the left achieved far better results in the 1960s than in the 1950s. It was as if capitalist successes—accelerated economic growth and greater wealth—had led to a radicalization of the political climate rather than its reverse. Nevertheless, the shift towards the left should not be over-emphasized.

In the first place the European electorates exhibited remarkable stability. The total share of the vote which parties of the left—socialist, social-democratic, and communist—obtained in the 1960s was roughly the same as that obtained during the 1950s, as Table 2.1 makes clear. The left's progress towards government was the result not of electoral gains but of its ability to find coalition partners. In Britain, where the electoral system makes coalition governments difficult, the Labour Party was able to win the 1964 and 1966 elections not because it did better than in 1951, but because the Conservative Party lost votes to the Liberal Party. Labour, in fact, had obtained a larger percentage of the vote in 1951 (when it lost) than at any other time before or since, including 1997. Italian, Belgian, Finnish, Austrian, and German socialists gained office because they had been able to form governments with parties on their right. Political alliances had shifted while the electorate stood still.

TABLE 2.1 The left's average share of the vote (%, rounded)

Country	1950–9	1960–9	Country	1950–9	1960–9
Austria	48	45	Italy	42	45
Belgium	40	35	Netherlands	35	29
Denmark	42	48	Norway	52	51
Finland	48	48	Sweden	50	53
France	42	43	United Kingdom	46	46
FRG	31	39	Average for decade	43.27	43.87

In the second place the gains made by the left were not translated into radical structural reforms. This disappointed many of its most committed supporters, who had expected substantial changes in economic policy. In reality the left's room for manoeuvre was severely restricted. It could obtain power only through coalition and/or without frightening marginal voters (as in the UK). This entailed an acceptance that the basic economic arrangements of society should be left unchanged. High growth, by making the majority more prosperous, lessened the pressures for redistribution of wealth and power. Socialists came to terms with the capitalist order. Some announced it openly, as did the SPD at their Bad Godesberg congress in 1959; others did it tacitly to avoid offending their most committed followers.

Contrary to common perceptions, high taxes did not correlate with socialism in power. It is true that they were high in social-democratic Sweden, but so were they in the conservative Netherlands. The entry of the PSI into the Italian government made no difference to the very low levels of taxation in Italy. Belgian tax rates (constantly increasing) were not affected by the presence or absence from power of the socialists. The increase in Austrian taxation occurred mainly in the period of coalition between the SPÖ and the ÖVP (when they could not be punished by the electorate). In Britain taxation did increase under Labour in 1964–70, though to just below the level it had been under the Conservatives in 1957.[10]

Another common perception for which there is no evidence is that the left spends lavishly on social services while reducing defence expenditure. In fact throughout the 1960s the proportion of expenditure on defence decreased everywhere, while that on social services increased. And this was true in social-democratic Sweden and Denmark as well as in the conservative Netherlands and Gaullist France.[11] In other words, the 1960s represented a shift to the left in economic and social policy throughout Western Europe: stabilization of the welfare state, full employment, transfer of public spending from defence to social spending. That this could be achieved by both centre-right and centre-left coalitions suggests that policy shifts depend not simply on the political ideology of the parties in power,

---

[10] See data in P. Flora (ed.), *State, Economy and Society in Western Europe 1815–1975: A Data Handbook*, (London: Macmillan 1983) i. 262.

[11] Ibid., ch. 8.

but on wider social and economic circumstances, such as the wealth and prosperity of a country.

Much has been made of the student unrest of the late 1960s as the harbinger of wider political change. The unrest itself was rather circumscribed. It was high and intense only in France in May 1968 and only because of the lengthy general strike that followed it. It had no immediate political effect except the dissolution of parliament, elections, and the return of the previous government with a massively increased majority. It is true that one year later de Gaulle was forced to resign, having lost a referendum on institutional reform. Gaullism, however, proved longer-lasting than its founder. The students' and workers' movement had weakened the old general and demonstrated that he was not politically invincible, but had failed to modify in any way the structures of the Fifth Republic. Elsewhere the movement was much more subdued (Germany) or virtually non-existent (Britain).

In Italy, however, the student movement was the catalyst for the longest wave of working-class militancy ever recorded in post-war Europe: the Hot Autumn of 1969. This contributed to social and institutional reforms which the centre-left governments of the 1960s had been unable to achieve. In the early 1970s power in Italy was devolved to the regions, a highly redistributive system of wage indexation (the *scala mobile*) was introduced, while a workers' charter (*statuto dei lavoratori*) entrenched unprecedented labour rights in the workplace; divorce was legalized and family law modernized.

The longer-term consequences of the student movement in Europe were probably more far-reaching than its immediate political effects. Some of the student groups degenerated into left-wing terrorist organizations, but were of little importance except perhaps in Germany (the Baader-Meinhof band) and, above all, in Italy (the Red Brigade). By the mid-1980s they had all been comprehensively defeated. Otherwise terrorism remained a prerogative of right-wing groups, as in Italy, or the expression of extreme nationalism—as in Northern Ireland and the Basque country. It is more fruitful to regard the student movement not as the cause of subsequent transformations but as part of a wider change in values in the mid- to late 1960s, as the post-war generation grew to adulthood. These new cohorts were distinctive from their parents and grandparents. They were more numerous, thanks to the baby boom of the late 1940s.

They were richer, thanks to the capitalist growth of the late 1950s and early 1960s. They were more culturally autonomous, having formed the first mass teenage consumer market in history. They were better educated, thanks to the formidable expansion of education. They were less worried about their future, thanks to a long peace and full employment. They were less sexually restricted because their own parents had experienced, during the war, a fragmentation of traditional values and because contraceptives for women, especially the Pill, had become widely available.

Few of the conditions favouring such youthful discontent existed in Eastern and Central Europe: a consumer society able to supply a teenage market was either rudimentary (Hungary, Czechoslovakia, and the GDR) or non-existent. Overt repression made it difficult, if not impossible, to organize free from party control. A student movement did emerge in Prague in 1968, but, unlike any of its Western counterparts, it was entirely supportive of the new reforming communists led by Alexander Dubček, who had wrested the leadership of the Czech Communist Party from the pro-Soviet group of Antonín Novotný. Its new Action Programme of 5 April 1968 criticized the previous rulers and advocated major reforms: wider scope for market relations, more representative political institutions, and greater tolerance of dissent. The party prudently reaffirmed its loyalty to the USSR and its commitment to the Warsaw Pact. In spite of these precautions, aimed at avoiding a repetition of the Hungarian events of 1956, Soviet troops marched into Czechoslovakia on 20 August and re-established a pro-Soviet administration.

This destroyed the possibility of 'socialism with a human face'. It now seemed that any significant reform of communism could only originate within the Soviet Union itself—which is what Gorbachev attempted in the 1980s, though far too late to save the system. Some of the economic reforms mooted by Dubček were partly inspired by Soviet plans outlined in the late 1950s and early 1960s. These aimed at introducing some elements of market mechanism into the determination of prices, while giving managers greater freedom of decision. The removal of Khrushchev in 1964 and his replacement by the far less innovative leadership of Leonid Brezhnev ended this experiment. What the Russians themselves later called 'the period of stagnation' aspired to freeze the whole of Eastern and Central Europe.

The convergence of Western Europe 1970–1991

The 1970s and 1980s, compared to the previous two decades, witnessed the most comprehensive changes in post-war Europe. The resulting state system exhibited astonishing convergence, unparalleled in history: by 1991 liberal democracy and the mixed economy had become the norm throughout most of Europe. The most salient features of this period can be grasped under the concept of closure, or 'end of an era'. It was the end of the Bretton Woods system (1971–3). It was the end of the right-wing dictatorships in Greece, Spain, and Portugal (1974–6). It was the end of the dominance of the Keynesian assumption that national policies of macroeconomics management could safeguard nation states against prolonged recessions and excessive unemployment. Above all, it was the end of communism in Europe, and of the cold war (1989–91).

Last but not least, new values swept through most of Western Europe: in the fifteen years or so from the late 1960s to the early 1980s divorce and abortion became legal, capital punishment was abolished, homosexuality was no longer an offence, censorship barriers were much reduced, and discrimination against women was made illegal. European convergence did not proceed simply by removing economic impediments to trade or establishing new political institutions. It was advanced by a largely unplanned drive towards the harmonization of social rights and values. A common definition of modernity emerged which defined a civilized society as one where self-expression, including sexuality, was an important individual right and where women should not be unquestioningly subordinated to men. This helped to bridge the cultural gap between countries like Portugal, Greece, and Spain and the well-established democracies in the north. Religious authorities were forced to concede to modern ideas, as they had for well over one hundred years. The resistance they put up was timid: they too were in the midst of a major redefinition of their role in the modern world.

One by one the pillars of post-war boom collapsed. The fixed convertibility of the dollar into gold—the cornerstone of the Bretton Woods system—disintegrated on 15 August 1971. Then, in December that year, the dollar was devalued, and on 19 March 1973 it was decided to allow exchange rates to float, thus effectively terminating the Bretton Woods system.

This coincided with the end of another pillar of the long boom, cheap oil. The rise in oil prices was so drastic and dramatic (it coincided with the 1973 Yom Kippur War between Egypt and Israel) that in the popular imagination the great inflationary spiral of the 1970s was seen as a direct consequence of OPEC's decision to raise the price of oil. In fact the length of the recession suggests that, at most, the OPEC crisis was a trigger or catalyst of a wider predicament.

The rise in oil prices created difficulties for all West European countries but particularly for Greece, Spain, and Portugal, as did the waning of US power after its defeat in Vietnam and the resignation of Nixon in the wake of the Watergate scandal. Each of the dictatorships had a different history, yet all collapsed in the mid-1970s. The first to collapse, in 1974, was Portugal, the oldest regime (1926). Later in the same year it was the turn of the Greek colonels, who had taken over in 1967. The last to go was that of the dictator Francisco Franco, extant since his victory in 1939. All three had been under increasing pressure to modernize, reform, and liberalize, not only by their increasingly discontented intelligentsia, but by their own bourgeoisie, anxious to be accepted into the European Community. In Spain the catalyst of change was the death of Franco, and the decision of his designated successor, King Juan Carlos, to become the guarantor and promoter of a peaceful transition to democratic rule. In Portugal the end of the regime was achieved thanks to a coup led by left-wing officers radicalized by a lengthy and unwinnable war in the country's African colonies. In Greece a failed foreign adventure, the Cyprus affair of the summer of 1974, precipitated the fall of the colonels.

In all three instances a mediating political figure belonging to the old order appeared to guarantee a relatively painless changeover: General António de Spínola in Portugal, King Juan Carlos and his prime minister, Adolfo Suárez, in Spain, and Kostantinos Karamanlis in Greece. Socialists, unlike the communists, played only a minor role in the clandestine struggle against dictatorship in Portugal and in Spain (after the civil war). They had been virtually non-existent in Greece before the military takeover. In all these countries socialist parties eventually emerged as the dominant national political force, easily displacing the communists. The three socialist politicians associated with this unquestionable success—Mário Soares in Portugal, Andreas Papandreou in Greece, and Felipe González in Spain—either were themselves the founders of their parties (Papandreou and Soares) or had taken it over shortly before the end of the regime (González). These 'new' men were the great victors of the transition, the representatives of a novel brand of Mediterranean socialism that emerged just as some of the well-established British and German parties were about to enter a long period of opposition.

Southern communists too were on the move. The Italian Communist Party, the PCI—by far the largest in Western Europe—had for years expressed its dissatisfaction at Soviet tutelage and had condemned Moscow's intervention in Czechoslovakia. Under the leadership of Enrico Berlinguer it sought to acquire that international and national legitimacy whose absence had for long impeded its access to power. Its new strategy uncannily retraced the steps taken earlier by the German social democrats. The SPD had accepted NATO in 1960. Berlinguer did the same in 1976. The SPD first entered government as a junior coalition partner of the Christian Democrats. Berlinguer offered to do the same, suggesting, in 1973, a 'historic compromise' with the DC. Massive electoral gains in 1975 and 1976 and a more flexible approach by the DC seemed, wrongly as it turned out, to open the way for a return to power of the tripartite coalition that had collapsed in 1947.

The left appeared to be advancing throughout the 1970s. It was now widely accepted that the inflation prevailing at the time could be controlled only in concert with the trade unions, whose cooperation the parties of the left were the best placed to obtain. Countries with moderate trade unions and powerful social-democratic parties, such as Germany, Austria, and Sweden, had relatively low levels of inflation, though this was true also of Belgium and the Netherlands, where social democrats were not particularly strong. It was assumed by most political opinion-makers that modern market economies could best be managed through regular negotiation between employers' associations, trade unions, and governments.

Throughout the 1970s unemployment was still regarded by conservatives as well as socialists as a greater threat to social stability than the rapidly developing inflation. The British Conservative government under Edward Heath, elected in 1970, started with the idea that a retreat of the state from the economy would lead to the vigorous development of market forces. It soon returned to the fold, frightened by a seemingly unstoppable rise in unemployment. However, it failed to secure the cooperation of the trade unions, and in the 1974 elections, fought during a lengthy miners' strike, narrowly lost to Labour. This seemed to confirm the widely held view that West European economies could not be governed successfully if the unions were disregarded.

The existence of powerful social and economic constraints reducing the differences between right and left were further confirmed in 1976, when a coalition of 'bourgeois' parties gained power in Sweden for the first time in the post-war period. Far from signalling a departure in economic policy, they soon proved as enthusiastic about preserving the Swedish model of full employment as their defeated social-democratic opponents.

It was in West Germany, above all, that the hegemony of social democracy in the 1970s appeared to be unchallengeable. In 1972 the SPD's share of the vote had overtaken, for the first time in post-war history, the CDU. Germany's powerful economic machine enabled the government to withstand some of the negative effects of its own interdependence with the global economy, so that it outperformed its main competitors in terms of inflation rates and balance of payments. Understandably, the SPD claimed that it had uncovered the secret of economic management. The slogan of *Modell Deutschland* was born. This model possessed three distinguishing features: an industrial policy aimed at managing the decline of the old industries and the promotion of the new high-technology, knowledge-based industries; a social policy aimed at ensuring that this transition would not have negative social effects; and a corporatist policy aimed at achieving a consensual outlook between employers and trade unions.[12] The contrast with strike-prone Britain could not have been more profound. Between 1973 and 1979 German inflation averaged 4.7 per cent, less than half the OECD-Europe average (11.9 per cent), while that of Britain hovered at a spectacular 15.6 per cent. While German social democrats gloated, in Britain the Labour government appeared to be presiding over the final decline of the British

---

[12] Josef Esser and Wolfgang Fach, '"Social Market" and Modernization Policy: West Germany', in Kenneth Dyson and Stephen Wilks (eds.), *Industrial Crisis* (Oxford: Blackwell 1983), 103.

economy, as its special relationship with the trade unions (the 'social contract') collapsed under a wave of strikes in the winter of 1978–9, paving the way for the victory of Margaret Thatcher's Conservative Party.

In spite of its undoubted achievements in withstanding the first oil shock, the SPD was unable to withstand the second (1979). Unemployment grew, while the Bundesbank pursued its own restrictive policy, which compounded the problem. In 1982 the SPD's allies the Free Democrats (FDP) changed sides, enabling the CDU to return to government, where they remained for sixteen years.

By the 1980s the left was in retreat in Germany and in Britain. In Southern Europe it was more successful. For the first time in the postwar period the French left found itself united and in power. The historic supremacy of the communists within the French left had been reversed. The candidate of the socialists, François Mitterrand, became president in 1981. His rule lasted fourteen years (he was re-elected in 1988), the longest in the history of republican France. The Socialist Party (PS) secured an absolute majority and remained in power until 1993 except for a brief span (1986–8) when a socialist president (Mitterrand) shared power (*la cohabitation*) with a Gaullist prime minister (Jacques Chirac). The socialists started their period in power with a bang: they nationalized large sectors of finance and manufacturing, reflated the economy, and decentralized power. However, the ensuing inflation and balance of power deficit forced them to change tack. The fact that a strong economy such as that of France had found its independence seriously curtailed by international constraints helps to explain why the socialist governments of González in Spain and Papandreou in Greece disappointed their more radical supporters. Nevertheless, the three countries, particularly Spain, bridged much of the economic and social gap that had separated them from the richer countries of the north.

In Italy the Italian communists were forced to abandon the strategy of the 'historic compromise'. Their smaller rivals, the socialists, chose to strengthen their own alliance with Christian democracy, thus keeping their communist rivals in permanent opposition. Their leader, Bettino Craxi, was prime minister from August 1983 to March 1987—by Italian standards a lengthy period. Little was achieved, however, by the Italian socialists, beyond their contribution to the growth of corruption.

National peculiarities aside, Western Europe continued to converge, a process facilitated by the development of a new post-social-democratic outlook. Just as the ideological pioneers of post-war social democracy had been the British Labour governments of 1945–51, the pathbreakers of the revival of neo-liberalism were the British Conservative governments led by Margaret Thatcher (1979–90) and her somewhat less charismatic successor, John Major (1990–7).

Ideological consistency can hardly ever be found in governing parties. The weight of traditions, the requirements of electoral politics, and the pressures of external constraints force the staunchest ideologues to water their wine. Thatcherism followed this rule. Its overt commitment to market forces coexisted with a passionate defence of traditional values. Nevertheless, Thatcher's Britain established in a somewhat extreme form the basic operational principles of practical neo-liberalism: the fight against inflation became the overall priority of economic policy; unemployment was regarded as a tolerable evil—indeed, in some quarters it was viewed as an ally in the containment of trade union power and in the fight against inflation; the growth in public spending had to be curtailed and, if possible, halted; direct taxation was to be reduced, even though this meant increasing indirect taxes; public-sector companies were to be privatized wherever possible; the welfare state had to be reformed so as to contain costs; the development of market forces should be facilitated by making markets more flexible—often a euphemism for eliminating employment protection legislation.

By the early 1990s this new *Zeitgeist* was well in place throughout Western Europe. Social democrats, Christian democrats, and 'one-nation' conservatives such as the French Gaullists, though unwilling and unable to match the free-market rhetoric of unadulterated Thatcherism, had accepted parts of the neo-liberal platform. Socialists moved rapidly towards the centre ground; many of them had never left it. As traditional social democracy found itself under growing attack in the West, in the East more momentous changes were taking place.

The end of communism in Europe

The appointment of Mikhail Gorbachev as secretary-general of the Communist Party of the USSR (CPSU) in 1985 heralded five years of unprecedented reforms. These led to the dismantling and collapse of communism throughout Eastern and Central Europe. Gorbachev appeared quite different from the grey men who had preceded him, although the need for radical change had long been discussed within the Soviet establishment. Paradoxically it was the enormity of the change required that prevented its implementation before the late 1980s. Political elites are always cautious, ready to innovate only when they assume they can control the consequences of new policies. As early as the mid-1960s it had become apparent to many insiders that there was a serious decline in economic performance. Standards in housing, services, and material production, instead of rising, as the people expected and official propaganda announced ineffectually, were in steady decline.[13] Labour productivity remained depressed, life expectancy plunged—unprecedentedly in an industrial economy. Corruption became widespread, especially in the Asian republics of the USSR. Military spending became ever more unsustainable as the country desperately attempted to keep up with the US military machine. Other communist economies, with the exception of Hungary, were not performing much better.

Overt opposition to the regime was confined to relatively small circles of dissident intellectuals, well-known in the West, but rather ineffectual in the East. Paradoxically the changes which led to the end of communism were initiated by the very forces that the ruling ideology itself had glorified: the organized working class (as in Poland) and the vanguard party of the vanguard country: the CPSU.

By 1985 it had become recognized by almost the entire Soviet establishment that Western market capitalism was superior to the so-called planned economies. Gorbachev's nomination was, in some

---

[13] Z. A. B. Zeman, *The Making and Breaking of Communist Europe* (Oxford: Blackwell, 1991), 267 ff.

respects, the 'ideological . . . revenge of the Sixties' generation' and of the 'liberal communism' of the Khrushchev era.[14]

Similar views had become commonplace elsewhere in the Eastern bloc since the Prague Spring, and nowhere more than in Poland, which had become so heavily indebted to the West that by 1980 it could barely meet its obligations. Major sectors of Polish manufacturing had become dependent on Western supplies. A parallel dollar economy had developed. An increasingly bankrupt communist administration was compelled to increase meat prices in 1976, but widespread unrest forced them to cave in. The government's loss of legitimacy was further confirmed in 1979, when the newly elected Polish pope, John Paul II (Karol Wojtyla), visited the country, drawing enthusiastic crowds.

In July 1980 the government, by then desperate, tried once again to impose a price rise. This unleashed massive strikes in August 1980. The manifest weakness of the regime enabled the creation of a new trade union movement, Solidarity. Led by Lech Wałesa, it spread rapidly from the Lenin shipyard in Gdańsk. By September 1980, according to the unions themselves, membership had expanded to 3 million. By October 1981 it stood at 9.4 million out of a total workforce of 12.5 million in the nationalized sector of the economy.[15] In practice the monopoly of power of the party had been broken. It was obvious to the Soviet Politburo that the 'infection' would soon spread. Solidarity threatened not merely Soviet power but also that of communist leaders in the rest of the Eastern bloc, especially in the GDR and in Czechoslovakia. The Polish communists reached a temporary compromise with Solidarity, leading to its formal recognition as a 'registered' trade union (November 1980). But the union continued to challenge communist rule until, perhaps fearing direct Soviet intervention, the government established martial law, arrested Wałesa, and banned Solidarity.

The Polish events were the most acute symptom of the wider crisis facing the Soviet bloc and, in particular, the USSR. The rise of Gorbachev must be seen as a last-ditch attempt to solve problems which had been accumulating over many years. At first it was believed that the socialist essence of the system could be preserved by introducing

---

[14] Boris Kagarlisky, 'The Importance of Being Marxist', *New Left Review*, 178 (Nov–Dec. 1989), 29.

[15] Oliver MacDonald, 'The Polish Vortex', *New Left Review*, 139 (May–July 1983), 17.

elements of democracy and openness (glasnost), allowing greater room for market forces, and combating corruption (perestroika). Gorbachev's exhortations were not widely endorsed by a diffident population. By June 1988 he had come to the conclusion that only a massive redefinition of Soviet democracy would shake up the system. He announced that there would be free elections to a revamped parliament. That decision sealed the fate of perestroika. The system could no longer be reformed. The elections of March 1989 produced a multiplicity of power centres, both in Russia itself, where Boris Yeltsin emerged as Gorbachev's main rival, and in the other Soviet republics, where former communists recycled themselves as democrats and/or nationalists. Gorbachev had lost control. In the summer of 1991 a botched attempt by conservatives to take over the country led directly to the declaration by Boris Yeltsin, now president of the Russian Republic, of Russia's independence. In practice the USSR had ceased to exist.

By then communism had already collapsed in most of Eastern and Central Europe. Political parties had been legalized in Hungary in January 1989. In April it was the turn of Solidarity, which went on to win all the seats bar one in the new Polish senate (albeit on a very low turnout). In May the Czech dissident writer Václav Havel was freed; later he became the first post-communist president. In September the border between Hungary and Austria was opened, enabling East Germans to reach West Germany via Austria. The Berlin Wall, no longer an effective barrier, was breached in November, paving the way for the reunification of Germany in October 1990. By the end of 1989 the so-called Iron Curtain had been demolished. Communist power was at an end.

Western Europe stood, bemused, watching the events unfold. The 'war' between East and West had remained 'cold' throughout, and the West had won it without firing a single shot.

Germany emerged as the dominant country of the new Europe, thanks to its size, wealth, and geographical position. The German chancellor, Helmut Kohl, proceeded to reassure his Western allies. Germany would not take advantage of its new power. It would not go it alone. The country's fate was indissolubly linked to that of the European Community. Integration proceeded with a new sense of urgency as the member countries signed the Maastricht Treaty on 7 February 1992. Its object was economic and social cohesion through the establishment of economic and monetary union.

The fifteen members of the Community, now called the European Union, were the richest countries in Europe (along with Iceland, Norway, and Switzerland, still outside the EU). They constituted the largest single market in the world. Their social problems—unemployment, welfare reform, growing poverty, social exclusion—though endlessly discussed by Western political parties jockeying for power, were regarded by the citizens of the former communist countries as mild ailments compared with their own lamentable conditions. It is thus not surprising if they assumed that a rapid transition to market economies on the basis of the neo-liberal principles then dominant in the West would produce the thriving consumer society they so ardently desired.

They were to be disappointed. In the years between 1989 and 1997 real gross domestic product decreased throughout the former Eastern bloc. In Russia and in the former Yugoslavia it nearly halved. In the same period the number of crimes recorded doubled in Russia and Hungary, trebled in the Czech Republic, and increased sixfold in Bulgaria and Romania.[16] Wages decreased everywhere except in the Czech Republic. Much of this was due to the collapse of Comecon trade and the burden of debt repayment. Moreover, they faced EU trade barriers. What the former communist countries produced was of little interest to the West; what they wished to import from the West they could not afford. Their main resource was cheap labour, and so they became highly dependent on inward investments from the West. To obtain them, however, they had to demolish the rigid labour markets and the pattern of strong social protection inherited from the previous communist regimes. This was a recipe for instability.

The former communist parties had recycled themselves as new social-democratic parties, accepting many of the principles of Western social democracy. In Poland and Hungary communist parties had promoted market forces well before the collapse of communism. In Poland, Hungary, Slovakia, Romania, and Bulgaria (but not in the Czech Republic after 1996) they became the main parties of the left in the first wave of democratic elections. This suggests that communism

---

[16] Michael Haynes and Rumy Husan, 'The State and Market in the Transition Economies: Critical Remarks in the Light of Past History and the Current Experience', *Journal of European Economic History*, 27/3 (Winter 1998), 637–9.

did have a popular basis, though a minority one, in most of the former Eastern bloc countries, unlike the supporters of the former right-wing regimes of Spain, Portugal, and Greece, who were electorally pulverized in all subsequent elections.[17]

By the end of the century the new political systems that emerged in the former communist countries resembled those of continental Western Europe: a centre-left bloc of parties facing a centre-right bloc, an electoral system with an element of proportionality, a written constitution, and an expanding private sector. Their external policies shared a central objective: a more or less rapid integration into the EU and the Atlantic Alliance. Indeed, in 1998 Poland, Hungary, and the Czech Republic had been accepted inside the Atlantic Alliance. Entry into the EU is likely to prove a far more complex and protracted operation.

Clouds over Europe's future

The fall of the Berlin Wall and the peaceful transition to post-communism appeared to have heralded an optimistic future for Europe. It seemed as if the alignment of all post-communist societies with the social and economic model of the West was only a matter of time. But the Western countries had considerable problems of their own.

In the first place their own model of social cohesion was under threat partly because of high levels of unemployment and partly because the perceived recalcitrance of taxpayers had led the main political parties to compete over who would be the most enthusiastic tax-cutter. West European states were under substantial pressure to align themselves, in turn, to the US model, with its low level of unemployment but high inequalities and disturbing social problems. It was probably because of this widely perceived threat to the welfare states that had protected them for so long that the electorates of most West European countries turned to the parties of the left. By the end

---

[17] See Peter Gowan, 'The Post Communist Socialists in Eastern and Central Europe', in Donald Sassoon (ed.), *Looking Left: European Socialism after the Cold War* (London: Tauris, 1997), 143–76.

of the century almost all the member states of the EU had centre-left governments and socialist prime ministers, including for the first time in history, the four largest countries, Germany, Great Britain, France, and Italy.

Secondly, business and enterprise had become more popular than ever before. It was now accepted that there was nothing shameful in uninhibited money-making (a preconception shared by the traditional left as well as by the traditional right). But the turn towards a more robust kind of capitalism had been accompanied by a remarkable growth in political corruption. Countries where this had been relatively rare in the recent past, such as Britain, were forced to set up mechanisms to combat it. Italy, where political corruption had been endemic, saw such an escalation of corruption that the resulting unparalleled wave of scandals resulted in the collapse of most of the parties that had dominated the country since the war (1992–4). 'Sleaze' of one sort or the other had also permeated the European Commission, which was forced to resign en masse in 1999.

Thirdly, while the main political parties of Western Europe remained firmly committed to maintaining and protecting democratic rule in all its aspects, there was a substantial growth in the electoral support for far-right xenophobic parties. Protected by its electoral system, Britain appeared to escape this trend, at the cost, however, of witnessing a development of Little England nationalism within the Conservative Party. In Italy the post-fascist Alleanza Nazionale, a pariah party until the early 1990s, was even able to enter the government of Silvio Berlusconi of 1994–6, though it did refrain from overt xenophobia. Others were far less inhibited, notably the two strongest far-right parties in Europe: the Austrian Freedom Party led by Jörg Haider and the French Front National led by Jean-Marie Le Pen.

Fourthly, there was a recrudescence of nationalism and regionalist movements which threatened the existence of the hitherto stable European nation states. In Britain Scottish and, to a lesser extent, Welsh nationalism had forced the Labour Party (in power after 1997) to support devolution and a degree of autonomy. In Spain Catalan nationalism was similarly placated (with, in addition, generous financial provisions). In Belgium, Flanders and Wallonia became separate entities in most domestic political matters. In Italy the growth of a populist northern movement, the Lega Nord, forced all political parties to envisage devolving more power to the regions. Such developments tended to break down national solidarity as the citizens of the more prosperous areas (Flanders, Catalonia, northern Italy) were increasingly reluctant to see any further transfer of resources towards the poorer areas.

Such problems were far more severe in Eastern Europe as nationalism, no longer contained by the universalist aspirations or pretensions of communism, resurfaced. Important minorities felt threatened. It appeared as if the defence of the rights of Russian-speakers in some of the Baltic republics and in the Ukraine might become a rallying-cry for Russian nationalists. In Hungary 10 per cent of the population was not Magyar, while 4 million Hungarians lived as minorities in other countries. This potentially explosive mixture coexisted with a strong desire to be admitted into the developed capitalist order, to 'join the West', in order to enjoy the security of higher standards of living and democratic rights. Nowhere was this more evident than in the former Yugoslavia.

Yugoslavia was the least 'communist' of the socialist countries. Thanks to tourism, emigration, and government borrowing from the international financial community, its population was well acquainted with Western lifestyles. In the early 1990s the richer areas, Slovenia and Croatia, began to move towards separation, encouraged by the West and by the nationalist demagogy of the Serbian leader, Slobodan Milošović. The doctrine of an ethnic state re-emerged. Consequently, all members of ethnic minorities were liable to become second-class citizens from one day to the next. A pattern of ethnic cleansing emerged. This was relatively effortless in Slovenia, whose population was fairly homogeneous. It was far more complex for Croatia, which eventually expelled its own Serbian minority. It was virtually impossible for Bosnia, which became a war zone between contending Croatians, Serbs, and Bosnian Muslims. Once Croatia and Slovenia had become independent in 1991, with the support of the West, Bosnia could not risk remaining part of a Yugoslavia dominated by Serbia, but its own independence was opposed by its own Serb minority, who sought to control as much land as possible—encouraged by Serbia. In Kosovo, an autonomous province of Serbia until 1989, when Milošović revoked its special statute, the Albanian majority became increasingly alarmed. Fear of being a minority in a country where ethnicity had become the main form of identity helps to explain the extraordinary violence that pervaded a region at peace since 1945.

The West, in the guise of NATO, was dragged into these Balkan disputes, without an overall strategy. The Atlantic Alliance, originally aimed at containing Soviet power, found itself rapidly forced to police the debris of the defeated empire. In fifty years of existence it had not fired a single bullet against communism. It now found itself involved in policing activities, peace-keeping missions, and even armed combat (as was the case in Kosovo in 1999), without ascertaining whether the Balkan crisis could be speedily and definitively resolved without destabilizing the entire region.

Growing nationalism is not the only threat to European prosperity and stability. The continuing economic and political degeneration of the Russian Federation, unless stopped, may turn out to constitute a greater peril than ever was posed by the USSR. The solution of the Russian question remains the most important task facing Europe in the twenty-first century.

In the second half of the twentieth century the United States and Western Europe were able to resolve the German question by contributing to its successful economic recovery and success. German political stability became a guarantee for a lasting peace. Unless some solution is found for Russia, and its people are made to feel secure and prosperous, it is doubtful whether the rest of Europe can look to the future without foreboding.

3

Social history

Hartmut Kaelble

European societies in the second half of the twentieth century were characterized by extraordinary, to some extent intended, social dynamics within a hot peace. This period had some quite particular social features, especially compared to the turbulent first half of the twentieth century.

First, this was an unusually long period of peace in Europe, but it lay in the shadow of one of the most catastrophic wars in European history, and also under the threat of intensive rearmament and of military conflicts in former European colonies. European society was first seen by Europeans through the lens of their experience of wartime, and was highly appreciated as a peacetime society. At the same time, peace was rarely seen as assured.

Secondly, because it was a lasting peace, this was an unusually dynamic period in social and other respects—far more dynamic than former periods of peacetime. The most distinctive economic boom of modern times was an essential part of this period, and the economic depression that followed was perhaps also the most dynamic in modern times. These social dynamics embraced all aspects of society: work and family, migration and inequality, values and institutions, state intervention and cities. More importantly, they embraced almost all European countries, and were not confined to the modernized areas of Europe. Hence, most younger Europeans in 2000 found it difficult to understand the life of their predecessors in 1945.

Thirdly, the Eastern part of Europe passed through one of the most far-reaching, ultimately unsuccessful, experiments in establishing and controlling a new society from above by centralized power. This experiment was begun in an earlier era, but only now did it become a worldwide phenomenon—not only in parts of Europe, but also in parts of Asia, Africa, and even America. Even in Western Europe, where the communist experiment was not established, it had a strong indirect impact, partly as a model of society and polity, but especially as a deterrent. As a consequence, Europe was never so clearly and fundamentally divided into two contrasting, antagonistic parts as in the second half of the twentieth century. What Europe as a whole meant in social terms as well as in other terms was rarely as unclear and fluid as it was then.

Fourthly, relations between society and politics changed profoundly in the minds of Europeans as well as in actual policies. Society became more central to politics in Eastern as well as Western Europe. The intervention of government in society was by no means new, but it took on new financial and legal dimensions and started to regulate the life of citizens much more intensively than before.

Finally, the relationship between societies in Europe and outside it changed profoundly. In 1945 Europe was for many Europeans still the hub of the world, the most advanced and civilized society, the pioneering model, and large parts of the world were still European colonies. In 2000 it was clear to most Europeans that their societies were dependent on worldwide trends, often called globalization, which Europe could influence but not control. Europe had become a quiet backwater of the world.

In most of these aspects, however, the end of the century does not look like a fundamental watershed, and it is not yet clear how long the trends of the second half of the twentieth century will last.

Was there a distinct Europe in social terms during this period? Around 1950 divisions rather than unity tended to prevail. Europe was divided in several respects. On the one hand there was the modern, industrialized, dynamic inner core, and, on the other, there was the more backward, still agrarian, more immobile periphery in Southern and Eastern Europe, and, in the extreme west and north, in Ireland and northern Scandinavia. In addition, Europe was divided by the social and economic after-effects of the Second World War. Some countries, such as Spain, Portugal, Sweden, Switzerland, and Ireland, had been left almost untouched by the war. A larger group of countries suffered from occupation by Nazi Germany and from direct warfare—the East and South-east European countries even more so than West or North European countries—while one single European country suffered heavily from warfare without being occupied: Great

Britain. A further group of countries, the aggressors, not only suffered from the economic and social after-effects of the war, but also faced the moral problem of their part in the war. More than any other country, this was true of Germany, whose government had started the war and had committed war crimes and genocide against the civil populations of the occupied countries. In addition, Europe was divided into two contradictory political and social systems: market-oriented, partly democratic Western Europe under the influence of the United States, and communist Eastern Europe under the control of the USSR. Finally, one often forgets that Europe until the 1950s and 1960s was still divided into colonial and non-colonial powers. In the colonial societies the future of bright and ambitious young men often lay beyond the borders of Europe in India, Algeria, Indonesia, or Africa. Social contact was often closer with countries outside Europe than within it.

It is important to note that these dividing lines did not coincide, but rather cut across one another. For all these reasons it was difficult for contemporaries to imagine Europe as a unity in social terms. However, because of the dynamics of the second half of the twentieth century and the upheaval of 1989–91 these internal European contrasts became less distinct, and Europe as a whole gradually gained more social and cultural contours in common.

The society we left behind: mid-twentieth-century Europe

Important elements of European societies around the middle of the twentieth century have become difficult to understand for Europeans today because of the social dynamics since then. Hence, before treating the processes of change in more detail, we need to recall what was unfamiliar about mid-twentieth-century European societies. At least nine social aspects that are now lost were still important for those societies.

Types of work which are now marginal were still important. Europe was still predominantly agrarian. To be sure, important European countries such as Britain, Germany, Belgium, Switzerland,

Austria, and Sweden, had already become industrial societies in the nineteenth century. But in Europe as a whole agriculture rather than industry was still the largest employment sector around 1950. According to estimates of the International Labour Office, 70 million of the working population of 180 million Europeans (not including the USSR) were active in agriculture, but only 61 million in industry.[1] Large European countries such as Spain, Italy, and Poland were still agrarian countries. In France the agrarian sector was not clearly smaller than the industrial sector. Moreover, to a substantial degree labour still meant family work on farms, in crafts, in retailing, in transport. Married couples worked together, often with their children or teenagers, and frequently with other family members. This was labour without a salary, without professional training, outside the labour market, outside modern labour relations, and outside the social security system. In addition, work around 1950 was still predominantly hard physical labour. Manual work was still widespread. Machines played a visible role, but even this kind of work was often physically exhausting. This was true of many workplaces, in mining and construction, for artisans and householders, for peasants and lorry drivers. Work-related disability and disease still noticeably shortened life expectancy. Many European cultural traditions such as painting and sculpture, heroic as well as critical, often portrayed male and female workers engaged in hard physical work.

The various mid-twentieth-century European family models were different from those of the present day. Men still played the dominant role in the family and the concept of a division of labour between the emotional, loving, tender mother and the strict, rational, breadwinning, father still prevailed in most European countries. Mothers rarely worked outside the family home in paid employment. The family structure was still seen as based on lifelong marriage with several children. Individual private space within the family was still very limited outside the small well-to-do sections of European societies. In many families neither parents nor children had a room of their own. At the same time, lack of space within the home was still compensated for by free social space outside, on streets and squares full of pedestrians, much less endangered by traffic than today. Life

---

[1] International Labour Office, *Economically Active Population*, 5 vols., 3rd edn. (Geneva: ILO 1986), v. 9, 123.

still took its traditional course, with a phase of intensive relations within the family, without kindergarten, up to the age of 6 or 7; schooling only until the age of 14; entry into the world of work; the beginnings of adulthood with military service for men and marriage for women; a long phase of parenthood; rarely an empty nest, i.e. a phase in which the parents were still alive after the children had left the family home. The family still played a crucial part in guaranteeing social security. However, in all these respects variations between European countries and regions were still enormous.

Life in Europe was still, to a substantial degree, based in the countryside or in small rural towns. Of course, urban industrial society was firmly established in inner Europe, and on average, about a third of the population of Western Europe lived in towns or cities of more than 20,000 inhabitants. But in Europe as a whole—not only in the periphery, but also in specific regions of industrialized countries—traditional rural life still existed: villages still consisted mainly of peasants or agricultural workers or fishermen. Rural upper classes consisting not only of large landowners but also of clergymen, doctors, teachers, foresters, were still powerful at least in local social terms. Agrarian work often meant living predominantly on the farm, with social contact almost exclusively with peasants and very few contacts at all in some regions and on isolated farms; and having little education beyond a few years of elementary school or no education at all. The exodus from rural areas that had been going on for decades rarely left deserted villages in its wake. Contrasts in lifestyle between rural and urban life were still enormous. Often urban dwellers still considered their national society to be predominantly rural, and still kept social links with rural kinship networks. To be sure, this rural society had changed dramatically, but it was not yet endangered by the threat of rural industrialization; or the urbanization of rural life, not just because of proximity to cities, but because of long-distance commuting; or changes brought about by the communication, transport, and consumption revolutions and by tourism and the rise of second homes.

In the industrialized European heartlands class societies still prevailed. Social distinctions were sharp between the middle classes and the working classes in matters of clothing, food, housing, leisure, property ownership, public space, and urban residential areas. Social networks and social solidarity, educational opportunities, and

upward social mobility rarely crossed class barriers. Class consciousness was strong among workers as well as in the middle classes. Social
class, however, was not the only social distinction that mattered a
great deal more than it does today. Social distinctions were deep, and
interconnections still rare between different religious milieus in
multidenominational countries such as Great Britain, the Netherlands, Germany, Switzerland, Czechoslovakia, Hungary, and Yugoslavia; between nationalities; between immigrants or refugees and
natives; and between family clans in small cities and villages. Europeans still largely accepted a strict conformity of lifestyle and values
within their various milieus.

European societies around 1950 were still societies of scarcity. This
was not just an after-effect of the war, but a general characteristic of
the continent up to the middle of the twentieth century. For the large
majority of Europeans the supply of consumer goods, as well as consumer values, were still far from those of an affluent society, though
the traditional cyclical hunger crises were gone during normal peacetime. Worn-out clothing was not thrown away, but mended. Durable
goods were usually produced for long time spans. The values of most
Europeans were oriented towards the prevention of waste. Hence,
European visitors to the United States had difficulty with the emerging American values of affluence. A European psychologist and emigrant to the United States, Erna Barschak, wrote in 1947 of American
affluence: 'The oversupply of food may explain, but can not justify,
the huge waste . . . I could not get accustomed to the half-full plates,
the leftover pieces of bread, butter, salads, eggs, which the indifferent
waitress cleared away.'[2]

The everyday perspective of the large majority of Europeans outside the upper classes was often still restricted to one locality or
region. Communication and mobility over longer distances was
much more restricted than today. The letter was still the most
important means of communication beyond personal encounters.
The telephone was used only by a small minority, varying from country to country, with only about five telephones per 100 inhabitants on
average. Except for the upper classes and special occupations or specific age groups, long-distance travel and holidays were also still rare.
Under normal circumstances most people had personal experience of

---

[2] E. Barschak, *Erlebnisse in USA* (Zurich: Pan Verlag 1947), 241–2.

no more than a small part of their country—often only the region in which they lived. Consumption rarely opened up a larger geographical perspective. Regional and national consumption styles were usually limited to the region or nation, and were rarely exported. Hence, consumption styles were much less cosmopolitan than they are now. Except for special commodities, food, clothing, furniture, and durable goods still came from domestic or very local producers. Many consumer goods were bought directly from the local producer. Nationwide and international commercialization was still limited, as were technical systems of food preservation, such as refrigerators, freezers, and deep freeze transportation. European life was far more local and regional, much less internationally open and cosmopolitan, than today.

Europe was still a continent of emigration, the last major wave occurring immediately after the Second World War. Several million emigrated, mainly to the Americas, between 1945 and 1950. Immigration into European countries came almost exclusively from other European countries, mainly from peripheral regions into the industrialized core of Europe. Immigration from outside Europe, from the Islamic part of the Mediterranean, or from European colonies overseas, generally faced no major legal obstacles as yet, but nevertheless hardly existed; contemporary Europeans could barely imagine it. One major reason was demography. In most European societies during peacetime birth rates were still higher than death rates, and natural population growth still prevailed.

Life in Europe was also much less secure. To be sure, social security systems were invented decades ago and partially established, especially in the northern parts of Europe, but only certain sectors of the national populations were in fact protected by such systems. It is estimated that only a third of the active population in Western Europe was covered by public pension insurance schemes, about a third by health insurance, and about the same by unemployment insurance. The majority still depended upon traditional charity institutions if they fell into poverty. Life was less secure in a more fundamental sense, too. Death was still more all-pervasive, not only during the war, but also in the ensuing peacetime. Not only was life expectancy clearly shorter than today; infant mortality was also far higher—on average about four times as high as it is currently.

The main periods of social history since 1945

Social history since 1945 can be subdivided into four periods: the immediate post-war era characterized by the after-effects of the Second World War; the era of economic prosperity from the 1950s to the early 1970s; the era of economic difficulties that followed; and the era following the political upheavals of 1989–91.

The post-war era

The immediate post-war era was characterized in large parts of Europe by extremely difficult living conditions, by hunger, over-crowded housing, by death, disability, or psychological disease, by enforced mobility, by the incapacity of collapsed economic markets and public services, and by a deep moral crisis especially in the Axis countries, strongest by far in Germany. Europe was often seen as a declining or even destroyed civilization.

It is crucial to an understanding of post-war European societies to realize that the direct social after-effects of the Second World War in many ways ran contrary to the general tenor of mid-twentieth-century European life described in the preceding section. This is what made post-war societies exceptional and, in the minds of contemporary Europeans, difficult to accept. In European societies affected by the war normal work was often devalued. Black market activities, smuggling, and unconventional ways of procuring food, clothing, and fuel became more important. For various reasons the family model also did not work as it had done. The role of mothers, and also of young people, became more important because of new material constraints and because of the absence or death of fathers. Divorce, illegitimacy, and prostitution became more frequent.

Enforced mobility transformed many formerly stable local European societies. Millions of Europeans were on the move: displaced persons, refugees, returning prisoners of war, detainees of concentration camps, forced labourers, returning soldiers, families who had been moved away from urban areas during the war or whose homes had been destroyed, dispersed family members in search of each other. In substantial parts of Europe indigenous local people had to accept incomers of different religious denominations, nationalities, customs, and dialects. Millions of Europeans, especially the men, had seen other countries as soldiers, as prisoners of war, as forced labourers.

The after-effects of war in some ways also challenged class societies. Class distinctions and other social hierarchies often could not be maintained in a situation characterized by scarcity of food, fuel, clothing, and housing. Nor could the traditional local separation of religious milieus be maintained. Established social security systems faced the huge and unknown task of providing a minimum standard of living for families adversely affected by the war: widows, orphans, the physically and psychologically disabled.

Thus the after-effects of war consisted not only of scarcity or lack of food, clothing, fuel, housing, and of destroyed families, but also of an enforced loss of crucial aspects of life. Most contemporaries saw this loss as temporary and wanted to return to the former state of society as rapidly as possible. Historians have debated whether the later social transformations were in fact caused by the direct after-effects of the war, or by the dynamics of the period after the immediate post-war era, to which I shall turn in a moment.

But the post-war era also had its dynamics. Crucial social reforms were started in this period in various countries. In Britain, France, the Scandinavian countries, the Netherlands, and Belgium the modern welfare state was initiated, with reforms of the health system and pension funds. Later on these reforms became the model for other European countries. In various countries this was also a period of fundamental reforms to the education system. As can be seen in Chapter 4, it was the beginning of a new international economic system, and new national economic policies were established, variously giving a stronger role to the state, as in France, or to the market, as in Germany. The most far-reaching dynamic of the immediate post-war period was the establishment of lasting democracies, especially in Germany and Italy, and for some years also in Central European countries such as Poland, Czechoslovakia, and Hungary. After the deep crisis of the early 1940s, when only one in six Europeans lived in a democracy, the immediate post-war period was also a period of new hope.

The era of prosperity

In total contrast to the post-war era was the subsequent era of prosperity, a contrast which contemporaries often saw as a 'miracle', as the 'glorious fifties', as a 'revolution'. The era of extraordinary prosperity, the economic causes and effects of which are treated in Chapter 4, was not simply another cyclical long economic upswing, as had occurred several times before in modern European economic history. It was characterized by uniquely high rates of economic growth and affected not just the industrialized areas of Europe, but the whole continent. The timing of the boom was not identical all over Europe, starting as it did in the late 1940s in major industrial societies, and coming rather later to the periphery. The social characteristics of the era of prosperity are also unique.

One social characteristic was the unique and unprecedented rise in real earnings and incomes. Never before or since have real wages and real income grown so substantially. To be sure, there were large variations between countries, occupations, and genders, and between active and retired people. The unprecedented general rise in real incomes led to fundamental changes in styles of consumption, patterns of income distribution, class distinctions, and industrial relations, topics to which we shall return. It contributed to the stabilization of democracy in Western Europe, and also to a temporary stability of the regimes in Eastern Europe.

A second social characteristic of this period of prosperity was the unusually high demand for labour. It was a time of full employment in a more comprehensive sense than ever before or since. Although unemployment rates did not fall to the same level everywhere, and often remained high in peripheral regions of Europe, on the whole they fell below American levels. This had far-reaching consequences. Family-oriented work on small farms, in small artisan shops, and in retailing was markedly reduced in most European countries. Many family members left the family business for better-paid, more secure, and more independent jobs on the general labour market, and more and more mothers started to work outside the home in paid employment. By the end of the era of prosperity this applied to a majority of mothers. Female patterns of work changed from being limited largely to the period before marriage and motherhood to including a second period of paid work after the first few years of motherhood. The demand for labour also led to a distinct rise in labour migration into the industrial European countries not only from the European periphery, but also from the Islamic part of the Mediterranean and from the former European colonies. Finally, because of the demand for highly qualified labour, as well as the increase in private incomes and private education, levels of education rose substantially, at least among the younger generations. Rates of illiteracy were reduced on the European periphery, and numbers completing higher education or achieving other further education qualifications started to accelerate.

A third characteristic of the era of prosperity was the unprecedented rise in tax revenues. State budgets increased more rapidly than ever before or since. In West European countries they were between seven and twenty times as large in 1975 as they had been in 1950.[3] The power of the state increased, with various social consequences. The modern welfare state was established and welfare expenditure gathered pace. In Scandinavian countries it was more than twenty times as high in 1975 as in 1950, and in Britain and Switzerland at least ten times as high in nominal terms. Moreover, the expansion of cities—with the construction of new urban areas or entire new cities, and of new city-centre public buildings and urban motorway systems—was easily financed. The integration not only of millions of post-war refugees, but also of millions of Europeans returning from the colonies, was less difficult than it would have been in a period of depression. Finally, governments could respond to the rising demand for education at all levels by investing heavily in public education, in nurseries and primary and secondary schools, as well as in universities.

A final characteristic of the era of prosperity was a widespread optimism. The longer prosperity lasted, the more it was seen not as exceptional, but as normality after a disastrous first half of the century. This optimism was not shared by all, but social policies and large sections of society were strongly influenced by this general mood. Private investment in the future was made more readily—investment in homes, in durable goods, in the education of children and their upward social mobility. Government policies, in multiple

[3] See P. Flora, *State, Society and Economy in Western Europe, 1815–1975*, 2 vols. (Frankfurt: Campus Verlag 1983), i. 255 ff.

ways, aimed at the creation of a new society with better living and working conditions. Social planning became a new field of activity for politicians at the municipal as well as the national level. Futurology as a scientific discipline was established and became popular. In the 1960s even fundamentalist opposition movements, the new social movements, believed in the possibility of the future creation of a better society.

The era of economic difficulties

During the 1970s the era of prosperity gradually came to an end. Most symbolic of this decline was an event in the international economy, the oil shock of 1973–4, but the main indicators of economic difficulties were domestic. Inflation and the gradual end of the rise in real incomes were the first signs, followed by a crisis in public spending and a visible rise in unemployment. However, in social terms this era was not simply another economic depression like the Great Depression of the 1930s. Rather, it was an unusual combination of economic crisis, with low rather than negative growth rates, and distinctive social changes. Whether crisis or change prevailed was a highly controversial question among contemporaries and will probably remain controversial among future historians.

In all major fields of social history this combination of crisis and social change was characteristic of the period. The European family entered a new phase, with a rise in divorce rates, illegitimate births, single-person households, one-parent families, working mothers and grandmothers, and with a decline in birth rates. On one interpretation this was a period of temporary crisis for the traditional family model, with endangered relationships between spouses and between parents and children, with overburdened mothers and grandmothers, irresponsible fathers, and a decline of family support for individuals. On another interpretation this signified the definitive end of the monopoly of a single family model and the rise of a richer variety of family forms.

The history of work in Europe also entered a new period. Unemployment increased for unskilled and highly skilled workers alike, for women as well as for men, for immigrants as well as for indigenous people. In the 1980s Europe became a continent of unemployment, with much higher rates than the United States or

Japan. Only a minority of European countries kept or regained lower unemployment rates. On one interpretation this was a deep crisis of the European labour market which could be solved either by government intervention or by adaptation to a new economic situation. On another interpretation this was an indicator of a fundamental change in the role of work, from being an activity central to life towards an oscillation between an unclear future of paid employment and/or other socially valuable activities within the family and in the community at large.

The welfare state, too, entered a period of financial crisis, as well as a crisis of efficiency and of political acceptance. On one interpretation this indicated a crisis in which the welfare state faced new challenges in relation to family and work, to which it had to adapt while maintaining the general goal of making life more secure for all citizens through public institutions. Another interpretation saw this as signifying the ultimate decline of the welfare state, indicating a need for new instruments of private and non-state welfare institutions and social provision. Other fields of society such as education, the city and urban life, social solidarity, immigration, and the idea of progress and conceptions of the future also entered a new era. Again, the new forms could be viewed as either constituting a crisis to be solved or heralding a transition to a fundamentally different sort of society.

The era since the upheaval of 1989–1991

This era is much less distinct from the previous one in social respects than it is in political history. The basic social characteristics of the earlier period—the ambivalence of crisis and change—have persisted. Major tendencies of social change remained clearly visible, including the predominance of the service sector, the emergence of new types of work, high unemployment rates, changes in the family, the crisis of the welfare state, and the rise of non-European immigration. This said, one should bear in mind the qualification that historians have great difficulty in discriminating between major and minor tendencies in their own time.

Nevertheless, the period since 1989–91 also has the characteristics of a new era. In Eastern Europe the period since 1989–91 has of course been one of fundamental, sometimes even traumatic, change in all dimensions of society. The fall in birth rates and the rise in rates of divorce, and the lowering of life expectancy in various countries, indicate important transitions in the nature of the family the contours of which are not yet fully clear. The earlier predominance of industrial labour has to a large extent been replaced by predominance of the service sector in a brutally rapid transformation. The labour-centred society has ended. Unemployment and enforced professional reorientation have become common, among women more than men. Work migration into Western Europe has become a new option. Opportunities for education have expanded, often more rapidly than before. Social security systems have been transformed, but often poorly financed by government and hence with important shortcomings for a section of their clients, as the drop in life expectancy in various countries indicates. Consumption patterns shifted in a few years from being premissed on a scarcity of goods to a full supply, but with reduced, sometimes even declining, incomes among a substantial number of East Europeans. Social inequality has increased and become more visible. The new economic situation has been welcomed by one section of the population as offering new and much better chances, but has been experienced in terms of individual disorientation by another, smaller section, with large variations from country to country.

To be sure, for Western Europe the upheaval of 1989–91 did not have major social-structural consequences, especially beyond the countries on the former border between Eastern and Western Europe, i.e. Italy, Austria, Germany, Finland, and Sweden. However, at least three important indirect consequences of 1989–91 can be observed even in Western Europe.

First, the whole of Europe again became an imagined social and cultural space. Western and Eastern Europe as separate social and cultural entities gradually disappeared from the minds of Europeans, although sometimes more slowly than one would have expected. Mobility across the whole of Europe for business people, technical experts, tourists, and intellectuals rapidly increased in all directions. Business people, technicians, and intellectuals from the West started to live in the East, often working in influential positions and living under economic conditions far better than those of the endogenous populations. In various European metropolitan areas immigration from Eastern Europe led to new European minorities, both rich minorities and transient labour minorities.

A new, intensive debate emerged, focusing on questions of the nature of Europe, specific European values, institutions, and civil society, and the geographic borders of Europe; to a substantial degree this was not only a debate about politics and economics. Moreover, in the whole of Europe the character of public debates about social affairs, state intervention, and the welfare state changed with the rapid decline or total reshaping of former communist parties and the widespread discrediting of radical forms of (state) socialism. Traditional lines of separation between political camps disappeared, and concepts that before had been strictly colonized by one political camp could be used much more freely by all.

Thirdly, as a consequence of the upheaval of 1989–91 the European Union became in many ways more powerful than before through the Maastricht and Amsterdam Treaties. This was also the case for social and cultural affairs. The power of the EU increased in the area of coordination of social policy, and by the inclusion of fundamental social rights in the European treaties. A so-called third pillar of the EU (besides economic and foreign policy) was established, dealing with immigration and police affairs. Although it varied from country to country, a policy of European cultural identity began, with the establishment of a European flag, passport, car number plates, separate or no controls for EU citizens at the borders and in the airports, and the European city of culture. The establishment of a European currency also had implications for this new European identity, and with the policy of enlargement, the rising power of the EU will become important for more than its fifteen member countries.

The processes of change

Throughout these different eras, during prosperity as well as during depression, the second half of the twentieth century was a period of persistent and fundamental change. It was a period not of a single change, but rather of a series of successive changes. Institutions, attitudes, and structures that became fashionable in the 1960s or 1970s were often replaced; attitudes towards change also altered not once, but changed several times between 1945 and 1999. The multitude of these changes is presented here in the following sections dealing with work, family and demography, consumption, social classes and inequality, values, urban growth and immigration, and the welfare state.

Changes in work

Work changed dramatically during the second half of the twentieth century, although at the beginning of the twenty-first century there is a widespread feeling that even more fundamental changes lie ahead. To put it briefly, in the second half of the twentieth century there was a change from a dual European society, with two different working sectors, towards a more homogeneous work society. The dual society was characterized by a combination of two major contrasting sections. A predominantly agrarian or artisanal sector, with much family-based work, often only basic education, sometimes vocational training, and often precarious but highly respected economic independence and traditional family work values coexisted alongside a modern work sector which was mostly hierarchical, almost exclusively male in the middle and higher ranks, predominantly industrial, with lifelong professional activities, low unemployment rates, advanced social security, and highly organized industrial relations. This dual society was gradually displaced by a more homogeneous work society characterized by more work in the service sector, more women in important jobs, less hierarchical and more fluid professional life courses, continuous lifelong training, higher unemployment rates, less security, and more diversified industrial relations.

By the end of the Second World War the largest employment sector was still agriculture. In Europe as a whole industry only became the largest employment sector in the 1950s and 1960s, in part because of industrialization on the periphery of Western Europe, in Italy, Spain, Ireland, and Finland, and in part because of the industrialization of communist Central and Eastern Europe, especially Poland, Romania, Bulgaria, and Yugoslavia. In the industrial societies of the European heartlands this was a second summer of industrial society, with the continuation of mining and the steel industry, and of the chemical and electronics industries, but also with the new growth industry, the motorcar corporations and their suppliers. The model of industrial society prevailed in Western as well as Eastern Europe. Economic growth and prosperity was seen as depending fully upon the rise of industrial labour. Europe was in fact almost the only society in the world that was industrial in the full sense, i.e. whose industrial sector was the largest employment sector. In all other modern societies the service sector was the largest employment sector, and had always been larger than the industrial sector.

By the 1970s and 1980s Europe as a whole had also become a service society, mainly due to the rise in public services and economic services (commerce, communications and transport, banking, insurance, consulting, the professions). It is important to note that this service society penetrated rural areas much more than the industrial society had done, and rendered them less distinctive than before. This trend, however, was largely confined to Western Europe. In Central and Eastern Europe until 1989–91 industrial societies persisted, with Czechoslovakia and the GDR as the oldest and most distinctly industrial societies. The service sector only became predominant in this part of Europe after 1989–91, in a brutally rapid transformation creating substantial unemployment among former industrial workers. In Europe as a whole it is as yet unclear whether the model of industrial society still prevails or whether some new form of service society will predominate in the public arena and in politics.

Superficially, patterns of female employment do not appear to have changed dramatically during this period. Overall female labour activity rates remained roughly constant, or at least did not show any substantial increases. But below the surface several crucial changes occurred in the second half of the twentieth century. This is the period of the rise of working mothers. This process can be seen in most European countries, in Eastern even more than in Western Europe, in Northern more than in Southern Europe. The female cycle of work changed from a model in which work was given up at marriage to one that was similar to that of males. During this period a new feature unique to Europe emerged. In no other modern society in the world were female activity rates lower than here. In other big industrial societies—in the United States, Japan, let alone the USSR—female activity rates were visibly higher. This mainly had to do with female work in Western Europe as a whole, regardless of large differences between relatively high activity rates in Scandinavia and Britain, and low activity rates in Southern Europe. Only in the 1990s, with the rise in female activity rates in Western Europe, did this

European phenomenon seem to have disappeared. Moreover, appreciation of women's work changed fundamentally during the second half of the twentieth century. At the beginning of the period women worked largely because of external pressures, in the post-war period to avoid poverty, in the era of prosperity to finance the new consumption patterns, to which we shall return. Gradually, however, work outside the household began to be seen as a normal focus of life for women as well as for men, as a means of developing one's personality and planning one's life. By the end of the century patterns of female and male work had not become identical, but they were definitely more similar than they had been around the middle of the century.

More dramatic for male as well as female work were changes in the basic character of work. To be sure, the nature of work varied enormously according to the large variety of activities in different European countries. The history of the transformation of labour refers primarily to work in the more advanced economic sectors, rather than to the whole variety of types of labour. With this qualification in mind, one can say that in the earlier part of the second half of the twentieth century there was a move away from handicrafts and individual work supported by machines, and from autonomous work groups or family-oriented work, towards what is often called 'Tayloristic' and hierarchical work. This was characterized by a range of features: more complex workplaces with a more rigid division of labour, often in connection with conveyor belts or assembly lines; a strict and complex hierarchy in factories and offices; often simple, sometimes mindless work requiring only relatively low qualifications in the lower ranks; primarily lifelong occupational activities and low unemployment; male dominance in the middle and higher echelons of the hierarchy; visible social distinctions between unskilled labour, skilled labour, clerks, and managerial personnel; mass trade unions and highly organized industrial relations and strikes; advanced systems of social security, usually based on distinct hierarchies of pay and the assumption of lifelong occupation. This Tayloristic and hierarchical work had already emerged in the inter-war period, but continued to become more important in the three decades or so after 1945. For sociologists of work of the 1970s this was the culmination of history.

During the last two or three decades of the twentieth century transformations in the character of work ran in yet another direction. Fully automated production lines and computerized offices emerged. These systems replaced mindless repetitive work, which became too expensive. The installation, control, continuous alteration, and repair of these systems was the main content of the new type of work. It was done by highly qualified labour with continuously changing workplaces and often also with continuously changing work. Fixed, long-term work contracts tended to be replaced by specific task-oriented contracts. Work and continuous training were closely intertwined. Lifelong steady work became rarer. Flexibility, innovation, imagination, achievement, replaced former virtues such as punctuality, loyalty, obedience, reliability. Changing jobs and changing occupations became more frequent; cycles of work became more discontinuous and less predictable. Unemployment also became more frequent.

Hence, new requirements for social security systems emerged, while mass unionization of these types of worker was more difficult. Mass trade unions and mass strikes tended to decline in many European countries and were replaced by more spontaneous, more limited, even individual forms of labour conflicts. Industrial relations became less highly organized, and more decentralized and local. Some contemporary social scientists even predict that paid work outside the household is losing its central place in the life of Europeans and will be replaced by other activities still to be chosen and established. Other social scientists argue that the most traumatic indicator of these changes, the spectacular rise of unemployment, can be found only in Europe since the 1980s and did not occur in some European countries. Hence, under more favourable conditions work could keep its central position in the life of Europeans, though in a fundamentally changed form.

Changes in the nature of the family

The European family also changed dramatically during the second half of the twentieth century, again with large variations between countries that cannot be covered in detail here. However, the predominant earlier model of the European family, with contrasting roles for men and women, late and lifelong marriage, relatively high birth rates, and strong bonds of intimacy among family members, did not change directly into the new pattern characterized by wide diversity of family models. Change came in several steps. Moreover, diverse forms of the family were quite distinct within Europe, differing between those countries that were strongly affected by the war and countries less affected, and later on between Western Europe and the communist countries in Eastern Europe, but also between the more rapid changes in the northern part of Western Europe and the slower changes in the southern part. Finally, distinctive elements persisted in the European family model that differed from those of non-European societies: a late age of marriage for women as well as men; the rarity of the three-generation household; and intimacy within the nuclear family in comparison with their relations to the extended family and the surrounding society.

Directly after the end of the war the traditional family model came under strong pressure in the countries affected by the war. A new type of mother-centred family emerged with husbands killed in the war or returning physically or mentally ill. Substantial numbers of marriages broke down after years of separation because of the war. Divorce rates increased dramatically, as did illegitimate births and unformalized partnerships or common-law marriages. Young people who had to make a living on their own became more independent within the family. But at the same time the family became one of the few remaining stable institutions in a society in which normal economic markets and public services were often in decline and public authorities discredited. Hence, at least in Western Europe, families tried to return to traditional values with limited modification relating to the role of women. In countries less affected by the war changes within the family were very limited. One has to bear in mind, however, that this traditional model of the family was still largely restricted to the middle and lower-middle classes, and was adhered to very much less in peasant and working-class milieus.

The era of prosperity in the 1950s and 1960s gave another strong impetus for change in the family all across Europe. Rising real wages, the enormous demand for labour, increased public budgets, and the arrival of modern mass consumption strongly affected the family in various ways.

Roles within the family changed. Wives became more independent, in part because more mothers worked and had an income of their own, but also because, at least in Western Europe, modern mass consumption was in many ways directly targeted at wives as consumers. This increased independence of wives was supported in some countries by reforms in civil and constitutional law. Young people, and later on also children, became more independent, since they were identified as special markets for consumer goods. Youth consumer culture—books, records, journals, furniture, clothing—was invented. Larger homes offered more room for individual space within the family. Expectations in marriage and childhood also changed. The love-centred marriage and the child-centred family became predominant and could more easily be afforded. The economic marriage declined with the decline of family-oriented work. As a consequence, at the end of the era divorce rates increased when marriages failed to fulfil the high expectations, and birth rates dropped since expectations for child-rearing were raised. All this, however, occurred with clear differences between Eastern Europe (where birth rates remained higher) and Western Europe, but also between the northern part of Europe, with high rates of divorce, and Southern Europe, with much lower rates of divorce and relatively high birth rates.

Moreover, the intimacy of the family was clearly reduced. Activities outside the family for children and young people started earlier and became more important. Kindergartens and nurseries slowly became prevalent in Western and Eastern Europe. The day school at elementary as well as secondary levels was introduced in the era of prosperity in many European countries, and reduced family life during the day. Working mothers were also absent during the day. Family life was reduced to evenings, weekends, and holidays. Crucial family events such as birth and death were located in hospitals, outside the family space.

Change, however, was ambivalent. At the beginning of the era of prosperity Europeans returned to the traditional model of the European family. This was especially clear in countries affected by the war. Marriages became more frequent, a baby boom took place, divorce and illegitimacy declined. In the longer run the intimacy of the family was also reinforced in new ways. The home became more central to life. The rise of the television, of do-it-yourself, the enlarged space in the home, led to new home-centred activities. The living room as an everyday room with a sideboard, coffee table, two chairs, and a sofa became standard in European homes. Weekend shopping by car and the rise of holidays for most Europeans also became new family activities. The return to the home was also enforced by the decline of public social life in the street, by the arrival of the car, and by the building of huge blocks of flats. Moreover, the family model, which was primarily a middle-class model, also became more prevalent in the working class and in rural society. The family policies of governments, churches, and political parties, at least in Western Europe, centred around this family model and supported it by government intervention and the invention of family policy in the modern sense. Publicity followed this model. Western social scientists at the time mostly saw this 'modern' family as the culmination of family history and the model for the rest of the world.

The European family changed again in the years of economic difficulty during the 1970s and 1980s, though this era in family history does not stand in total contrast to the era of prosperity. The trends described for the era of prosperity mostly continued. Various trends in the 1970s and 1980s had already started in the 1960s or developed out of earlier trends. The main new tendency was the large variety of family forms and the end of the predominance of the traditional family model. The traditional model did not disappear, but it existed only alongside other family models, including elements such as partnership before parenthood; unformalized stable partnership with children; the one-parent family, mostly with a mother, much more rarely with a father; the household with children from two or more marriages; single status without marriage throughout life rather than merely through short-term transitions; the marriage of elderly people; formalized homosexual partnerships. Some of these new family forms had existed earlier. Single status throughout life was the choice not only of monks and nuns, but also, until the nineteenth century, of many rural workers or urban journeymen lacking sufficient income for a family. One-parent families have been mentioned as a consequence of wars. But the emergence of these new family forms during the 1970s and 1980s was the result not of external constraints, but rather of intentional new choices. They emerged partly because of the rise in incomes of men as well as women, partly because of the rise of the welfare state in the full sense, but partly also because of changes in the value system which became oriented more towards the values of individual happiness and individual achievement. On the whole policies followed rather than created the new variety of family forms. One can argue that the political events of 1968 were not an initial push, but a mirror of changes in values already taking place during the late 1960s.

The new diversity of family forms was seen by some observers as a decline of the family. However, a dissolution of the family did not occur between the 1970s and the 1990s. Family ties remained strong or became even stronger. Under the Central and East European communist regimes the role of the family was unintentionally reinforced and remained the main network of mutual social and political trust. In West European societies family ties also remained important for individuals. The vast majority of Europeans saw the family as the most important centre of life besides work. The models of the love-centred marriage and the child-centred family were by no means weakened by the larger variety of family forms. With the extension in the years of schooling and higher rates of further education, teenagers and young adults stayed longer in the family home and depended upon their parents for longer. With rising unemployment and job insecurity family support became crucial for the individual in moral as well as in material terms. With the rise in numbers of working mothers, grandparents became more important even for the nuclear family. At the same time in the 'third age' of physical decline, the family, especially daughters and daughters-in-law, remained the major source of help and was often not replaced by welfare institutions. To be sure, the European family became more diversified and more difficult to understand, but it remained indispensable.

The rise of mass consumerism

The arrival of mass consumerism is perhaps the major watershed in European social history between the middle and end of the twentieth century. Mass consumerism began to arrive in Western Europe in the 1950s—late compared to the United States because of the two world wars, but earlier than in Eastern Europe, where it was started by governments only in the 1970s and 1980s. Within Western Europe mass consumerism also came later in the south, in Spain, Portugal, and Greece, and also in Ireland. Mass consumerism was a slow and gradual process. It comprised and was premissed on several changes in European societies.

First of all, mass consumption was only possible under conditions of rising purchasing power among private households. Hence, the era of prosperity from the 1950s, with its extraordinary rise in real private incomes, formed the real basis of the beginnings of mass consumption in Europe. Private households not only received higher real incomes; the structure of household expenditure also changed. Expenditure on food and clothing increased in absolute terms, but private incomes grew so fast that, in comparative terms, this expenditure decreased relative to total income, and other expenditure—such as transport, housing, and durable goods—claimed a higher share of total income. Cars, refrigerators, furniture, radios, and television sets could gradually be afforded by the vast majority of households.

Moreover, the rising demands of mass consumerism could only be met by commercialization. Direct contacts between consumers and producers—peasants, tailors, carpenters—was gradually replaced by commerce. Many new durable goods were never sold directly by producers to consumers.

Commercialization in the mass consumer society also led to the expansion of big commerce, i.e. department stores, supermarkets, mail-order firms, large specialized commerce. At first commerce was still established in city centres; later on, with the arrival of the car, it was based more frequently in commercial centres outside cities and rural towns.

Mass consumerism also entailed fundamental changes in consumer attitudes. Consumers had to change from products made for individual tastes, sizes, and needs to products standardized in terms of measures, quality, and usage. Publicity and hire purchase arrangements, which had barely existed before, became crucial elements of consumption. The wealth of goods also led to new attitudes: waste became a new public issue.

European mass consumerism also included the breakdown of national and regional autarchy and an opening up of international consumption patterns. Holiday travel made the average consumer more familiar with consumption in other European countries, and sometimes in non-European countries, despite some tendencies towards the formation of national tourist ghettos abroad. The creation of the European Common Market, and later on the European Union, by European governments, and the creation of the European consumer by European enterprises, led to an internationalization of European consumption styles, despite slogans such as 'Buy British' or

'Von deutschen Landen frisch auf den Tisch' ('Fresh onto the table from German lands'). The communications revolution, the car and the motorway networks, the plane and the new system of rapid trains, the automatic telephone system, fax, email, and Internet internationalized the everyday life and consumption of Europeans. The concept of economic autarchy which had been applied by Hitler and by the communist regimes became totally unrealistic. Internationalization of consumption was no longer an idealistic utopian goal, but became an intrinsic part of everyday life in Europe.

In addition, mass consumerism altered the symbolic social function of goods. Before its arrival consumer goods were often used as instruments of social distinction. The European middle class drew the lines according to car ownership, plane travel or travel to foreign countries, suits and fashion outfits, make-up, or consumption of meat, wine, white bread, or butter. Mass consumption blurred these lines of distinction, which were replaced by more subtle distinctions that were often difficult for outsiders to understand. Consumption had also often been used for maintaining regional or national distinctions. Mass consumption either removed these distinctions by standardizing goods for all national and regional markets, or specific regional and national goods were sold on the larger European market. Consumption became a European mix of Italian pizzas, French cheese, Swedish furniture, German cars, and Dutch flowers. Traditional patterns of consumption also drew a distinct line between urban and rural societies below the level of elites. Mass consumption gradually eliminated this specificity of rural society, which had been one of the most important lines of social distinction in European history. Peasants started to buy the same commodities as the urban population, the same cars, television sets, furniture, clothing, even food. To be sure, social distinctions were not fully eliminated by mass consumerism. But they became more subtle, more ambivalent, more difficult to understand, and they often changed more rapidly.

Finally, the arrival of mass consumerism in Europe also aroused strong opposition—stronger in Europe than in the United States or in Japan. In the early years of mass consumerism opposition came primarily from the then small circles of the educated elites, intellectuals, professors, journalists. They opposed what they saw as a threat to individualism, as conformism, as egalitarianism in mass consumption. They were often afraid of a decline in refined and

cultivated taste, of an elimination of social distinctions by mass consumerism. America was often perceived and rejected as a symbol of
mass consumerism. During the 1970s and 1980s a different type of
opposition emerged, though with links to the former elite opposition.
It was more organized in social movements, and often integrated in
mass parties. It was much less elitist, and dealt more with the ordinary mass consumer. It opposed mass consumerism because it saw it as
a threat to standards of quality for different products, as well as a
threat to individual health and to the environment.

In Eastern Europe emerging mass consumerism was fundamentally different from that in Western Europe. Mass consumerism
not only came here later; it was also different in character. Consumer
goods were distributed not by the market, but—except for a limited
number of agricultural products and black market goods—by centralized planning. Consumer attitudes were basically different from
the West. In the West, with an abundance of goods, consumption was
limited by individual income. In the East, with an abundance of
money, consumption was limited by scarcity of goods, especially of
durable goods.

The basic goals of the consumption policy of communist governments changed over time. In the 1950s and 1960s they wanted to
establish a fundamentally different form of socialist consumption,
but later on they simply tried to catch up with Western consumption
and to meet popular expectations. This could only be reached by
raising productivity, and Eastern governments hoped to achieve this
by raising levels of consumption and thus reinforcing the motivation
to work. East European governments applied a policy of contrasting
prices: low and highly subsidized prices for goods fulfilling basic
needs such as food, housing, transport, medical care, education; and
high prices for durable or luxury goods. This consumption policy,
however, did not work out in the end. Motivation to work did not
rise sufficiently. At the same time the necessary investment to raise
productivity was difficult to find, because a great deal of capital
had to be spent on the huge subsidies for basic goods, whose
prices in turn, could not be raised in face of the fierce opposition of a disappointed population. People protested regularly
against price rises in Poland, and in other East European countries.
In fact, the failure of these consumption policies in Eastern Europe
was one of the major dead ends of communism, and a major

domestic reason for the eventual breakdown of the communist regimes.

The arrival of mass consumerism has clearly contributed to more distinct contours of European society in several ways. Exchanges between European societies increased dramatically—exchanges of goods, people, lifestyles. European societies became more interconnected and somewhat less mutually unintelligible. They also became more interconnected by the critique of mass consumerism. Moreover, European mass consumption in many ways became a model for the periphery in Southern and Eastern Europe, as well as for countries outside Europe. European mass consumption was a major element in the internal and external attractiveness of Europe, alongside human rights and European integration. It became attractive perhaps because it was part of an insecure and perpetually questioned European identity, rather than part of a grand imperial concept. Finally, European mass consumerism had a profile of its own and was not simply Americanization. To be sure, Americanization did take place in the period directly after the Second World War, when living standards were much more advanced in the United States than in Europe, and when American society became a highly controversial model for Europeans. It is also true that American products predominated in specific markets such as cinema and television, fast food, and beverages such as Coca-Cola. But, on the other hand, most major symbols of European mass consumerism had been invented as well as produced in Europe. This was true for the car, ready-made clothes, fast food, holiday resorts, department stores, motorways, prefabricated homes and furniture, design, publicity. Moreover, the idea of Americanization often owed more to a European way of discussing modernity by calling new trends 'American' in order to render them either more repellent or more attractive. In addition, the internationalization of consumerism was often an Asian as much as an American achievement, and last but not least also frequently a European achievement.

From class society to individualism

A slowly forgotten social change in the second half of the twentieth century was the disappearance of one the most important European social features of the late nineteenth and early twentieth centuries, the

European social class system: not only the working class, but also the bourgeoisie, the lower middle class, the landed aristocracy, the peasants.

The crucial classes around the middle of the twentieth century have been briefly described above: the working class and the bourgeoisie. They existed, however, in the full sense only in the industrialized heartlands of Europe: especially in Britain, Germany, France, Austria, Switzerland, Belgium, Bohemia, to a much lesser extent in more recently industrialized countries such as Scandinavia and Hungary, and only locally in the South and East European periphery. This distinctive social feature of European society declined slowly in most respects.

Social-class milieus disappeared as a social network at the local level with intensive social contacts and intermarriages. They gradually receded as a visible lifestyle with distinctive clothing, food, housing, and leisure, and with conflicts with the other main social classes in the political arena as well as in everyday life. They also slowly receded as a specific system of social and political values and culture. To be sure, many elements of these lifestyles in eating and drinking, clothing, buildings, music, and theatre survived, but they mostly became arbitrary and in general lost their symbolic function of creating a distinct social milieu.

Neither the causes nor the extent of this disappearance were the same in the different European countries. In Germany and Austria the Nazi period was especially destructive of the working-class milieu as well as of the other social milieus. In East Germany and Bohemia communist regimes put an end to the classical social-class milieus in a specific way. In Britain the working class milieu and in France the bourgeoisie declined less obviously and more slowly than elsewhere in Europe. But on the whole these class milieus declined in Europe for general reasons too. First, because of the increase in real wages and the rise of the modern welfare state during the era of prosperity, a crucial element of the working-class social milieu, local social solidarity in poverty, was less in demand. At the same time the rise of the welfare state offered social security for all citizens, and thus weakened a crucial element of the distinctiveness of the middle and lower-middle classes, security through property ownership. Social scientists can show that disparities in income and property ownership itself also became somewhat smaller. The enormous expansion of education and of educational opportunity for children of all social classes made secondary and higher education less of an instrument of distinction between the working and the middle class. The expansion of cities and the planning of new urban districts or even whole new towns, as well as urban renewal in city centres, gradually reduced the traditional spatial separation of social milieus in the cities from the late nineteenth and early twentieth centuries. The rise in mass consumerism, in standardized goods and services for all citizens, also gradually diluted specific social-class styles in clothing, housing, leisure, food, and drink. It created a new commercialized mix of middle-class suits and make-up, of lower-class pizzas and jeans, of middle-class butter and proletarian beer, of middle-class sofas and proletarian football. Early initiatives failed to create class-specific radio and television, travel and sport. A new local culture of festive events emerged—carnival, district events, town jubilees—which was not linked to specific social milieus. Changes in the nature of work, the decline of industry and, within industry, the decline of traditional repetitive, hard, hierarchical work and increasing numbers of female and immigrant workers in low-paid jobs, also diluted the social milieus that had been predominantly male and indigenous.

In Eastern Europe a different type of society emerged. Here the European class system was eliminated in a much more brutal way than in Western Europe. The economic section of the bourgeoisie was to a great extent rapidly destroyed, dispossessed, sometimes even detained or forced to emigrate, sometimes provisionally maintained for its special expertise. The professional section of the bourgeoisie gradually lost its former autonomy and social distinction. Income was often drastically reduced, as was the possibility of transferring cultural capital to descendants, though with spectacular exceptions. Intellectuals lost their former role as autonomous critics of political and economic power. With important exceptions, such as Poland, the peasantry was gradually eliminated and replaced by large and centrally controlled agricultural enterprise, often against the quiet resistance of rural society. The traditional working class also changed with the disappearance of its counterpart, the bourgeoisie. Industrial conflict now turned into conflict with government; thus it became more political and at the same time faced more repression. It often also turned into food protests because of the consumption policies of communist governments. Educational opportunity and upward social mobility increased dramatically in the late 1940s and 1950s with the destruction of the bourgeoisie and the rise of a new political elite, and also with the rapid expansion of secondary and higher education in most East European countries. But in the 1970s and 1980s educational opportunity became more limited than in most West European societies, and recruitment to top positions in politics as well as the economy became roughly similar to the West or even more gerontocratic.

A different, more individualistic way of life emerged in most European societies during the 1970s and 1980s, which has been much discussed by social scientists. This new value system and lifestyle came about gradually, was not always clearly visible, and did not develop in all European countries. It was characterized by changes in values, particularly the rise of post-materialistic values, giving a higher priority to self-fulfilment, social contacts, participation, and individual rights, and lower priority to material well-being and order. Conformity of lifestyles weakened. As we have seen, new varieties of family forms emerged. Collective conformity of styles was replaced by more individual mixtures of different elements of lifestyles. At the same time small, local linkages to the family, the neighbourhood, and the community became more important. New identities and identity policies emerged: the ethnic identities of immigrants from outside Europe, regional and local identities within European countries, gender identities, minority identities. New youth cultures emerged, as described in Chapter 5.

In addition, loyalties to big institutions such as the nation, the church, the trade unions, and the professions became weaker. In a significant number of European countries a previously strong pride in the nation became weaker over the long run, with a stabilization, in some European countries even a reversal, in the 1980s. Attitudes of mutual respect and confidence generally became more important in relations between European countries. Europeans became more committed to human rights and to international peace.

This individualistic pattern also affected relations with the church, though with distinct variations within Europe. Individualism was a factor in reinforcing long-term secularization, though religiosity as such and the belief in God declined less distinctly, and participation in religious sects even increased. Membership in the big churches and attendance at traditional church services had fallen in many

European countries, though attendance had remained high in Poland, Ireland, Austria, Italy, Spain, and Portugal. Individualistic values were more advanced in Protestant Northern European countries and in Protestant environments, but were also advanced in bidenominational countries such as West Germany. Membership in church associations on the whole became weaker in countries that were predominantly Catholic or Protestant, less so in bidenominational countries such as the Netherlands, West Germany, Britain, and Northern Ireland. The impact of individualism on Islamic Europeans is as yet unexplored.

Commitment to trade unions also became weaker during the rise of individualism. Trade union membership declined in various European countries and in Western Europe as a whole over the long term, with France as the country with the weakest membership rate. This overall trend was not really compensated for by sustained high trade union membership rates in the small Nordic countries; nor by high union membership levels in Eastern Europe before 1989, since the functions of centrally controlled trade unions under communism were very different, and in any event they lost a substantial proportion of members after the upheavals of 1989–91. With the decline of trade unions an important characteristic of European society, the strength of the trade unions, weakened as compared with the United States and Japan. As part of the rise of individualism, however, new social movements focusing on issues such as the environment, gender, and peace visibly increased from the late 1970s and 1980s in various European countries, with widely different impacts on party politics. Non-governmental organizations became more powerful in national as well as in European politics.

The era of more individualistic lifestyles was also characterized by new forms of social inequality and social exclusion. Disparities in income and property ownership started to increase again in Western Europe and, after 1989–91, even more so in Eastern Europe. New forms of poverty emerged. The new poor were not the traditional labourers and elderly people, but immigrants, the long-term unemployed, one-parent families, drug addicts. The number of homeless adults and young people increased. This poverty was less visible and less concentrated in specific social classes and specific urban districts. It was to some extent more transient for individuals, sometimes affecting only a limited period of family life or working life. But this new poverty became a genuine and important problem. The modern European welfare state, which had emerged in an era of prosperity with stable and predictable life courses, was often not capable of meeting needs in an appropriate way.

Urban growth and immigration

Urban growth and immigration were also not continuous processes throughout the second half of the twentieth century. The modernity of 1950 was very different from the European modernity of 1970 and different again from that of 1990. In many ways the social history of European cities after 1945 took place under the influence of the Second World War. The destruction of city centres in London, Rotterdam, Berlin, Warsaw, Budapest, and many other cities, together with the turmoil of millions of displaced persons, returning soldiers, refugees, dispersed families in search of each other, led to overcrowded cities and often depressing housing and living conditions. This was also true of European cities superficially untouched by the destruction of the war. The Frenchman Jean-Laurent Bost wrote in 1946, on returning from a visit to the United States: 'In Europe we no longer know any lively big cities. We no longer know cities overcrowded by taxis, cars, pedestrians; we no longer know luxurious and full department stores . . . All the cities in France, especially Paris, are more or less dead'.[4]

Europe entered a new period of rapid urban growth in the 1950s and 1960s, caused by population growth as well as migration from rural areas and international immigration. To be sure, this was not the first period of rapid urban growth in Europe. The last period of expansion of the cities in the late nineteenth and early twentieth century was characterized by even more impressive urban growth rates. It was also a more overwhelming experience for most Europeans, since widespread urban growth at that time was totally new and led to an unknown society. Nevertheless, the period of growth of the 1950s and 1960s was peculiar in various respects.

First, urban growth in the 1950s and 1960s was not confined to the industrialized areas of the European core. It became a European process in the full sense, including also the periphery of Europe, in

---

[4] J.-L. Bost, *Trois mois aux États-Unis* (Paris: édition de minuit 1946), 130–1.

countries such as Spain, Portugal, southern Italy, Greece, Bulgaria, Poland, Finland, and Ireland. Urban growth in these countries was often even more rapid than in the older industrial societies in the heartlands of Europe. In this way former contrasts between rural and urbanized areas were reduced; Europe became somewhat more homogeneous.

This was also the period of big urban planning premissed on an optimistic belief in the creation of a new, more mobile, healthier, and more functional urban society. The planning of huge urban areas— Greater London, the agglomeration of Paris, the Dutch Randstad, in Germany the area of the Ruhr—was based on new conceptions of communication, hygiene, industrialized construction, and the functional segregation of cities into residential, industrial, commercial, and administrative districts. As a result, this was the period of the construction of new cities; the total demolition of those old inner-city blocks that had survived the war and reconstruction with high-rise buildings; the loss of street fronts; inner-city motorways and dual carriageways; new commercial centres; and the separation of industrial, business, and residential districts. The large financial resources of the cities in the era of prosperity were crucial for large-scale planning.

This period was also characterized by further internationalization of city planning. An international concept from the inter-war period, the Charter of Athens, became highly influential and weakened national patterns of city planning. Urban architecture was extensively employed, not to hide modern urban life behind historically designed façades, but rather to break consciously with nineteenth-century cities even in architectural style, favouring instead flat, functional façades and high-rise buildings. All this led to the homogenization of European cities. Late nineteenth- and early twentieth-century European cities such as London, Paris, Berlin, and Florence were still distinctive as far as their urban architecture was concerned. But the new city planning and the new architectural style of the 1950s and 1960s was similar everywhere. The underlying concepts had often been developed in the inter-war period or even earlier, but they were only now applied widely. However, contrasts between Eastern and Western Europe in city planning and architectural style were more distinctive than they later became. Inner-city planning in particular was clearly different in Eastern Europe from the West, strongly oriented towards political purposes, creating huge open spaces for large political demonstrations and spectacular buildings in the city centre as symbols of communist power.

In the 1950s and 1960s the social structure of the cities also changed. It has been mentioned that in the expanding new urban districts of the big cities and in the new cities segregation between the social classes became much less distinct. This was often the case in the reconstructed city centres that had been destroyed by the war or demolished in inner-city renewal programmes. Urban working-class districts also started to change slowly with rising immigration. This immigration was not new. It had already begun in the second half of the nineteenth century with European immigrants, mostly young single people from the periphery of the continent, especially from Italy, Spain, Portugal, Yugoslavia, Greece, and Ireland, and then also from Central and Eastern Europe. But this immigration now became larger than before and was therefore more visible in the city centres.

What had been modern in the 1950s and 1960s gradually became traditional in the fundamentally different period from the 1970s to the 1990s. Urban growth became less notable, and a process of de-urbanization could even be observed in some European countries (outside Southern and Eastern Europe), though much less distinctly than in the United States. Rates of urban growth in Europe as a whole clearly fell behind the expansion of the city worldwide. At the end of the twentieth century only two European cities (London and Paris) ranked among the twenty largest cities of the world, compared to five European cities around 1950.

Nevertheless, this also became the period of the urbanization of rural society in Europe, although this had already begun during the era of prosperity. In villages the farming population declined. The social structure of many villages, even beyond the suburban environs or city green belts, became more similar to that of urban areas, or villages became annexes of urban society with the growth of second homes or as centres of tourism. Standards of living and lifestyles also became very similar in rural and urban areas. The pillars of mass consumption—cars, television sets, refrigerators, sofas, frozen and canned food—gradually arrived in rural as well as urban areas. The rising service and communication society was rural as well as urban. Small rural towns offered the same banking and insurance services, schools, supermarkets, garden and do-it-yourself centres as urban areas, and the same forms of communication by car, telephone, fax, Internet, and email. A major century-old distinction of European society, the distinction between urban and rural life, started to disappear in most European regions. In this respect, too, Europe became more homogeneous.

In addition, in this period conditions for big urban planning became less favourable. The budgets of the municipal administrations and government in general became more limited or even entered into full-blown crisis. Perhaps more important was rising discontent with the large-scale planning of the 1950s and 1960s, with its concomitant destruction of public social space by the high priority given to transport, the combination of open space with human isolation in residential tower blocks, the destruction of existing social networks and communities by radical demolition of entire urban areas, and the lack of local political influence of citizens on large-scale planning issues. This period of urban development was characterized by new urban policies: by inner-city renewal rather than the growth of new suburbs; renovation rather than demolition of inner-city areas; the establishment of pedestrian zones and public transport systems rather than new highways for cars; by placing new value on city centres as well as residential areas and out-of-town commercial centres; new urban cultural policies, in museums, theatres, festivals, congress centres, universities and polytechnics, railway stations, arcades. All this was by no means successful all over Europe, but it was attempted all over Western Europe.

During this period East Europeans gradually gave up the idea of a distinctive socialist city. Urban expansion, which still continued in most communist countries, took place in similar forms, with basically similar achievements and failures, as in Western Europe. Again, Europe became more homogeneous even as far as the appearance of cities was concerned. Hence, the evaluation of the achievements and costs of urbanization will be a general European question of urban history.

However, in one respect, that of immigration into the cities, contrasts between West and East European cities increased up to the upheaval of 1989–91, and even remained thereafter. Immigration into West European cities changed from the 1970s onwards. As a consequence also of earlier tendencies, two new types of immigrant established themselves in West European cities alongside traditional working-class immigrants from the European periphery.

On the one hand, there was visible immigration from non-European countries, partly from the eastern and southern Islamic part of the Mediterranean, and partly from former African, Asian, and Caribbean European colonies. European immigration laws and policies gradually became more selective towards this type of immigrant, especially compared to the fully free mobility for the colonial population that had obtained until the 1950s, but also compared to the massive recruitment of non-European labour from the Mediterranean until the early 1970s. As a consequence, labour immigration turned into family immigration. European immigrant communities gradually became complete societies, with all sorts of activities rather than merely being communities of workers. The longer these migrants lived in Europe, the more this turned into long-term immigration rather than mere labour migration. European urban life became more colourful, with a larger variety of restaurants, shops, entertainments, religious life, sometimes with separate ethnic cultures, sometimes also with ethnic upward social mobility especially in sports, music, business, and politics. Policies towards these immigrants varied greatly in different West European countries.

On the other hand, an almost invisible type of immigrant came from the other member states of the European Union. Policies towards these immigrants became less selective. They gradually received full economic citizenship rights, though not yet full political rights. The number of these immigrants increased further from the 1970s, with the rising number of member states. These immigrants were also active in all sorts of professions. They never developed separate ethnically based communities and, hence, remained almost invisible.

Because of these waves of immigration, West European cities became more and more different from East European cities. After 1989–91, however, a new bridge emerged with the East European migration to West European cities.

The rise of the modern welfare state

The modern welfare state emerged only after the Second World War, although substantial public social services had already developed earlier in various European countries. The modern welfare state had four main principles: first, the guarantee of a *minimum* of material well-being, especially in income, housing, and education; secondly, the guarantee of this minimum of well-being for *everybody* regardless of class, gender, ethnic, or geographical origin; thirdly, a legal *right* to this guarantee, which could be upheld in court, rather than mere acts of charity; finally, the guarantee in *specific situations* such as illness, invalidity resulting from accidents at work, poverty in old age, unemployment, lack of education, lack of housing, regardless of the risks of specific groups.

The general acceptance of these four principles developed only in the second half of the twentieth century, for various reasons. A clear conception of the modern welfare state was prevalent only from the 1930s and 1940s, particularly in Britain and Sweden. A broad consensus between the basic political tendencies—conservatives, liberals, socialists, and communists—about the need for a modern welfare state emerged only after the Second World War. In this period of deep crisis and poverty in Europe, as a consequence of the war, government intervention was more necessary than before. Moreover, the unique period of economic growth, with an exceptionally rapid rise in public revenues as well as private income during the 1950s and the 1960s, was a crucial precondition for the financing of the modern welfare state.

To be sure, welfare state policies did not lead to a uniform European system of social security. Institutions remained different in different countries, and Europeans migrating from one country to another experienced fundamental contrasts in social security systems, even in the 1990s. However, some common European characteristics of the modern welfare state existed. Sooner or later, by reforms of social assistance, a minimum level of income was guaranteed. A system of public social insurance was established or expanded in all four major fields: protection against invalidity resulting from accidents at work, the costs of medical treatment for the whole family of the employed, poverty in old age, and unemployment. The modern idea of the old-age pension was accepted, on which an elderly person could live quite independently of any support from family members, and old-age pensions increased to well above the poverty line. In some countries a free public health service was founded. The total active population, or at least the large majority, benefited from public social insurance.

Expenditure on public social insurance expanded dramatically in almost all West European countries, especially from the 1950s onwards. By the 1970s it was ten to twenty times higher than in the period immediately after the Second World War. So within a quarter of a century a new system of social security had been established, the modern welfare state, new in its goals and principles, new in its financial dimensions, new in its comprehensiveness for all citizens, and new in its centralized organization. This concept of the welfare state was a European invention. The welfare state was most advanced in Europe and constituted a central element of the European model.

Divergences in the modern welfare state emerged between Western and Eastern Europe from the late 1940s on. First of all, the East European welfare state *de facto* did not have to care for protection against unemployment poverty, since employment was guaranteed in most East European societies. In addition, the organization of public social insurance was clearly different in Eastern Europe. It was not only that it was often more centralized than in Western Europe. A separation between social insurances caring for wage-earners, on the one hand, and social insurances caring for members of the professions, farmers, independent craftsmen, retail traders, and retired people, on the other, was made for ideological reasons, seeking to privilege the working class in a wider sense. The centrally controlled trade unions often became the most important organizations for social insurance.

Moreover, the costs of public social insurance were presented to the public in a different way. In Western Europe the costs of public insurance were more visible, either within the public budget, or as a budget of independent social security organizations, or as financial contributions by individual wage-earners and the individual enterprise, with great variations between the individual West European countries. In the East European countries the welfare state was fully integrated into the state budget; the costs of the welfare state were unclear, and were also not as widely discussed as in the West because of the lack of an independent political public. Finally, the role of the client of the welfare state in Western Europe was very different from that in Eastern Europe. Once again, with clear variations, the West European welfare state activated the client, who often had to choose between various possibilities of individual social security and to put demands to the welfare bureaucracy. The idea of the client of the welfare state in Eastern Europe was much more that of a passive client who received, more or less automatically, the service of the welfare bureaucracy. This passive role of the client also made it more difficult to protest against unjust decisions on the part of the welfare bureaucracy.

During the 1970s and 1980s the welfare state in Western and in Eastern Europe went into a crisis, which was again, however, different in the two parts of Europe. However, the crisis of the welfare state was similar across all West European countries. It had three dimensions.

It was first a financial crisis. After the unique, extremely rapid growth of welfare expenditure the welfare state reached its financial limits. Public expenditure, especially for health and old-age pensions, could not grow in the same way as it had done before the deep financial crisis of public budgets.

Moreover, the crisis of the welfare state was a crisis of efficiency. The optimistic goal of the golden years of the modern welfare state for securing all aspects of life turned out to be unrealistic. A new type of poverty emerged in the 1970s and 1980s which was difficult to fight with the instruments of the welfare state: the poverty of the one-parent family, the long-term unemployed, the immigrants, for whom the welfare state rarely cared because it was based upon the idea of a regular working life. It also turned out that the welfare state could not cope with the huge health costs in the third age—the age of physical decline. The housing policies of the modern welfare state ran into difficulties, partly because the supply of housing at affordable rents became inadequate, and partly because the planning of new cities turned out not to have always taken into account the basic needs of human beings.

Finally, the crisis of the welfare state was a political crisis. It faced a fundamental critique from all political camps: the free-marketeering critique of the destruction of private initiative and innovation, hindering mobility and flexibility in the labour force, a critique for which especially the (Conservative) British government stood; the anti-bureaucratic critique of the welfare state, arguing that the welfare state bureaucracies did not take into account the needs and interests of the client; the anti-corporatist critique, which argued that the huge public insurance schemes were part of a system of concentration of power of big business, big unions, and big bureaucracy, a political system which was not open enough for reforms and which tended towards political immobility. This intensive public critique of the welfare state, however, did not lead to fundamental reforms of the welfare state, or even to a substantial reduction of the public social expenditure. But the optimistic image of the welfare state was lost.

The crisis of the welfare state did not exist in Eastern Europe in this sense. There was no intensive public debate, mainly because governments did not accept public debate in general, but also because it was difficult to isolate and calculate the cost of the welfare state in Eastern Europe, and even governments probably did not know the exact cost. It is, however, highly probable that welfare state subsidies in Eastern Europe were higher in relation to economic performance. But the lack of a political alarm bell for the financial difficulties of the welfare state might have been one of the reasons why the East European regimes broke down.

Conclusion

European society after 1945 went through dramatic social changes—often several successive waves of change. European social history after 1945 was also a period of real changes, rather than the invention of new social models and concepts as was the case in the late eighteenth century or the late nineteenth and early twentieth century. Social change was more widely accepted. It was experienced much less as traumatic upheaval or the fundamental loss of a better society than had been the case during the nineteenth century. Protests and social movements against social change in general aimed at change for the better rather than a return to the past. Social change affected all important dimensions of life, work as well as family, social class as well as consumption, urban life as well as the welfare state, and religion. It was so dramatic that most Europeans today have difficulty in understanding the lives of their counterparts in mid-twentieth-century Europe. The main factors giving impetus and momentum to social change included unprecedented economic prosperity, especially in the 1950s and 1960s; rapid technological advances; the desire for change among most Europeans, even when the optimism of the 1950s and 1960s had worn off; the perception of reforms as a positive goal shared by all governments; the expansion of education; and the communications revolution, which accelerated the transfer of ideas to much larger parts of the population than ever before. At least in the western part of Europe social change was also more widely accepted than in the nineteenth and early twentieth century, since most people profited from it and since it did not put into question widely accepted social principles such as democracy, the market economy, and social security.

In contrast to former periods, social change also did not divide Europe into a modern centre and a traditional periphery. It occurred in most European countries and in the vast majority of regions. As a consequence, the second half of the twentieth century was in general a period of convergence. To be sure, European societies remained distinctly different. Some new differences even emerged in the second half of the twentieth century. But at the beginning of the twenty-first century European societies were less different from one another than they had been in the middle of the twentieth century. National differences in Europe were also, in general, less enthusiastically perceived as signs of national superiority.

This convergence of European societies was to a certain extent part of a worldwide trend towards convergence. In certain fields and in some periods it was also a consequence of the Americanization of European society. But on the whole it went beyond mere globalization and cannot be explained simply as an imitation of American concepts and lifestyles.

Various factors worked in the direction of a specific European convergence of societies. Industrialization and growth of the service sector in the whole of Europe rather than just in parts of it, a peculiarity of the second half of the twentieth century, led to basically similar work societies in Europe. Patterns of increasing state intervention, which followed similar basic models and which were also opposed in a similar way, led to more similarities in some dimensions of European societies, though to similarities of the results of policies rather than to similarities of institutions. Rising international mobility by travel to other European countries, by work, education, and recreation in other European countries, by increased trade especially of consumer goods, and also the new intensity of international communications, led to a more intimate knowledge of concepts of lifestyles and social institutions of other European countries, to more transfers between European countries, and hence also reinforced the rapprochement of European societies. The convergence of European national politics and policies described in other chapters of this book was an important context for the convergence of European societies. The slowly emerging European public sphere, predominantly still a public sphere of experts, also promoted intellectual exchange and rapprochement of concepts. The policy of the EU, especially with the membership of large parts of Western Europe from the 1980s, was also a factor of convergence, through the mobilization of Europeans as well as the sometimes controversial policies of European harmonization of goods and rules. No doubt the upheaval of 1989–91 and the end of the division of Europe into West and East was also a driving force towards convergence, including a convergence of structures as well as of minds and mentalities.

All these trends did not and probably never will abolish national and regional peculiarities, one of the strong points of Europe. But these peculiarities became more accessible for other Europeans, more open to a process of mutual learning, understanding, and appreciation, and the basis for the construction of a Europe beyond national isolation and beyond the military supremacy of one country over the others as in Nazi Europe.

4

Economy

Barry Eichengreen

The second half of the twentieth century was a period of unparalleled growth in Europe which transformed the lives of its people almost beyond recognition. In 1950 many Europeans heated their houses with coal, cooled their food with ice, and relied on what we might euphemistically call rudimentary forms of indoor plumbing. Today their lives are eased by natural-gas furnaces, microwave ovens, and electronic gadgets that boggle the mind. Over the intervening years real gross domestic product per capita (what the output produced by the typical European will buy) more than tripled in the countries of the continent's West and doubled in the countries of its East. The quality of life improved even more than these simple measures would imply. Hours worked per year declined by more than a third, permitting an enormous increase in leisure time. Life expectancy lengthened, reflecting improved living standards and advances in medical technology. Everything was not sweetness and light, of course. Unemployment worsened over the period, and with it feelings of alienation and insecurity. Tax burdens soared, leaving many Europeans feeling that they were supporting expensive government programmes from which they derived little benefit. But by any objective standard, the growth of the past half-century has left Europeans enormously better off today than half a century ago.

Not all parts of Europe shared equally in this prosperity, of course, and not all portions of the half-century were marked by equally rapid growth. Southern Europe grew faster than Northern Europe, Western Europe faster than Eastern Europe. Growth was faster in the two decades before 1973 than the two decades after. This deterioration was most dramatic in the East, where it culminated in the crisis of central planning and the collapse of the Soviet bloc. But notwithstanding this diversity, the post-war period is rightly regarded as a golden age of economic growth.

Two conditions stimulated growth continent-wide in the second half of the twentieth century. One was the backlog of unexploited technological and organizational knowledge at the beginning of the period. The decades between the First and Second World Wars were a period of economic instability and crisis, but they were also decades of significant technological progress. While the economic slump of the 1930s was hardly a propitious environment for commercializing these advances, new knowledge could be stored for future use. The Second World War was a hothouse for technological advance, the military having to innovate to survive; it produced advances in jet engines, radar, and computing, to cite three examples. After 1945 these developments could be put to peacetime use.

The other factor shaping economic growth continent-wide was the great power conflict. How European societies organized their economies was the most important determinant of their subsequent economic performance. The cold war had a decisive impact on that choice: it moved Western Europe towards market capitalism and Eastern Europe towards state socialism. The principal features of the international economic environment—the Marshall Plan, the Bretton Woods international monetary system, and the General Agreement on Tariffs and Trade—were all shaped by the US–Soviet conflict.

Together, the technological backlog and the cold war drove European economic growth over the second half of the twentieth century. To these two actions there were two reactions—two ways in which Europe responded to these external stimuli. One was the transition from extensive to intensive growth. By extensive growth economists mean growing on the basis of known technologies—raising output by putting more people to work at familiar tasks, and raising labour productivity by building more factories along the lines of existing factories. Intensive growth refers, in contrast, to growth through innovation. Europe relied more heavily on extensive growth before 1973 and more heavily on intensive growth thereafter. Extensive growth was facilitated by the backlog of technology; it was less important to innovate so long as there were known technologies still to be acquired and commercialized.[1] Extensive growth was easy so long as there were elastic supplies of labour—refugees from the East, repatriates from the colonies, and under-employed workers from the agricultural periphery—who could be added to the industrial labour force without putting upward pressure on wages.

Similarly, extensive growth was what planned economies organized on Soviet lines did best. The government decided how many factories to build, directed banks to mobilize the resources, and limited consumption to what was left over. It decided what foreign technologies to acquire, whether through licensing or espionage. It is not surprising, then, that the centrally planned economies of Eastern Europe performed best in the age of extensive growth.

The more successfully European countries pursued this model of extensive growth, the more quickly they exhausted the backlog of technological and organizational knowledge. And as that backlog was exhausted, they were forced to switch to intensive, innovation-based growth. The centrally planned economies were least good at innovation, since new knowledge typically bubbled up from below instead of raining down from above. More than any other activity, it responded to incentives, something which in the planned economies was in decidedly short supply. This weakness came back to haunt them once the technological pantry was bare and innovation became the order of the day.

Europe's second response was integration. While related to the wider process of 'globalization', the particular manifestation of this trend was different in Europe. Integration has meant regional integration, and the process was driven more by policy and less by technology than elsewhere. European integration mirrored the great power conflict: the United States encouraged its West European allies to cultivate closer political ties, while the Soviet Union prohibited the participation of East European countries which may have been tempted to collaborate in Western integration initiatives. It reflected the transition from extensive to intensive growth in so far as the

[1] While it is tempting to associate intensive growth with the growth of total factor productivity (productivity not associated with increases in capital and labour inputs), extensive growth with the growth of capital and labour inputs, this would not be correct for our period. Extensive growth in Europe after the Second World War took place in part by acquiring and commercializing new technologies, as explained in the text. This meant that it was associated with significant increases in total factor productivity.

Single European Act of 1986 and the Maastricht Treaty of 1991 were meant as remedies to mounting unemployment and slowing growth.

The remainder of this chapter seeks to elaborate these themes. The first section provides an eagle's-eye view of post-war economic trends. The next describes the initial conditions: the state of Europe after the Second World War. The following two sections contrast the periods of extensive and intensive growth. The last, in concluding, provides a brief reconnaissance of the state of the European economy.

Overview of post-war economic trends

An eagle-eye's view of Europe's growth since 1950 appears in Table 4.1. It contains figures for the rate of growth of gross domestic product (GDP) over various sub-periods. Between 1950 and 1973 the twelve West European economies for which consistent data are available grew more than twice as fast as over the more than a century and a half since 1820. Thus, what is referred to in the introduction as the golden age of economic growth stands out clearly. The following

TABLE 4.1 *Phases of growth of GDP in areas of Europe, 1820–1992* (average annual compound growth rate)

Area	1820–70	1870–1913	1913–50	1950–73	1973–92	1820–1992
Eastern Europe[a]	1.6	2.4	1.6	4.7	−0.4	2.0
Western Europe[b]	1.7	2.1	1.4	4.7	2.2	2.2
Southern Europe[c]	1.0	1.5	1.3	6.3	3.1	2.1
World	1.0	2.1	1.9	4.9	3.0	2.2

Notes

a   Eastern Europe is defined here to include Bulgaria, Czechoslovakia, Hungary, Poland, Romania, Yugoslavia, and the USSR.

b   Western Europe includes Austria, Belgium, Denmark, Finland, France, Germany, Italy, the Netherlands, Norway, Sweden, Switzerland, and the UK. This group could also be referred to as Northern Europe but for the inclusion of Italy.

c   Southern Europe is defined for present purposes as Greece, Spain, Portugal, Turkey, and (no misprint) Ireland.

Source: Angus Maddison, *Monitoring the World Economy 1820–1992* (Paris: OECD, 1995).

sub-period, from 1973 to 1992, in contrast, is rather typical: Western Europe's growth averaged 2.2 per cent per annum over both that sub-period and the entire 172 years since 1820.

The same fluctuations are evident in Southern Europe and in Ireland, although the pattern of acceleration and deceleration is if anything even more pronounced. While growth over the entire period since 1820 is essentially the same as in Western Europe, the post-war acceleration is more dramatic. Growth is fully three times as fast in 1950–73 as over the longer period. While Southern Europe experienced a post-1973 slowdown much like that of Europe as a whole, growth remains 50 per cent faster in 1973–92 than the period average. Even more than in Western Europe, then, the second half of the twentieth century stands out.

The data for Eastern Europe also show growth accelerating after 1950 and decelerating after 1973. Output expands at the same rate as in Western Europe in the years of extensive growth (4.7 per cent per annum), but the absolute increase relative to the period average is faster, reflecting Eastern Europe's tendency to lag behind the West in the nineteenth century. Growth decelerates after 1973—indeed, it actually turns negative, a shift evident in no other region.

Of our twelve West European economies extensive growth was fastest in Germany, Austria, and Italy (Table 4.2), reflecting the post-war *Wirtschaftswunder* (economic miracle) in Germany, Austria's economic and geographic proximity and structural resemblance to its larger neighbour, and Italy's—especially northern Italy's—success in catching up with the continent's high-income regions. It was slowest in the United Kingdom, a problem which by the 1970s had given rise to a literature on the country's economic failure.

Turning to Southern Europe, the golden age was brightest in Greece and Iberia, least so in Turkey and in Ireland (the Emerald Isle typically being conferred honorary membership in this group). More surprising is the fact that Ireland and Turkey were the best performers in Southern Europe in the years of intensive growth.

Growth of output per capita was strikingly uniform in Eastern Europe, reflecting the heavy hand of planning. In the years of extensive growth it was slowest in those countries that started out with the highest levels of output per person (Czechoslovakia and the USSR), fastest where initial output per capita was lowest (Bulgaria, Romania, and Yugoslavia). This suggests that central planning and state trading

TABLE 4.2 *Per capita real GDP growth in twenty-four countries, 1820–1992* (annual average compound growth rates)

Country	1820–70	1870–1913	1913–50	1950–73	1973–92
Eastern Europe					
Bulgaria	n.a.	n.a.	0.3	5.2	−1.4
Czechoslovakia	0.6	1.4	1.4	3.1	−0.1
Hungary	n.a.	1.2	0.5	3.6	0.0
Poland	n.a.	n.a.	n.a.	3.4	−0.6
Romania	n.a.	n.a.	n.a.	4.8	−1.6
USSR	0.6	0.9	1.8	3.4	−0.4
Yugoslavia	n.a.	n.a.	1.0	4.4	−0.5
Arithmetic average	n.a.	1.2	1.0	4.0	−0.8
Southern Europe					
Greece	n.a.	n.a.	0.5	6.2	1.5
Ireland	1.2	1.0	0.7	3.1	2.7
Portugal	n.a.	0.5	1.2	5.7	2.1
Spain	0.5	1.2	0.2	5.8	1.9
Turkey	n.a.	n.a.	0.8	3.3	2.6
Arithmetic average	n.a.	0.9	0.7	4.8	2.2
Western Europe					
Austria	0.7	1.5	0.2	4.9	2.2
Belgium	1.4	1.0	0.7	3.5	1.9
Denmark	0.9	1.6	1.6	3.1	1.6
Finland	0.8	1.4	1.9	4.3	1.6
France	0.8	1.5	1.1	4.0	1.7
Germany	1.1	1.6	0.3	5.0	2.1
Italy	0.6	1.3	0.8	5.0	2.4
Netherlands	1.1	0.9	1.1	3.4	1.4
Norway	0.5	1.3	2.1	3.2	2.9
Sweden	0.7	1.5	2.1	3.1	1.2
Switzerland	n.a.	1.5	2.1	3.1	0.8
UK	1.2	1.0	0.8	2.5	1.4
Arithmetic average	0.9	1.3	1.2	3.8	1.8

Note: n.a. = not available

Source: Maddison, *Monitoring the World Economy 1820–1992.*

were powerful engines for technological and organizational convergence. Strong uniformity is also evident after 1973, despite the divergent reform programmes of the different planned economies. Not only is the growth slowdown pronounced, but stagnation is region-wide.

These, then, are the facts to be explained. Explanation necessarily starts at the start, at the end of the Second World War.

Initial conditions

The Second World War was immensely destructive. It destroyed not just economic capacity—as people perished, factories and farms were bombed into rubble, and roads and bridges were laid to waste—but economic relations as well.

The task of reconstruction

Jean Lecerf provides the following inventory of war damage for France: 115 railway stations damaged or destroyed; 9,000 out of 12,000 locomotives unusable; all major canals, riverways, and ports unnavigable; nine out of ten motor vehicles out of commission.[2] But while this destruction was serious, much of it could be made good in short order. Roads and railways could be repaired. The results were not always beautiful, but they were functional; the speed with which physical damage could be reversed was a lesson of Allied experience with strategic bombing, whose impact on Germany had been less than anticipated. The same was true of roads, ports, and even factories; critical damage could be repaired quickly. While the housing stock took longer to replace, it was in some sense less essential to the resumption of production.

Less visible but more fundamentally disruptive was the interruption of normal modes of economic organization. The price mechanism that traditionally guided the allocation of resources had been superseded by rationing and controls. In the post-war environment of shortage these controls were retained. They were used to direct labour and raw materials as a way of maintaining the production of critical commodities. Wages were frozen, and workers were permitted to take only jobs advertised by official labour offices as a way of guiding manpower to priority uses. Governments froze the prices of essential consumer goods like food, fuel, and clothing, and rationed

---

[2] J. Lecerf, *La Percée de l'économie française* (Paris: Arthaud, 1963).

purchases. They regulated lending by the banks and forced them to absorb the public sector's emissions of debt. To prevent excess liquidity from spilling over into imports of luxury items and exhausting the central bank's hard-currency reserves, commodity imports and capital exports were strictly controlled.

At the conclusion of hostilities industrial production was no more than 40 per cent of pre-war levels in Belgium, France, and the Netherlands, and less than 20 per cent in Germany and Italy. From this difficult initial position it was possible to boost output quickly by restoring essential infrastructure and freeing resources for peacetime use. As early as 1947 Europe's industrial production had risen to 87 per cent of 1938 levels (Table 4.3). Agricultural output, while slower to recover, reached 80 per cent of pre-war levels by 1947–8.

TABLE 4.3 *Production in Western Europe* (1938 = 100)

Country	1947	1948	1949	1950	1951	Percentage increase 1951 over 1947
Turkey	153	154	162	165	163	7
Sweden	142	149	157	164	172	21
Ireland	120	135	154	170	176	46
Denmark	119	135	143	159	160	35
Norway	115	125	135	146	153	33
UK	110	120	129	140	145	32
Belgium	106	122	122	124	143	33
Luxembourg	—	132	132	139	168	—
France	99	111	122	123	138	39
Netherlands	94	114	127	140	147	56
Italy	93	99	109	125	143	54
Greece	69	76	90	114	130	88
Austria	55	85	114	134	148	269
Germany (Federal Republic)	34	50	72	91	106	312
All participating countries	87	99	112	124	135	55
All participating countries excl. Germany (Federal Republic)	105	119	130	138	145	37

Source: US President, *First Report to Congress on the Mutual Security Program* (31 Dec. 1951), 75; drawn from W. A. Brown and R. Opie, *American Foreign Assistance* (Washington, DC: Brookings Institution, 1953), 249.

The transition to sustained growth

This was the easy part, achieved by repairing obvious damage and putting idle resources back to work. The more difficult task was to sustain the expansion. Here there were three obstacles: ambitious (some would say overly ambitious) public investment programmes, price controls, and political uncertainty.

A lesson widely drawn from the war was the importance of investment, industrial investment in particular. The Allies and the Nazis had engaged in a deadly industrial race, in which success was measured in tons of iron and steel and thousands of tanks, battleships, and aircraft produced. In the end the United States determined the outcome by bringing to bear its formidable industrial capacity. Restoring economic vitality after the war consequently came to be seen as the task of repairing industrial capacity and industrial competitiveness. 'The psychology of 1945', as Adams[3] referred to this mindset, attached priority to growth, specifically industrial growth.

Recovery was thus driven by public spending on the repair and expansion of industrial capacity. Priority was given, on both competitiveness and national-security grounds, to heavy industries like iron and steel. Thus, the Monnet Plan, the modernization programme unveiled by the French government in 1947, emphasized investment in transport, energy, and iron and steel. The problem was that Europe itself produced only limited quantities of the capital goods that were inputs into this process. This was especially so as long as the occupying powers limited German industrial production, that country having been a major producer and exporter of capital goods.

Industrial inputs might be purchased from the United States, but only for hard currency. And by 1947 Europe had largely exhausted its dollar reserves. Merchandise exports could be used to finance imported inputs only to a limited extent, since imports had to come first to provide the raw materials necessary for industrial production. And borrowing abroad was infeasible, given the uncertain political situation and the disastrous legacy of inter-war loans.

The second obstacle to sustained growth was price controls themselves. So long as the prices of consumer goods were frozen below free-market levels, producers had little incentive to bring their goods

---

[3] William James Adams, *Restructuring the French Economy* (Washington, DC: Brookings Institution, 1989).

to market. Farmers stored their grain rather than marketing it. They fattened their pigs instead of slaughtering them. Unable to purchase consumer goods, workers spent their time not at the factory but cultivating garden plots and foraging in the countryside. The problem worsened as governments continued running deficits and printing money, aggravating the disparity between black-market and controlled prices. Officials resorted to threats against those accused of hoarding. The Ramadier government in France attacked speculators, those traditional French bugbears, for withholding stocks, but to no avail.

The solution—decontrolling prices and allowing the market to operate—was straightforward in principle but difficult in practice. So long as budgets remained in deficit and governments printed money to bridge the revenue gap, decontrol implied inflation. This made tax increases and expenditure reductions preconditions for price decontrol. And in the fractious post-war political environment, no consensus prevailed on the composition of the requisite adjustments.

This points to the third obstacle to sustained growth, namely policy uncertainty. Communists occupied important positions in early post-war Italian and French governments. In Denmark the Communist Party had similarly proven popular in the first post-war elections, leading to a weak minority government incapable of implementing a stabilization. The British government, which included Labourites of radical persuasion, had embarked on an ambitious programme of industrial nationalization. In Germany uncertainty emanated from the policies of the Allied occupiers, whose goals included limiting industrial production, dismantling factories, and breaking up cartels and large enterprises. The single largest political party, the SPD, advocated the socialization of industry and the maintenance of controls. It was not clear that governments in any of these countries would respect private property, resist the temptation to impose confiscatory taxes, and let the free-enterprise system work.

This uncertainty increased the value of waiting. Entrepreneurs held off investing until learning more about the status of private property. Investors hesitated to purchase securities, not knowing whether their dividends would be taxed away. Banks hesitated to lend, not knowing whether their principal would be inflated away.

The role of the Marshall Plan

The Marshall Plan, launched by the United States in 1947, removed these three obstacles simultaneously. By providing $13 billion of US government grants over four years, it relaxed the balance-of-payments constraint on growth. It thus unravelled the Gordian knot of having to first export in order to import but being unable to import without first exporting. Europe's strategy of investment-led growth was sustained.

In addition, the Marshall Plan provided incentives for governments to embrace the market. Countries accepting US aid had to sign bilateral pacts agreeing to decontrol prices, stabilize their exchange rates, and balance their budgets. In other words, they had to put in place the prerequisites for a functioning market economy. The United States made the disbursal of Marshall aid conditional on progress towards meeting these goals. The plan thus helped to resolve political uncertainty by tipping the balance of political power in favour of centrist parties. US officials made clear their reluctance to favour far-left governments with Marshall aid. This strengthened the hand of mainstream politicians, who could point to the loss of US grants as an additional cost of opposing their programmes. In both France and Italy the announcement of the Marshall Plan was accompanied by the exit of communist ministers from the governing coalition. In Denmark it was followed by a major setback for the communists in the October 1947 elections.

In a sense the Marshall Plan defined the conflict between East and West as the choice between plan and market. The Soviet Union was invited to participate (although historians have questioned the sincerity of America's offer). Moscow refused, on the grounds that no foreign power could tell it how to run its economy. Czechoslovakia and Poland attempted to accept the US invitation but were overruled by Stalin, who instead placed their economies firmly under his thumb.

In the West the response to price decontrol was immediate. Stores empty one day were overflowing the next as goods flooded out of hoards. Now that workers had goods to buy, absenteeism fell. The supply of raw materials from mines and farms provided industry with inputs needed to expand production. As budget deficits were cut and monetary printing presses slowed, external disequilibria were reduced. It became possible to begin lifting import restrictions and for European nations to exploit more fully their comparative advantage in international markets.

A final effect of the Marshall Plan was to encourage European integration. The US offer was contingent upon the recipients' willingness to devise a collective strategy for utilizing the funds. In their more idealistic moments the Marshall Planners saw their initiative as encouraging the formation of a 'United States of Europe', in which economic and political integration made war inconceivable. More concretely, European integration was a way of reconciling other countries, France in particular, to higher levels of German industrial production and of disarming those who insisted on 'pastoralizing' the German economy. By locking Germany into Europe and promoting the development of institutions of transnational governance, it permitted Paris to agree to the elimination of ceilings on German industrial production. By substituting American aid, it encouraged the French to drop their claims to German reparations. These concessions were essential for the success of the German monetary reform of 1948, under which the monetary overhang was eliminated, debts were cancelled, and goods flooded back into the shops. Had production ceilings and reparations remained in place, these measures would not have succeeded in restoring the incentive to produce and in igniting a dramatic increase in output. But with these obstacles removed, the post-war German economic miracle, or *Wirtschaftswunder*, could get under way. Since Germany was at the heart of the European economy, that heart could now beat more strongly. The geopolitical threat from the East could be repelled by the return of prosperity.

The age of extensive growth

The emphasis the Marshall Planners placed on European integration had an economic as well as political rationale, namely as a means of stimulating Europe's trade. Before 1950 the economies of Western Europe suffocated under a stifling blanket of trade restrictions. To husband their precious hard currency for purchases from the dollar area, each country sought to restrict its imports from each other country to the value of receipts in its currency. Pairs of governments drew up lists of commodities for which they would issue import licences up to agreed limits. Under these restrictive arrangements intra-European trade remained little more than two-thirds of pre-war levels in the first half of 1948, by which time the volume of Europe's exports to other continents had already surpassed 1938 volumes.

Of course, some trade was better than no trade. 'In the period immediately following the war, bilateral agreements permitted the rapid rebuilding of trade relations,' as a team of United Nations experts put it.[4] But bilateral agreements, once in place, made more difficult the next step of placing Europe's trade on a free-market footing. This required allowing payments to be settled multilaterally (for Britain's exports to France to be used to finance its purchases from Belgium, for example). But no country could take this step unilaterally. If it offered to liberalize but the others failed to follow, it would see its market flooded with imports but still lack access for its exports, a combination which spelled dire consequences for the balance of payments. The abortive attempt to make sterling convertible for current account transactions in 1947 (as required of the British under the terms of a $3.75 billion American loan) had to be reversed after five weeks of disastrous reserve losses, illustrating the problem.

Before 1950 efforts to coordinate the transition to freer intra-European trade proved unavailing. With inflation running hot in France and Greece and the prospect of inflation in Germany and Austria once prices were decontrolled, surplus countries hesitated to agree to a clearing mechanism with credits for deficits for fear that inflation- and deficit-prone participants would immediately absorb whatever credits were collectively offered. Bilateralism did not provoke a crisis so long as Marshall aid could be used to finance intra-European trade imbalances as well as imbalances in relation to the dollar area. But by 1949 the end of the Marshall Plan was in sight. A new sense of urgency prompted renewed negotiations.

[4] United Nations, *Economic Survey of Europe in 1948* (Geneva: UN, 1950), 98.

The European payments union and first steps towards collective governance

The result was the European Payments Union (EPU). The EPU was initially conceived as a two-year transitional arrangement at the end of which the participating countries would restore convertibility for transactions on current account (for trade in goods and services). In the event the transition proved more difficult than anticipated, and the EPU remained the structure for intra-European trade for nearly a decade. Under its provisions each country's net balances with each other country were reported at the end of each month to the Bank for International Settlements, the EPU's fiscal agent, which cancelled off-setting claims. Remaining balances were consolidated, leaving each country with liabilities or claims not on other countries but on the EPU as a whole. Hence, governments no longer cared with which other European country trade was conducted; all that mattered was the overall balance of debits and credits. Moreover, EPU membership entitled a participating country to credit from its partners, with which it could finance temporary deficits. Thus, not only did the EPU remove the need for countries to balance their trade with each other country, but it allowed them to run temporary deficits in relation to the group as a whole. The United States contributed $350 million of Marshall Plan funds towards the EPU's operation. The problem of coordinating the transition to current account convertibility was solved by requiring participants to accept the Organization for European Economic Cooperation's Code of Liberalization, a second, simultaneous agreement under which they agreed to removing import controls at a predetermined pace.

This initiative did much to grease the wheels. Intra-European trade rose from $10 billion in 1950 to $23 billion in 1959, significantly faster than output. It spurted ahead in 1950–1, coincident with the creation of the EPU. While much of that surge reflected the experience of one country, Germany, here too the EPU's role was critical. Tied as it was to the Marshall Plan, the EPU reassured other countries that Germany would use its economic power benignly and not renege on its commitment to free and open trade. More concretely, the EPU helped Germany surmount its 1950–1 balance-of-payments crisis. The outbreak of the Korean War drove up the prices of the primary commodities Germany imported, aggravating the country's external deficit and creating pressure to reverse recent trade liberalization measures. The EPU managing board provided extraordinary credits to bridge the gap and sent in a pair of experts, whose recommendations of temporary tax and discount rate increases lent those policies domestic political legitimacy. With these measures in place, restrictions on German imports could be moderated.

More important still, the EPU was a stepping-stone towards collective governance. The members of its managing board 'served as individuals performing a collective function, rather than as government representatives'.[5] The decision to extend extraordinary credits, for example, was taken collectively.

The next step towards collective governance, the European Coal and Steel Community (ECSC), was even more momentous. The motivating issue was the same—permitting the German iron and steel industry to expand without exciting fears that the country would rebuild its military-industrial complex. The solution was a joint high authority to provide transnational oversight of national investment plans for coal and steel. 'Membership required transference of sovereign powers to a new European authority,' in the words of the Community's historian.[6] In addition to the high authority, the treaty instituting the ECSC provided for a common assembly as a forum for discussion and a high court as an advocate for the high authority as regards the contracting states, anticipating the European Parliament and the European Court of Law. In these structures and not just in the fact that the contracting states became the six founding members of the EEC lay the true significance of the initiative.

Investment and the labour market

New technology, to find commercial use, had to be embodied in plant and equipment. That required investment. Gross investment averaged 22 per cent of income from 1949 to 1958, up a quarter from the

---

[5] Jacob J. Kaplan and Gunther Schleiminger, *The European Payments Union: Financial Diplomacy in the 1950s* (Oxford: Clarendon Press, 1989).

[6] John Gillingham, 'The European Coal and Steel Community: An Object Lesson:', in Barry Eichengreen (ed.), *Europe's Postwar Recovery* (Cambridge: Cambridge University Press, 1995), 151.

inter-war years.[7] Governments kept interest rates low and regulated the financial system to channel resources towards investment. But countries varied enormously in the efficiency with which they utilized these funds. In Germany an additional 3 percentage points of national income devoted to investment generated a full percentage point of additional growth. In Norway, in contrast, an additional percentage point of growth required an additional 9 percentage points of output devoted to investment. West Germany, of course, had been late to initiate the reconstruction of its industrial sector (due in part to the Allied controls described above), and it experienced a flood of immigrants from East Germany (some 3 million from 1950 until the Berlin Wall was finally erected in 1961); for both reasons a little investment translated into a lot of growth. Norway, in contrast, devoted a disproportionate share of its investment to projects like electrifying the north, an undertaking important more for political than economic reasons and one with little immediate pay-off in terms of growth.

More generally, all the countries with high returns on investment experienced high rates of growth of the labour force (excepting Portugal and Spain, which started out far below average levels of industrial efficiency). Conversely, the countries with the lowest returns on investment, notably Ireland, Norway, Sweden, the United Kingdom, and Finland, had the most slowly expanding labour supplies. Thus, the pay-off on investment was high where there was an expanding labour force with which more capital could be put to work. A further effect of a growing labour supply was to moderate the upward pressure on wages, allowing firms to plough back additional profits into investment.

In part the mechanism was the classic one of supply and demand. Where labour supplies were most elastic, upward pressure on wages was least. So long as refugees from the GDR flooded into West Germany, there was a reserve army of labour to be employed. German

---

[7] These estimates are for twenty-one European countries. They come from United Nations, *Economic Survey of Europe in 1961*, pt. 2: *Some Factors in Economic Growth in Europe during the 1950s* (Geneva: UN, 1964), as do all the statistics that follow on growth in the 1950s (except where explicitly noted otherwise). Angus Maddison ('Economic Policy and Performance in Europe, 1913–1970', in Carlo M. Cipolla (ed.), *The Fontana Economic History of Europe*, Vol. v, pt. 2 (Glasgow: Fontana, 1976)) calculates net fixed investment rates for Western Europe, estimating these as 9.6% in 1928–38 and 16.8% in 1950–70.

unemployment remained in the double digits until this influx was absorbed in the later 1950s; it is no surprise that wage pressure was moderate under these circumstances. The same mechanism operated in the Netherlands with the return of Dutch settlers from the East Indies (300,000 of whom represented 7 per cent of the labour force), and in Switzerland with the import of guest workers from Southern Europe. It operated in France and Italy with the migration of under-employed labour from agriculture to industry and services, relieving supply-side pressure on the tertiary sector.

The post-war social contract

But more than the iron laws of supply and demand explain the wage moderation of the post-war years. In addition, European societies developed corporatist structures to restrain wage growth and see that profits were ploughed into investment. Post-war governments asked unions to limit their wage demands to make profits available for modernization and capacity expansion. The problem was guarantee-ing that industrialists would in fact invest the profits they con-sequently received. Sceptical that more investment, faster growth, and higher living standards would result from self-denial, labour hesi-tated to make the requisite sacrifices. The danger was that unions would pursue wage increases, management would pay out profits as dividends, and investment and growth would suffer, as in the inter-war years.

Cooperation between capital and labour was cemented by a series of institutional bargains, some informal, some codified in law. One set of institutions monitored the compliance of the parties to their agreement to exchange wage moderation for the reinvestment of profits. German co-determination, giving labour oversight of firms' investment policies, allowed workers to monitor management's com-pliance with its commitment to invest. Works councils (required in shops with as few as five employees) played a similar information-disseminating role in small firms not covered by the co-determination law. In the Netherlands representatives of labour, management, and government worked together on *Publiek Rechtelijke Bedrijfsorganisatie,* (Public Work Board), hammering out agreements regarding the employment and investment policies of Dutch firms. Norway established planning councils and production committees to promote worker participation in management decisions. Union and industry representatives sat together on the boards of Belgian public and semi-public industrial and financial enterprises under the provisions of the 1948 Law on the Organization of Industry. Even in France, where labour relations were hardly smooth, labour–management committees were required by law for all enterprises employing fifty or more workers. Representatives were entitled to attend meetings of the board of directors and served as conduits for information about the investment policies of the enterprise. A 1946 Act required management to inform the committee and receive its opinion before finalizing investment decisions and (in the case of limited liability companies) to inform it of the profits made by the undertaking and permit it to audit the books. Labour was thereby reassured that capital was keeping its part of the bargain to invest the fruits of its wage restraint.

A second set of institutions created 'bonds' that would be lost in the event that either party reneged on the terms of its agreement. In Austria firms were promised industrial inputs at sub-market prices from public enterprises in return for following cooperative investment and dividend policies. The Swedish government regulated the payment of dividends by public companies and invited corporations to place up to 40 per cent of their profits into closed public accounts. Central banks helped to cement the corporatist bargain by pursuing investment-friendly monetary policies that encouraged firms to follow through on their commitment to invest.

A parallel set of government programmes bonded labour. In Belgium the first post-war government adopted a social security scheme in return for labour's adherence to the 1944 Social Pact limiting wage increases. The Norwegian government offered legislation mandating paid vacations and limiting the length of the working week in return for wage restraint. The Danish government offered an expanded system of sick pay in 1956, when the agreement to link wage increases to productivity negotiated during the reconstruction phase showed signs of breaking down. The German government indexed retirement incomes to living standards in the 1957 pension reform. The Austrian government extended tax and social insurance concessions to labour in return for wage moderation.

A third set of institutions coordinated bargains across firms and sectors. Coordination was necessary to solve problems of collective action in so far as wage moderation in one sector increased the profits available for investment economy-wide. Increasingly, bargaining was centralized in the hands of a trade union federation and national employers' association, and governments intervened to harmonize the terms of the bargains reached by different unions and employers.

Post-war imperatives elicited this response because of the existence of powerful collectivist predispositions. Building institutions to free Europe's citizens from the tyranny of the market was encouraged by nineteenth-century Roman Catholic theology and twentieth-century Christian Democratic ideology. It became a goal of the socialist and working-class parties whose electoral base expanded after the Second World War. Further encouragement was lent by the American administrators of the Marshall Plan, who had seen their own economy turn, if briefly, in a corporatist direction under the National Industrial Recovery Act. And the desirability of relying less on the market and more on government and on extra-market cooperation was the general lesson drawn from the collapse of the market economy in the 1930s.

The dawn of the golden age

Table 4.4 summarizes the performance of the principal economies of Western Europe in the 1950s, decomposing growth into the contributions of capital, labour, and technological progress.[8] Countries are ranked by their rate of output growth. Germany's position at the top of the league results from the unusually rapid rate of growth of inputs, reflecting exceptionally fast growth of the labour supply and high investment rates, but also the country's unusually rapid growth of productivity. Technological progress is also strikingly rapid in Italy, reflecting that country's success at closing the gap with Europe's high-income countries. Britain's poor performance reflects both low investment rates and disappointing productivity growth. France stands out for the stagnation of its labour force. While French policy-makers were much concerned about this 'Malthusianism', the country's impressive productivity performance (behind only that of Germany and Italy) sustained more than respectable overall rates of growth.

---

[8] Based on a Cobb–Douglas production function with a coefficient of 0.7 for the labour force.

TABLE 4.4 *The contribution to growth of GDP in nine West European countries of labour, capital, and technical progress, 1949–1959*

Country	Compound annual percentage rate of growth			Estimated contribution to growth of GDP of:			ICOR
	Labour force	Capital stock	GDP trend	Labour	Capital	Technical progress	
West Germany[a]	1.6	6.0	7.4	1.1	1.8	4.5	2.6
Italy	1.1	3.2	5.9	0.8	1.0	4.1	2.1
Yugoslavia	1.1	4.9	5.5	0.8	1.5	3.2	2.5
Netherlands	1.2	4.8	4.8	0.8	1.4	2.6	4.0
France	0.1	3.4	4.5	0.1	1.0	3.4	2.9
Norway	0.3	4.6	3.4	0.2	1.4	1.8	8.5
Sweden	0.5	2.0	3.4	0.3	0.6	2.5	4.1
Belgium	0.3	2.6	3.0	0.2	0.8	2.0	2.8
United Kingdom	0.6	3.1	2.4	0.4	0.9	1.1	3.7

[a] 1950–9.

Source: Extract from United Nations, *Economic Survey of Europe in 1961*, pt. 2: *Some factors in Economic Growth in Europe during the 1950s*.

The average worker was only half as productive in agriculture as industry. The principal exceptions were the United Kingdom, where a century of free trade had forced farmers to rationalize their operations, and the Benelux countries, which specialized in high-value-added dairy and truck farming. Part of the explanation for the rapid growth of productivity in the 1950s was thus the shift of employment from low-productivity agriculture to higher-productivity manufacturing and services. The share of employment in agriculture fell by 9 percentage points in Germany, 8 points in Italy, and 7 points in Norway. Farmers were a powerful lobby, and government protected their interests, but the agricultural sector was still allowed to contract in relative if not absolute terms as a necessary concomitant of the post-war productivity miracle.

Eastern Europe and the planned economy

Eastern Europe was even more heavily agricultural. Only one country there, East Germany, had a larger share of its labour force in industry than agriculture. Together with the same productivity gap between manufacturing and farming as in Western Europe, this helps to account for the East's relatively low per capita incomes at the start of the period. State planning offices saw the expansion of industry as the most direct way of raising labour productivity. Consequently, East European agriculture did not receive government support comparable to that enjoyed by the farmers of the West. To the contrary: the planners set artificially low prices for agricultural goods, artificially high ones for manufactures; together with differences in output per worker, this caused the output of the typical industrial worker to be valued at three times that of his agricultural counterpart. This skewed price structure reflected the desire to encourage industry relative to agriculture. In Hungary, Poland, and Bulgaria the entire increase in labour supply over the course of the 1950s went into sectors other than agriculture. In East Germany and Czechoslovakia the structural shift was even more dramatic, with agricultural employment declining 20 per cent. Conventional calculations indicate that structural change (the shift of resources out of agriculture and into industry and services) accounted for an even larger share of productivity growth in Eastern than Western Europe.

East European governments reported impressive rates of growth of net material product in the 1950s, on the order of 8 per cent in Hungary and Poland and 11 per cent in Bulgaria, even higher than the output growth rates associated with the West German *Wirtschaftswunder*. Not everything that was produced was of good quality, of course. The estimation of net material product was also subject to valuation problems due to the price distortions described above. These are both reasons for taking the published statistics with a grain of salt.

For what they are worth, those statistics point to investment as the engine of growth. Investment rates were not high by West European standards, but the rate of growth of the capital stock was rapid, reflecting the low level from which it started. Even more than in the West, this was the heyday of extensive growth—growth driven by investment. Priority was given to heavy industry and to the production of capital goods, especially after East–West tensions mounted with the outbreak of the Korean War.

By 1949 most major branches of industry and finance in Eastern Europe were owned and operated by the state. The first five-year plans were introduced in 1949–51 (aside from Yugoslavia, which adopted its in 1947). More factories were built in the image of existing factories. More workers were assigned to established tasks. A premium was placed on applying existing technologies and replicating existing facilities, not on innovation.

Achievements and limitations of central planning

The results were superficially impressive, but already in the 1950s there was trouble beneath the surface. While the region's endowment of skilled labour and the available backlog of proven technology provided obvious scope for increasing industrial production, cold war imperatives and Stalinist ideology led planners to push the process too far. Central and Eastern Europe had traditionally been the continent's breadbasket; the region was endowed with rich agricultural land, providing an economic logic for why it should continue to produce and export agricultural goods. Instead, agriculture was starved of resources: Czechoslovakia, Poland, and Yugoslavia first managed to match pre-war levels of grain production only in the last years of the 1950s. Similar problems resulted from the neglect of light industry, as in Hungary, where handicraft trades were abolished so that additional resources could be transferred to heavy industry.

Unlike the West, where increases in output translated into commensurate improvements in living standards, living standards in Eastern Europe stagnated. This too reflected over-concentration on heavy industry; much of what was produced by the industrial sector was used to satisfy that same sector's own appetite for inputs. Managers protected themselves against the risk of missing production targets by over-ordering raw materials, building excess capacity, and employing superfluous labour; the target-oriented plan provided few deterrents against wasting resources. Lagging living standards also reflected problems with what was produced in the consumer goods sector. Part of the rise in welfare in the West resulted from the growing variety of consumer goods delivered by the market economy; under planning, enterprises were only given targets for the volume of output; they reaped no reward for producing a wider variety of goods. It should come as no surprise that the Hungarian footwear industry in the early 1950s produced just sixteen types of shoe. And many of these goods were shoddy, quantity targets giving no reward for quality improvement. While public dissatisfaction and, in

Hungary, open revolt led to some reallocation of resources towards consumer goods sectors and to efforts to give enterprise managers a profit motive, the problem persisted.

These limited reforms set the tone for the 1960s. Following Stalin's death Moscow insisted less strongly on the maintenance of rigid Soviet-style planning. Growth decelerated between the second half of the 1950s and the first half of the 1960s, and planners, out of desperation, began to experiment with decentralizing the planning mechanism. Enterprise managers were given more freedom and rewards for economizing on the use of resources. Prices, albeit administered prices, were increasingly used to guide these decentralized decisions. The extent of these reforms varied: East Germany, Poland, and Romania were the least ambitious, Hungary and Yugoslavia the most. Still, it is striking that after barely a decade of experimentation with the command economy, elements of the market had begun to creep back in.

Decentralization did not extend to the management of innovation, the great weakness of the planned economies. East Germany established large-scale research centres within each of its *Kombinate* (industrial holding companies). In Czechoslovakia, where resources for research and development had been allotted to small as well as large enterprises, they were concentrated in the large ones in the hope that these would develop innovations with wide applicability. The National Office for Technological Development in Hungary allowed R & D activities to remain more decentralized but sought to coordinate better the tasks of the various research institutes.

Planning at home was incompatible with trading abroad. The prices set by the planners were different from those prevailing in the rest of the world, and free trade would have given enterprise managers conflicting incentives about which signals to follow. But neither was national self-sufficiency desirable, since different countries had different resource endowments and economic capabilities. The solution was to encourage trade within the Eastern bloc. The Council for Mutual Economic Assistance, or Comecon, was established in 1949 in reaction to the Marshall Plan. Comecon's founding members, Bulgaria, Czechoslovakia, Hungary, Poland, and Romania, together with the Soviet Union, were joined by East Germany in 1950. Moscow's idea was that Czechoslovakia and East Germany would specialize in industrial goods while countries like Romania concentrated on agriculture in an 'international socialist division of labour'. However, this was incompatible with the aspirations of the Romanian leadership, among others. Planners in each country sought to create an economy in which industry accounted for half of output and agriculture for a quarter or less.

Intra-bloc trade nonetheless expanded under the influence of Comecon, as the constituent economies shipped their slightly different goods back and forth. The share of East European imports drawn from East European sources was twice as high in the 1950s as it had been on the eve of the Second World War. Much of the rest of the region's trade was with the Soviet Union. Trade with Western Europe, where the East European economies' principal market had historically lain, declined to negligible levels.

Regional integration in Western Europe

The Eastern bloc's commitment to Comecon was strengthened by regional integration in the West. The establishment of the European Economic Community in 1958 and its creation of a free trade area encompassing France, Germany, Italy, and the Benelux countries in less than ten years was without question the most profound development affecting growth in the West in the 1960s. The stage for this initiative had been set by the progressive elimination of the dollar gap—that is, of Europe's structural deficit in relation to the United States. Important progress in this direction had already been achieved by the time the Marshall Plan was wound up in 1951. Further strengthening of Europe's payments position then allowed controls on current account transactions to be substantially removed in the mid-1950s. By 1958 the countries of Western Europe were ready to restore full current account convertibility. In turn, this made feasible the establishment of a free trade area.

Freer trade allowed the participating countries to specialize more completely in the production of goods in which they had a comparative advantage and to better exploit economies of scale and scope. It eroded the market power of monopolies and cartels, forcing sheltered producers to shape up or lose market share to imports. The impact was most dramatic in countries like France whose economies had been relatively well sheltered in the 1950s. There, the share of domestic consumption accounted for by imports doubled from 8 per cent in 1959 to 16 per cent in 1969; between 1959 and 1980 it increased by more than 10 percentage points in thirty-one out of forty-six industries.[9] The share of Western Europe's trade that stayed within the region expanded by a fifth in response to the removal of controls under the EPU and then the Common Market (Table 4.5). The share of the exports of the six EEC members that stayed within the bloc rose by fully half over the period (Table 4.6).

Empirical studies generally conclude that the EEC was trade-creating rather than trade-diverting, that it encouraged additional trade among its members rather than inducing them to trade with one another at the expense of the rest of the world. The General Agreement on Tariffs and Trade (GATT) deserves credit for this outcome; tariff reductions achieved under the Kennedy Round of GATT negotiations in 1964–7 meant that freer intra-European trade complemented rather than substituted for freer trade with the rest of the world.

The founding members of the EEC were limited to the six members of the ECSC. The United Kingdom declined to join following a debate in which it rejected the Franco-German view that the free trade area should be seen as the first step towards deeper political integration (just as it had rejected the Schuman Plan prompting the creation of the ECSC). Still, the attractions of freer trade were irresistible; seeking both to liberalize trade among themselves and to

TABLE 4.5 *Intra-trade as percentage of total exports*

Area	All commodities		Primary products		Manufactures	
	1955	1969	1955	1969	1955	1969
Europe	61	73	81	82	54	70
Eastern Europe	61	61	64	48	60	68
Western Europe	56	66	72	79	49	63
EEC	33	48	44	63	29	45
EFTA	18	24	31	30	14	23
EFTA (excl. UK)	14	21	8	15	18	22

Source: United Nations, *Economic Survey of Europe in 1971*, pt. I: *The European Economy from the 1950s to the 1970s* (New York: UN, 1972).

[9] Adams, *Restructuring the French Economy*, 156–7.

TABLE 4.6 *Europe and United States: total economy output, employment, and labour productivity* (annual percentage compound rates of growth)

Country	Output (GDP at 1963 factor cost)		Employment		Output per person employed	
	1950–2 to 1958–60	1958–60 to 1967–9	1950–2 to 1958–60	1958–60 to 1967–9	1950–2 to 1958–60	1958–60 to 1960–9
Bulgaria	6.4	7.4	0.7	0.4	5.7	7.0
Czechoslovakia	5.7	4.8	1.0	1.3	4.7	3.5
GDR	7.1	4.5	0.7	0.1	6.4	4.4
Hungary	4.1	5.5	1.2	0.7	2.9	4.8
Poland	6.2	6.0	1.7	1.9	4.4	4.0
Romania	6.3	8.0	1.4	0.4	4.8	7.6
Soviet Union	8.3	6.9	1.9	2.1	6.3	4.7
Eastern Europe	7.6	6.5	1.7	1.7	5.8	4.7
Austria	5.7	4.5	0.4	−0.2	5.3	4.7
Belgium	2.5	4.5	0.2	0.6	2.4	3.8
Denmark	3.2	4.7	1.0	1.2	2.2	3.4
Finland	4.3	4.6	1.0	0.9	3.3	3.7
France	4.3	5.5	0.0	0.7	4.4	4.8
FRG	7.5	5.1	2.2	0.3	5.2	4.8
Ireland	0.8	4.0	−1.6	0.1	2.5	3.9
Italy	5.3	5.5	0.7	0.2	4.6	5.3
Netherlands	4.5	5.5	1.1	1.2	3.4	4.3
Norway	3.0	4.9	0.0	0.6	3.1	4.3
Sweden	3.6	4.5	0.2	0.4	3.4	4.1
Switzerland	4.0	4.4	1.4	1.8	2.6	2.5
United Kingdom	2.4	2.9	0.5	0.4	1.8	2.5
Industrial Western Europe	4.5	4.7	0.8	0.5	3.6	4.2
Greece	5.6	6.3	0.9	1.0	4.7	5.3
Portugal	4.0	6.1	0.4	0.0	3.6	6.2
Spain	5.2	7.0	1.0	0.6	4.1	6.4
Turkey	5.1	5.2	..	..	..	..
Yugoslavia	6.4	6.1	0.5	1.1	5.9	5.0
Southern Europe	5.3	6.3	..	..	..	..
Southern Europe excl. Turkey	5.4	6.6	0.8	0.7	4.6	4.8
United States	2.8	4.6	0.5	2.1	2.3	2.4

Source: United Nations, *Economic Survey of Europe in 1971*, pt. 1: *The European Economy from the 1950s to the 1970s.*

negotiate favourable access to the EEC, Britain and six smaller European countries (Austria, Denmark, Norway, Portugal, Sweden, and Switzerland) responded by establishing the European Free Trade Area (or EFTA) in 1959, an entity whose more limited aspirations were evident in its name.

The apex of the golden age

In response to these stimuli, growth accelerated. The growth of output per employed person in Western Europe rose from 3.6 per cent per annum in the 1950s to an even more impressive 4.2 per cent in the 1960s (see Table 4.6). Investment was maintained at high levels, and most West European countries remained net importers of financial capital. Much of this foreign investment originated in the United States and was associated with technology transfer in sectors such as chemicals, computers, and transport equipment. Investment ratios rose compared to the earlier period, although this was insufficient to accelerate the growth of output still further because more investment was now needed to make good on depreciation of the capital stock and because a declining share of investment was devoted to industry (reflecting the demand for better housing and increased consumer durables on the part of now wealthier households).

All the while, the extensive growth model was sustained by the movement of workers to the industrial regions from Mediterranean Europe and North Africa. Only in Austria and West Germany, where extensive growth had been fastest, was there a clear slowing down between the 1950s and the 1960s. In Belgium, Denmark, France, and Norway there was a marked acceleration. Norway finally reaped returns on expensive infrastructure investments undertaken in earlier years. France, previously saddled by controls and cartels, benefited disproportionately from the liberalization of trade. Denmark, where trade liberalization in the 1950s had created serious problems for an industrial sector which had been generously protected since the 1930s, now reaped the benefits of industrial rationalization.

Growth accelerated to even higher levels in Southern Europe, as Greece, Portugal, and Spain began opening to Europe and the world. In Spain the pivotal event was the new tariff of 1960, under which half of all barriers to imports from OECD countries were removed. For Portugal it was joining EFTA. Greece negotiated an association agreement with the EEC (as did Spain). Opening these countries, rather than shunting them into the agricultural backwater as some feared, was associated with rapid growth of labour-intensive manufactures. In Spain, for example, industrial production expanded at an annual rate of 10.2 per cent, the service sector by 6.7 per cent, and agriculture by a mere 2.3 per cent per year between 1960 and 1973, as labour was shifted from low-productivity agriculture to high-productivity manufacturing and capital goods were imported from abroad.[10] This was extensive growth redux. With Austrian and German growth declining from higher levels and the pace picking up in these other countries, expansion by 4.5 per cent per annum, fully twice the historical average, became the European norm.

Britain remained the sick man of Europe, its output per worker growing by only 2.5 per cent per annum. The corporatist bargain of wage restraint for high investment had never taken hold there. Early industrialization had bequeathed deeply ingrained distinctions between different trades and a fragmented system of industrial relations. Employers were forced to negotiate with a bewildering array of craft-based trade unions which resisted efforts to coordinate an economy-wide wage bargain. While employers made a number of attempts to cooperate in a more systematic way, they had no identifiable counterpart on the union side. Inadequate coordination meant poor wage restraint and disappointing profits, weakening the incentive to invest. British investment rates in the era of extensive growth (1950–69) were the lowest of any West European country.[11]

The government sought to wring additional output out of its capacity-constrained economy by running it at high levels of demand. This demand periodically spilled out into inflation and balance-of-payments deficits, forcing the authorities to raise interest rates in order to slam on the brakes. This policy of 'stop–go' and the unstable financial conditions with which it was associated hardly encouraged investment.

---

[10] Joseph Harrison, *The Spanish Economy from the Civil War to the European Community* (London: Macmillan, 1993), 23.

[11] United Nations, *Economic Survey of Europe in 1971*, pt. 1: *The European Economy from the 1950s to the 1970s*, 14. This point should be qualified by noting that consistent data on investment are difficult to assemble for Ireland in the 1950s, when its economic performance was similarly poor.

The balance of payments and other problems

Following a 'growth recession' at the end of the 1950s, the European economy expanded steadily until 1966. The upswing disguised several disturbing tendencies, including growing labour militancy and a propensity for demand stimulus to show up in inflation rather than employment. And with inflationary pressure came balance-of-payments problems. Inflation rendered exports less competitive. The post-war social compact made no allowance of nominal wage reductions; a serious deterioration in a country's competitive position could be reversed only by devaluing its currency. Although the Bretton Woods international monetary system allowed countries to change their exchange rates against the US dollar in the event of a 'fundamental disequilibrium', it did not encourage them to do so. Governments were required to obtain approval from the International Monetary Fund, discouraging them from invoking the option for fear that their intentions might be leaked to the market. Frequent small devaluations might be undertaken without prior consent but threatened to undermine the credibility of the government's commitment to its parity and to excite destabilizing capital flows.

More generally, engineering an orderly devaluation became more difficult with the rise of international capital mobility, reflecting the recovery of capital markets from their inter-war doldrums. Rumours of a pending devaluation could provoke massive, destabilizing capital flows. Hence, governments were willing to contemplate the option only as a last resort. The only major devaluations in the period were by Britain in 1967 (which led to compensatory devaluations by Denmark, Finland, Ireland, and Spain) and France in 1969. Given how Bretton Woods arrangements encouraged governments to delay the decision, devaluation inevitably took place in an atmosphere of crisis that hardly inspired confidence. The 1971–3 collapse of the Bretton Woods system was precipitated by events outside Europe—in particular, by Washington DC's reluctance either to restrain domestic inflation or to alter the dollar exchange rate—but mounting balance-of-payments difficulties in Europe itself heightened these tensions.

The economics of intensive growth

As they moved through the 1950s and 1960s the West European economies gradually exhausted the technological backlog. They found it increasingly difficult to sustain growth through the simple multiplication of inputs of capital and labour. The Fordist model of dividing and conquering the labour process that had dominated the period of extensive growth gave way to flexible production based on microchip technologies and numerically controlled machine tools. The challenge now was to develop new products and new processes.

Here the United States had a leg-up. In 1963 it devoted 3.5 per cent of its GDP to R & D spending. Only in the United Kingdom was the R & D share of national income even half as high. Whereas the United States devoted nearly 8 per cent of government expenditure to R & D, in no European country was the comparable ratio even half as high.

European governments took steps over the 1960s to close the gap. The small states concentrated on applied research relevant to their existing industrial base, while larger ones, where more R & D spending was by government and less was privately financed, devoted a larger share to modern, science-based sectors. The European economies made good use of their limited resources: with the exception of the United Kingdom West European countries all managed to expand their shares of global exports of research-intensive goods between the mid-1950s and mid-1960s. An OECD study published in 1968 concluded that Europe's share of major innovations corresponded almost exactly to its share of OECD output.[12] While the United States was still the technological leader, Western Europe was increasingly well positioned for the transition to intensive growth.

Inflationary pressure and labour conflict

Intensive growth required investment, albeit of a different sort from earlier decades. In turn, this required maintenance of the post-war bargain of wage restraint in return for the reinvestment

[12] Organization for Economic Cooperation and Development, *Gaps in Technology* (Paris: OECD, 1968).

of profits. The acceleration of inflation in the late 1960s jeopardized the entire process. After two decades in which observers contemplated the 'withering away of the strike', work stoppages in support of wage demands erupted over much of Europe in 1968–9, threatening to relegate the post-war social compact to history's dustbin.

Several factors combined to aggravate friction in the labour market. Employment in agriculture having fallen to less than 15 per cent of employment continent-wide, elastic supplies of underemployed labour from the agricultural sector no longer served to cap industrial wage demands. Rates of unemployment fell to very low levels. Moreover, wage and price inflation showed disturbingly little tendency to subside even when unemployment rose, as in the recession of 1970–1, indicating that other factors must have also been at work. For one, memories of high unemployment faded as the older generation aged and retired. For another, willingness to sacrifice on behalf of post-war reconstruction gave way to demands for immediate gratification, and satisfying those demands could not be put off indefinitely. Finally, the Soviet threat was perceived as less immediate, removing one obvious incentive for labour and capital to pull together.

Were this not enough, with the weakening of the Bretton Woods system, inflationary expectations lost their anchor. So long as countries were committed to defending their exchange rate pegs, there was no possibility that they would succumb to policies of sustained inflation. Since bursts of inflation were only temporary, workers had relatively mild incentives to demand compensatory wage increases. The Bretton Woods system anchored expectations, moderating the impact of inflation on wages. But once that expectational anchor began to drag, unions had reason to fear that inflation, once ignited, would persist. Keynesian demand stimulus provoked increased wage demands and translated into additional inflation, not extra output and employment.

Each element that had contributed to the earlier climate of wage restraint thus weakened over the second half of the 1960s before breaking down completely in the 1970s. Wage increases won by strikers in 1968–9 were about twice those of the preceding three years. Money wages grew faster in 1969–73 than they had in 1962–9 in each of the nine European countries considered by Flanagan, Soskice, and

Ulman.[13] Real wages grew faster as well. And as wage growth accelerated, productivity growth slowed. The combined result was a sharp
fall in the share of profits in national income between 1965–9 and
1970–3.

Governments did what they could to contain inflation. In the
United Kingdom a statutory freeze (or 'standstill') on wages and
prices was in effect from July 1966 to June 1967, a period of severe
weakness in the British balance of payments. The Dutch authorities
imposed price controls from 1961 to the end of 1966, and employers
agreed to a voluntary extension of the programme subsequently.
Other European governments imposed similar measures.

These policies were 'not very successful', according to the authors
of the definitive post mortem on the subject, Ulman and Flanagan.[14]
Producers sought exceptions on grounds of exceptional increases in
costs. Efforts to enlist union federations in the anti-inflationary campaign met resistance. An agreement to restrain wages on the part of
the central labour federation might not extend to the population of
non-union workers. Negotiations at the plant level frequently vio-
lated caps set in economy-wide bargaining (in the phenomenon
known as wage drift).

The contradictions of corporatism

Given the limited effectiveness of controls, governments sought to
strengthen the social compact. Unions were promised increased
health and unemployment payments and social security stipends in
return for wage restraint. Financing these programmes was serious
business. Public expenditure as a share of gross domestic product
rose from 38 per cent in 1967–9 to 46 per cent in 1974–6.[15]

Where the institutions of corporatism were most advanced (typically, in the smaller European democracies), their reinforcement
limited the rise in labour costs and unemployment. Following the
wage explosion of 1974–5, wage increases slowed. Demand stimulus

[13] Robert J. Flanagan, David W. Soskice, and Lloyd Ulman, *Unionism, Economic
Stabilization, and Incomes Policies: European Experience* (Washington, DC: Brookings
Institution), table 1–1.

[14] Lloyd Ulman and Robert J. Flanagan, *Wage Restraint: A Study of Incomes Policy in
Western Europe* (Berkeley: University of California Press, 1971).

[15] Flanagan *et al.*, *Unionism, Economic Stabilization, and Incomes Policies.*

(fiscal expansion and accommodating monetary policy) was combined with agreements by the unions to keep wages below inflation, and with increases in public employment where necessary, to offset the impact of the first OPEC oil price shock on unemployment. In Austria and Sweden, where the relevant institutions were highly developed, wage moderation in combination with increased public employment and demand stimulus kept unemployment at a remarkably low 1.7 and 2 per cent of the labour force in 1973–9. In Germany, where the unions similarly restrained wages but macroeconomic policy was less stimulative, unemployment still averaged less than 3 per cent over the period. In Britain, Italy, and France, where corporatist institutions were less well developed and more difficult to reinforce, unemployment rates were consistently higher (as shown in Table 4.7).

The cost was inflation, which accelerated to 5 per cent in Germany, 6 per cent in Austria, and 11 per cent in Sweden. The average rate of West European inflation doubled from 5 per cent in 1960–73 to fully 10 per cent in 1973–9, placing growing strain on the consensus favouring wage restraint. As wages began to rise faster, more inflationary demand stimulus was needed to contain unemployment. Inflation accelerated and developed persistence.

And even where wage restraint together with Keynesian demand stimulus limited the rise in unemployment, it did not sustain

TABLE 4.7 *Unemployment and employment in selected European economies, 1973–9 and 1979–1983/5*

Country	(average annual unemployment rate)	
	1973–9	1979–85
Austria	1.7	3.0
Belgium	5.8	11.6
France	4.3	8.0
FRG	2.9	6.0
Italy	6.5	9.0
Japan	1.8	2.4
Netherlands	4.5	10.3
Norway	1.8	2.4
Sweden	2.0	2.7
Switzerland	0.4	0.6
United Kingdom	1.7	10.3

Source: Scharpf (1991).

economic growth at historical rates. Western Europe's gross national product grew only half as fast between the business cycle peaks of 1973 and 1979 as it had over the preceding two cycles. Output declined significantly in 1974 before wage restraint was achieved and the effects of Keynesian stimulus began to kick in, producing the most serious pan-European recession in two decades. Doubts that the authorities could reinforce the post-war social compact and respond with counter-cyclical policies meant that expectations did not react in stabilizing fashion; as a result, investment fell more sharply than it had in any previous post-war recession.[16] The decline in output, together with the employment-smoothing policies of firms, meant that labour productivity grew more slowly than over the typical post-war cycle. And with output growing slowly, even improved wage restraint in the second half of the seventies did not deliver the investment needed to return productivity growth to previous levels.

The acceleration of inflation also meant that when the economy was disturbed again at the end of the 1970s by the second OPEC oil price shock and then by monetary disinflation in the United States, United Kingdom, and Germany, it became more difficult to apply the same shopworn formula. Having already held wages below inflation, the unions were loath to do so again. Public employment having been raised significantly in response to the previous recession, budgetary burdens had grown, leaving less room for pursuing this avenue again. The social democratic–Keynesian cooperation that had contained European unemployment in the 1970s proved impossible to replicate.

With governments unable to reinforce it, the model began to crumble. By the mid-1980s corporatism was in retreat, albeit at different rates in different countries. Possessing neither a highly decentralized labour market like the United States nor highly concertized arrangements like those of earlier years, European countries found it increasingly difficult to mount a coordinated response to recessionary pressures. Between 1973–9 and 1979–85 unemployment rates Europe-wide rose by half again, and in some countries, such as Germany and the Netherlands, more than doubled.

Moreover, there is a sense in which the continent's subsequent difficulties were created or at least aggravated by these efforts to use

[16] Andrea Boltho (ed.), *The European Economy: Growth and Crisis* (Oxford: Oxford University Press, 1982).

the welfare state to reinforce the social contract. Non-wage labour costs shot upward as governments shifted the burden of financing social benefits onto employers, rendering firms reluctant to hire, and undermined their international competitive position. The tendency towards bloated public sectors originated in this period. Generous unemployment benefits which insulated the unemployed from pressure to search for work originated in these years. The policies which allowed workers to claim disability benefits freely and draw after-tax compensation of 90 per cent of their previous incomes almost indefinitely were products of this decade. These factors combined to render Europe's labour markets less flexible than they had been previously and less flexible than those of their foreign competitors. And the recipients of government largesse soon became formidable opponents to those who sought reform.

Finally, the expansion of public spending led to the accumulation of high levels of public debt. By the mid-1980s mounting debt problems led to fiscal retrenchment and radical public sector reform in Denmark and Ireland. In the rest of Europe it led to a protracted fiscal crisis with which governments are still attempting to cope.

Retreat into regionalism

The volatility of the global economy lent additional impetus to the process of European integration, as European governments sought to create for themselves an oasis of stability. This desire buttressed support in the United Kingdom for joining the EEC, intensifying the pressure for Ireland and Denmark to follow its lead. The first enlargement of the Community to encompass these countries was completed in 1973. The next challenge was to address the problem of exchange rate volatility produced by the collapse of Bretton Woods. Currency fluctuations threatened not only to excite inflationary expectations but also to jeopardize the Common Agricultural Policy (CAP) that provided the political glue holding the EEC together. Under the CAP domestic-currency support prices were set for a range of agricultural commodities in each member state. Exchange rate fluctuations disrupted the relationship between these prices in different countries and thereby the operation of the programme. More generally, there was the fear that uncontrolled exchange rate fluctuations would strengthen demands for protection against imports in countries with temporarily overvalued currencies, undermining the Common Market.

Europe's response was the Snake, adopted in the wake of the Smithsonian Agreement of December 1971, which had allowed a dramatic widening of currency bands against the dollar. Countries participating in the Snake agreed to hold their bilateral exchange rates within narrow margins and established short-term and very short-term financing facilities to extend credits to one another. Unfortunately, their desire for exchange rate stability was not accompanied by significant convergence of monetary and fiscal policies. This is not surprising, given the widely differential impact of the oil and commodity price shocks of the mid-1970s and divergent views of the appropriateness of an accommodating policy response. Countries following relatively inflationary policies were repeatedly driven from the Snake. The United Kingdom was first to withdraw, on 23 June 1972. Denmark withdrew a week later before returning in October. Italy withdrew in 1973. France was forced to float in January 1974 before rejoining in mid-1975 and then withdrawing again in March of the following year. Sweden withdrew in 1977, Norway in 1978. Only Germany and the Benelux countries remained associated throughout.

This disarray was disheartening. Moreover, an arrangement that failed to stabilize the French franc against the German mark was unlikely to remain viable for long. The French and German economies were at the heart of the European Community. And the desire to unite the two countries politically as well as economically remained a centrepiece of the integrationist project. French president Valéry Giscard d'Estaing and German chancellor Helmut Schmidt responded by proposing the creation of a new structure, which came to fruition in 1979 as the European Monetary System (EMS). The EMS was a better-appointed version of the Snake, reflecting the lessons drawn from the operation of its predecessor. The short- and very short-term financing facilities were enlarged. While the participants were still obligated to hold their currencies within narrow fluctuation bands, provision was made for them to devalue and revalue as a way of avoiding the kind of terminal difficulties that had led to French withdrawal from the Snake. And governments were permitted to retain capital controls to protect themselves from destabilizing capital flows.

None of the founding members of the EMS (eight of the nine EC member countries, excepting only the United Kingdom) was forced to withdraw over the course of the 1980s, in contrast with earlier experience with the Snake. In part this reflected the prevalence of controls, which had been tightened in the late 1970s and now offered countries like France and Italy room for manoeuvre. In part it reflected governments' willingness to realign: there were EMS realignments in September and November 1979, March and October 1981, February and June 1982, and March 1983. The election of a socialist government under François Mitterrand in 1981 led France to adopt expansionary monetary and fiscal policies which considerably increased the strains on the EMS, but the repercussions were limited to realignments in 1981, 1982, and 1983, and did not extend to French abandonment of the system.

Still, poor coordination of macroeconomic policies strained the EMS. Moreover, unilateral monetary and fiscal initiatives like those of the French socialists were ineffectual in achieving their goal of increased employment, given the inadequacy of wage restraint and the capital flight they now provoked. Eventually this led even socialist governments to abandon the pursuit of unilateral initiatives. Inflation and interest rates became better harmonized. Resort to realignment grew less frequent. The most restrictive capital controls could be relaxed.

Rising unemployment and integrationist response

The achievement of currency stability was gratifying, but it alone could not remedy the problem of unemployment, which by the mid-1980s cast a pall over Europe. Unemployment rates, having gone up in the early 1980s, showed disturbingly little tendency to come down. By the second half of the decade the problem was widely diagnosed as one of inadequately flexible wages, overly rigid work rules, and excessive non-wage labour costs. For employers the problem was how to eliminate these rigidities. For unions it became how to prevent 'social dumping' (competitive cuts in wages and work rules designed to import jobs and export unemployment to one's European neighbours), especially once Mrs Thatcher's government succeeded in curtailing the power of Britain's unions and remaking the country's labour markets along American lines.

A generation earlier, when conflict had cut along national rather than class lines, political leaders had sought a solution in European integration. The crisis of unemployment now elicited the same response. Deeper integration—adding the free movement of capital and labour to the already existing customs union—could create a unified economic zone as large as the United States of America, enabling European producers to better exploit economies of scale and scope and compete internationally. Harmonizing regulatory structures would simplify doing business. Eliminating excessive regulation and state aids and subsidies by empowering the European Commission to disallow unfair impediments to intra-European competition would further enhance Europe's international competitive position. Marrying deeper integration with a 'European social charter' under whose terms countries promised to maintain acceptable working conditions and avoid social dumping made this bargain acceptable to labour. A major step in this direction was the Single European Act (SEA) in 1986, under which the signatories agreed to create a single market free of internal barriers to trade no later than 1992. The year 1986 also saw the second enlargement of the Community to include Greece, Portugal, and Spain, an event which can be seen as responding to these same imperatives.

The Maastricht Treaty, hammered out in intergovernmental negotiations in 1990–1, and ratified by the member states over the course of 1992, was the next step in this process. The treaty contained a 'social chapter' promising labour protection against social dumping; in a sense this was the other half of the bargain that had allowed for the adoption of the SEA. Mrs Thatcher, having already remade the UK labour market along American lines, obtained an opt-out from this provision. At the core of the treaty was a commitment for the EC to move to monetary union (a single monetary policy, a European Central Bank, and a single currency) by the end of the decade. This too was an outgrowth of the SEA. Integral to the creation of an integrated internal market was the removal of capital controls. But the elimination of controls rendered the EMS more fragile than before. Countries were more directly exposed to destabilizing capital flows. The periodic realignments that had vented pressures and restored balance to the EMS now proved more difficult to effect, since the merest hint that a devaluation was on the cards could provoke a massive outflow of funds. After 1987 there were consequently no more realignments of EMS currencies.

But there were reasons to doubt that this situation was sustainable. A basic principle of international economics is the 'unholy trinity'—the incompatibility of fixed exchange rates, international capital mobility, and monetary independence. Now that the mobility of capital had been restored, European governments had to choose between fixed rates and independent policies. And the only way of credibly forsaking monetary independence was by going all the way to a common currency. For countries other than Germany, which were already forced to follow the Bundesbank, whose anti-inflationary credentials allowed it to set the tone for monetary policy Europe-wide, this strategy had the additional advantage of promising that they might regain some control of their monetary destinies. The alternative threatened to be exchange rate volatility of a sort that might jeopardize support for the single market.

The apostles of integration had in mind a smooth glide path to monetary union. They did not anticipate the turbulence soon to follow. In particular, they did not forecast the collapse of the centrally planned and centrally controlled economic and political systems of Eastern Europe and the Soviet Union or its implications for their own integrationist ambitions.

The crucible of integration

The West European country where the impact of events in Eastern Europe was most profound was Germany, where neither geography nor man-made barriers like the Wall could hold back immigration from the Democratic Republic to the Federal Republic. West German chancellor Helmut Kohl, never reluctant to take a leap, responded by proposing complete and immediate reunification of the two Germanies. Reunification responded to a deeply seated belief in Germany in the artificiality of the country's post-war division and for that matter of Europe itself. A weakened Soviet Union, concerned mainly to obtain NATO acceptance of its western borders and desperate for foreign aid, was in no position to object.

The unification of the two Germanies under the banner of the Federal Republic—with a single currency (the Deutsche Mark) and a single political system—did not automatically wipe away all social and economic ills. Unemployment and enterprise failures rose as consumer goods produced in the East were pushed off store shelves by brand-name goods from the West. In 1991 the new *Länder* accounted for 20 per cent of reunified Germany's combined labour force but less than 7 per cent of its combined GNP; average labour productivity computed in this way was three times higher in the West. A strong incentive for East–West migration remained, a fact that was hardly welcomed in the comfortable precincts of the West. Moreover, the cheap labour of the East posed a threat to the unions, who feared a low-wage *mezzogiorno* that would undercut their bargaining power.

The Bonn government responded by accepting the unions' demands that their bargaining coverage be extended to the new states of the East and that wages there be pushed up to West German levels. It provided fiscal transfers to the new states to keep their residents at home and to bring physical and social infrastructure, and hopefully productivity, up to Western levels. Transfers to the new *Länder* reached nearly two-thirds of those states' GDP in 1992 and 1993, extraordinary high levels by any standard. In a sense, the policy of high wages made these transfers inevitable in so far as it pushed up labour costs and aggravated the problem of transitional unemployment. Transfers meant deficits, given the reluctance of West Germans to pay higher taxes. Deficits meant higher interest rates, given the reluctance of the Bundesbank to run accommodating monetary policies, not just in Germany but throughout Europe (because the interest rates of different countries were hitched together by the pegged exchange rates of the EMS, upward pressure on their level was a pan-European phenomenon). And those higher interest rates aggravated unemployment continent-wide.

These conditions formed the backdrop to the crisis that disrupted the progress of Europe's monetary union project in the summer of 1992. The Maastricht Treaty required countries seeking to qualify for monetary union to hold their exchange rates within their narrow EMS bands and to adopt policies of budgetary austerity. But the more unemployment climbed, the more governments hesitated to bear the costs of austerity now in return for the reward of monetary unification later. A number of the countries concerned, Italy prominent among them, were already suffering from inadequate competitiveness, having failed to bring their inflation rates down to German levels. Now their central banks were forced to ratchet up interest rates to defend their currencies against speculators' bets that they might eventually be devalued. And higher interest rates worsened unemployment, which created additional doubts about whether governments would stay the course, requiring still higher interest rates to fend off the speculators.

Denmark's rejection of the Maastricht Treaty in a referendum on 2 June 1992 was the spark that ignited this combustible mixture. It raised the possibility that monetary union might not happen, in which case governments' incentive to continue pursuing tight, anti-inflationary monetary and fiscal policies would be removed. Anticipating that countries like Italy and the United Kingdom would respond by cutting interest rates and allowing their currencies to depreciate, speculators pounced. By the middle of September Italy and the United Kingdom had been driven out of the EMS. Spain, Portugal, and Ireland were forced to devalue, in some cases repeatedly. As the crisis dragged on into the spring and summer of 1993, even the French franc, one of the key currencies at the centre of the EMS, came under attack. The crisis came to a head in the final week in July. Over the last weekend of the month, under intense pressure, ministers and central bankers agreed to widen EMS bands from 2¼ to 15 per cent.

Now that exchange rates could vary over a wider interval, making currency speculation less of a one-way bet, speculators retired to the sidelines. Behind the cover of wide bands European financial markets settled down. Stimulated by the US economy's recovery from its own post-cold-war recession, Europe's economies began recovering too. Monetary unification got back on track. Governments began to make progress towards meeting the Maastricht requirement that they cut public-sector debts and deficits to qualify for monetary union, although some countries took more credible steps than others: serious fiscal retrenchment was undertaken by the Netherlands, Sweden, and Finland (the Scandinavians, along with Austria, having joined the European Community, now European Union, in the third enlargement in 1995), while Italy and France settled for more cosmetic steps.

All the while unemployment showed disturbingly little tendency to come down. As late as 1997 unemployment rates remained over 10 per cent, an order of magnitude higher than in the golden age of the

1960s and more than twice the rates of the United States. With the decline of corporatism, the legacy of strong unions and highly developed welfare states now meant mainly high wages, restrictive work rules, and burdensome non-wage costs. While high wages provided unions and employers an incentive to find ways of raising productivity in pace with costs, there were limits to this process. With lower labour costs stimulating the demand for labour in the United States, the US economy added as many jobs in a month as Europe added in a year. This created a growing awareness of the need to cut hiring and firing costs in order to make the European labour market more flexible. But while eliminating firing costs allowed firms to lay off redundant workers, firms were still reluctant to hire so long as reform remained incomplete. While cutting budget deficits reduced the burden on the private sector, interest rates did not come down so long as the permanence of those cuts remained in doubt, and employment was little stimulated.

Having gone half-way towards fiscal and labour market reform, Europe's governments were caught between the two banks of the river and in danger of being swept away by the current. Germany demanded fiscal consolidation of its potential partners in the monetary union on the theory that balanced budgets limited inflationary pressures. But fiscal consolidation meant painful public-spending cuts and, to the extent that it was half-hearted, did little to inspire confidence and bring down unemployment. For every European for whom Maastricht meant financial and political stability, there was another who associated it with unemployment.

The collapse of central planning

It was not only in the West that the final decades of the twentieth century were marked by growing difficulties. The contradictions of central planning had long been apparent. The growth of material product had decelerated between the 1950s and 1960s, reflecting a declining rate of productivity growth more than declining rates of growth of inputs. The extensive-growth strategy of throwing more capital at the problem encountered diminishing returns. Between 1971–5 and 1975–80 the incremental capital—output ratio (the additional investment share of national income necessary to produce an additional percentage point of growth) rose in every East European country for which data are available.

The centrally planned economies broke down completely at the end of the 1980s. Instead of growing, output shrank. With the planned economy unable to deliver the goods, political acquiescence gave way to disaffection and revolt, precipitating the collapse of the Soviet bloc, democratization, and the first hesitant steps towards market-oriented reform in 1990. The limitations of central planning had long been clear, notably the difficulty of formulating a plan that properly took into account the complex internal wiring of the modern industrial economy and the difficulty of eliciting effort in a system that provided few pecuniary incentives for performance. But these limitations became more apparent in the 1970s and 1980s as the advanced economies of the West evolved away from manufacturing towards services, and away from hierarchically controlled corporations and Fordist assembly lines towards the decentralized organization and flexible specialization made possible by the development of new information technologies. Technologies facilitating the free flow of information were of course precisely what the dictatorial regimes of Eastern Europe had a particular incentive to suppress. And hierarchical control was all the planners knew how to do.

The mystery is why difficulties already apparent in Eastern Europe in the 1950s and increasingly evident in the 1960s took twenty years to culminate in crisis conditions. How was growth maintained through the 1970s and into the 1980s, in other words, given that the easy returns to the extensive-growth strategy had been exhausted? Part of the answer may be that much of the growth recorded in this period was really a statistical artefact. Quite simply, the numbers were cooked. In addition, East European governments consumed irreplaceable resources to which they attached no value when producing industrial and agricultural goods. Steel and chemical plants polluted the environment to an extent that would not have been permitted in the West, where democracy ultimately held leaders accountable. In the East, meanwhile, recorded output was boosted by pollution that created serious health problems for residents, in a process that could not continue indefinitely.

To the extent that growth persisted, Eastern Europe had the West to thank. With the liberalization of financial markets in Western Europe and the United States and the need to recycle petro-dollars in the wake of the first OPEC oil price shock, Western money-centre banks sought new outlets for their liquidity abroad. They found them in Eastern Europe. The region's cumulative borrowing rose from $11 billion in 1972 to nearly $70 billion by the end of the 1970s. Foreign capital was essential for sustaining the extensive-growth strategy; without it, consumption would have been squeezed even more severely, making it necessary to cut back on investment to quell incipient unrest.

Foreign borrowing had the further advantage of providing access to Western equipment and technology. Imports of capital goods and technology licences were directly proportional to the volume of foreign loans, since East European exporters had little capacity to penetrate Western markets and earn additional revenues. New technologies developed in the West for the production of steel and chemicals were licensed, and some countries permitted the participation of Western companies in the development of production facilities. Machinery imports from the West as a share of total imports rose from less than 30 per cent in the mid-1960s to nearly 40 per cent in the second half of the 1970s.[17] Where electricity generation capacity had lagged behind the growth of industrial production, countries imported the equipment needed to modernize this sector. Countries that exported agricultural goods (like Hungary) imported farm equipment. Where the production of textiles, apparel, and leather was important, they imported machinery for those sectors. It is easy to see how these forms of Western assistance helped to sustain the East European system, and how the curtailment of loans when the debt crisis struck at the beginning of the 1980s so aggravated the economic difficulties of the East. The only mystery is why banks in the West remained gung-ho for so long.

The resumption of piecemeal reform also helped to sustain the planned economy by eliminating its most glaring inefficiencies. In contrast to earlier reforms, intended mainly to increase the efficiency of planning, reform in the 1980s grafted onto the command economy elements of the market system. Limited numbers of prices, notably in the farm sector, were allowed to respond to the balance of supply and

---

[17] Data for the Comecon six, from A. Koves, *The CMEA Countries in the World Economy* (Budapest: Akademiai Kiado, 1985), 84, cited in Derek H. Aldcroft and Steven Morewood, *Economic Change in Eastern Europe since 1918* (London: Routledge, 1995), 162.

demand. In some cases, members of agricultural cooperatives were permitted to farm individually. In East Germany *Kombinate* were given increasing autonomy. In countries like Poland and Hungary producers were permitted to keep a portion of their receipts in foreign exchange and to use it to finance imports of intermediate inputs and capital goods. In Hungary the central bank's monopoly on credit was eliminated, and enterprises were authorized to extend commercial credit to one another and to individuals.

In Eastern Europe as elsewhere economic freedom and political repression ultimately proved incompatible. It was not feasible to give residents increased freedom to decide how and where to work while strictly limiting what they said. As individuals made location and production decisions more freely, the dissemination of dissident material became widespread. Just as perestroika (restructuring) and glasnost (openness) went hand in hand in the Soviet Union, political liberalization sprang from the seed of economic liberalization throughout Eastern Europe. With the Soviet Union in no position to intervene as it had in Hungary and Czechoslovakia in times past, there was no external force to prevent one thing from leading to another.

The ultimate consequence of political liberalization was thus nothing less than the collapse of central planning. As long as the Stasi was a threatening presence in East Germany and the secret police were a force to be reckoned with throughout the region, workers could be intimidated into expending effort. With the growing challenges to political repression, intimidation as a motivating force was removed, and the absence of positive incentives became a fatal liability. In East Germany, where the government had long relied on secret-police intimidation, 1987 was a poor year for growth, but 1988 was worse, and 1989 was a disaster, the worst in nearly three decades. After the fall of the Wall little effective police presence remained to keep workers from walking off with machinery and tools. With political liberalization the central contradiction of state socialism became clear: property that officially belonged to everyone effectively belonged to no one. No one had an incentive to protect it.

Difficulties of the transition

Eastern Europe's subsequent transition to the market was anything but smooth. Between 1990 and 1992 output plummeted. The fall in real GDP varied across countries, from 18 per cent in Hungary and Poland to more than 30 per cent in Bulgaria and Romania. The transition from the planned to the market economy meant the reallocation of resources from the production of capital to consumer goods. It meant shifting resources from manufacturing to services. It was easier in the short run to curtail production by heavy industry simply by removing state subsidies than it was to conjure up new consumer goods industries, and service sectors. For all these reasons it is hardly surprising that output fell.

Western Europe had faced the same challenge after the Second World War—to scale back heavy industry and redeploy resources to the production of consumer goods and services—but had accomplished the task without enduring a post-war depression. One difference, to return to our previous discussion, was the Marshall Plan, which buttressed political stability and economic reform in the West and encouraged the reconstruction of Europe's trade. In the 1990s there was no Marshall Plan for Eastern Europe. Eastern Europe's trade, rather than being rebuilt, collapsed with the disintegration of Comecon and the Soviet Union. This last event removed the one residual source of demand for the military hardware and producers' goods churned out by the region's heavy industry.

Above all, reform which was concerted and comprehensive in the 1940s was piecemeal and hesitant in the 1990s. Decontrolling some prices but not others meant that sectors producing goods whose prices remained controlled could not afford increasingly expensive inputs from the rest of the economy. Cutting some state subsidies but not others (notably those extended to politically powerful heavy industry) allowed the economy to continue producing goods whose cost in terms of resources exceeded their market value, and meant a continued drain on the government budget. Finally, political and technical constraints prevented the rapid privatization of enterprise. Privatization required planning and execution, which took time. (Giving away state enterprise to the managers and workers, as was done to a greater extent in many former Soviet republics, was faster, but threatened to encourage asset stripping and create a populist backlash against reform.) So long as enterprise was still state-owned, managers had little incentive to make profits and avoid losses. This meant budget deficits, which meant pressure on the central bank for money finance and inflation, discouraging foreign investors.

TABLE 4.8 *Liberalization in post-communist countries* (World Bank index, except where indicated)

Country and classification	Year of most intense reform	Prior level	Change in year of most intense reform[a]	Change over next two years[a]	Level 1994	Level 1995
Non-socialist						
Radical reform						
Poland	1990	0.24	0.44	0.14	0.86	3.4
Czech Republic	1991	0.16	0.63	0.11	0.90	3.6
Slovakia	1991	0.16	0.63	0.07	0.86	3.4
Albania	1992	0.24	0.42	0.04	0.70	2.6
Gradual reform						
Hungary	1990	0.34	0.23	0.21	0.86	3.6
Bulgaria	1991	0.19	0.43	0.04	0.70	2.6
Ex-communist						
With democratization						
Romania	1990	0.00	0.22	0.23	0.71	2.6
Former Yugoslavia						
Macedonia	1990	0.41	0.21	0.06	0.78	2.7
Croatia	1990	0.41	0.21	0.10	0.86	2.9
Other						
Slovenia	1990	0.41	0.21	0.16	0.82	3.3

Notes:
The World Bank index is a weighted average of change from 0 to 1 along three dimensions: internal prices, external markets, and private-sector entry; it does not include the level of inflation. The EBRD index is used only in the last column.

[a] Difference in index levels.

Source: Anders Aslund, Peter Boone, and Simon Johnson, *How to Stabilize: Lessons from Post-Communist Countries,* Brookings Papers on Economic Activity 1 (Washington, DC: Brookings Institution, 1996), 217–314.

In practice, no country followed a 'big bang' strategy of instantaneous liberalization. Throughout Eastern Europe price decontrol, enterprise privatization, and fiscal consolidation proceeded gradually. Still, there was considerable variation in the speed and extent of reform, with Poland doing the most the quickest and Romania and Bulgaria doing the least. Where state subsidies were withdrawn most rapidly, there was nothing to prevent output from going into free fall. But rapid reform also put in place the preconditions for rapid

TABLE 4.9 *Output decline in post-communist countries* (World Bank index, except where indicated)

Country and classification	Year of most intense reform	Change from 1989 to year of most intense reform [a]	Change in year of most intense reform [a]	Level 2 years later	Level At end 1994	Level At end 1995
Non-socialist						
Radical reform						
Poland	1990	. . .	−11.6	84.3	91.9	97.4
Czech Republic	1991	−1.0	−14.2	78.6	80.7	83.8
Slovakia	1991	−2.5	−14.5	74.3	77.9	81.4
Albania	1992	−35.0	−7.2	72.1	72.1	77.7
Gradual reform						
Hungary	1990	. . .	−3.5	82.5	83.5	84.2
Bulgaria	1991	−9.1	−11.7	72.3	73.3	74.8
Ex-communist						
With democratization						
Romania	1990	. . .	−5.6	75.7	78.6	81.9
Former Yugoslavia						
Macedonia	1990	. . .	. . .	. . .	. . .	. . .
Croatia	1990	. . .	−8.5	67.8	66.2	68.5
Other						
Slovenia	1990	. . .	−3.4	82.8	88.5	92.9

Notes: Output is an index of GDP. 1989 = 100.
[a] Percentage change.

Source: Aslund *et al.*, *How to Stabilize: Lessons from Post-Communist Countries*.

recovery. By 1995 output had nearly recovered to 1989 levels in Hungary, Poland, and Slovenia, three formerly planned economies of Eastern Europe where liberalization had gone furthest.[18] Economically, radical reform front-loaded the costs (which took the form of a particularly virulent recession), but then paid healthy dividends (in a form of singularly rapid recovery). The question was whether the cold bath of radical transition, however invigorating economically, might provoke a political backlash against reform, leading previous progress to be rolled back.

[18] As measured by Martha de Melo, Cevdet Denizer, and Alan Gelb, *From Plan to Market: Patterns of Transition*, Policy Research Working Paper 1564 (Washington, DC: World Bank, 1996).

Retrospect and prospect

In virtually every economic sense, Europe today could not look more different from Europe after the Second World War. In the wake of the war its economy was based on heavy industry, heavy inputs of fixed investment, and a backlog of unexploited technology. Today Europe is a high-wage economy producing technologically and organizationally sophisticated goods and services using products and processes developed at home. Following the war the European economy was divided into closed national economies and riven by an East–West gap. Today Europe has taken a long step towards establishing a true single market. With the collapse of the Soviet bloc, the East–West divide has disappeared, leading the countries of Central and Eastern Europe to emulate the economic systems of their Western neighbours and to seek admission to the European Union. After the Second World War governments pursued national economic strategies that entailed manipulating markets and relying on the close collaboration of trade union federations and employers' associations. Today the market system has escaped the shackles in which it emerged from the war, devaluing the leverage of both governments and the social partners. In a world of footloose finance, where exit for capital is all but costless, individual countries in Europe as elsewhere find it increasingly difficult to rely on extensive regulation and Keynesian stabilization policy to manage and manipulate the market. The continent has responded by adopting more market-acquiescent policies like those of the United States and the United Kingdom, but at the same time by vesting additional power in the EU in the hope that a larger transnational entity can recapture some control from the market.

As this history makes clear, a powerful set of internal dynamics drove the development of the European economy in the second half of the twentieth century. By its nature, extensive growth could not continue indefinitely. By the 1970s the process was played out in both Western and Eastern Europe, and incentives arose to shift to intensive growth. In the West, where there existed a market system, this transition was navigated successfully, although not without a secular decline in the growth rate. In the East, where incentives were lacking, inability to respond to the imperatives of intensive growth led to nothing less than the collapse of central planning and the reintegration of the region into the West European economy.

A second source of internal dynamics emanated from the post-war social compact in which labour deferred wage increases in return for management ploughing profits back into investment. As European labour markets tightened in the 1960s and 1970s, it became increasingly difficult to maintain labour's acquiescence. Increased consumption could not be deferred indefinitely. More fundamentally, trading current sacrifices for future gains was attractive only so long as wage moderation and high investment promised significantly higher living standards in the future; as the technological backlog was played out in the late 1960s and early 1970s and the return on investment declined, the terms of this trade-off became less attractive, tempting the social partners to renege. West European governments sought to buttress the bargain by promising increased health and unemployment payments and increased social security stipends in return for wage restraint. While these policies succeeded in the short run, in the long run they gave rise to the high tax rates and generous benefits that provide the explanation for today's problem of high European unemployment.

The third source of dynamics was regional integration. For fully half a century this was European policy-makers' response to whatever problems they faced. The process was set in motion after the Second World War by an unusual conjuncture: nationalism had been discredited, there existed a strong indigenous strand of thought favouring integration, and the United States lent external support. Once started, the process fed on itself. The ECSC created a transnational policy elite and a set of institutions with the capacity to push through and manage a customs union. The Common Market, by increasing the volume of intra-European trade, then created a constituency for the single market. And the single market, which required the removal of capital controls, set on foot pressure for the creation of a single currency. These internal dynamics pushed Europe, albeit not without interruptions, towards progressively deeper integration.

In political economy as in physics, every action provokes a reaction. The rapid progress of European integration provokes a negative reaction from those who feel their autonomy threatened by a vast EU bureaucracy. The welfare state that held the post-war social compact in place through the 1970s and, in some cases, for longer is being scaled back in the hope that a more flexible labour market will bring lower unemployment. Optimism about Europe's innovative capacity has again succumbed to doubts about the continent's capacity to match the United States in the development and application of new information technologies. All that can be said with confidence is that this too will pass.

5

Culture

Axel Körner

Introduction: culture and society in post-1945 Europe

Culture, intellectual debate, and the arts are an abstract expression of ideas, of experiences and memories, of hopes and expectations, related to a specific moment in history. They reflect and anticipate political and social developments in society; they are a key to the perceptions of change and to the semantics of historical time, to the experience of continuities and discontinuities. That makes cultural development, in the context of this book, a most powerful witness of European history during the period concerned. An outline of cultural developments in Europe since 1945 contributes to the social, political, and economic history in that it presents not only the cultural 'events' themselves, but also subjective perceptions of social and political realities. Culture tells us about the way in which people reflect on historical change and what they expect from their future.

In a chapter which tries to give a broad overview of cultural developments in Europe it is difficult not to make inappropriate generalizations. One has to do justice to developments in Western and in Eastern Europe, while also paying attention to the concept of Central Europe. One has to consider the dictatorships in Spain, Portugal, and Greece and the liberal democracies of France and Britain; the experiences of the Mediterranean countries matter as much as those of the Scandinavian. A leading question therefore should be if there is, with regard to the period 1945–2000, such a thing as a European culture. Sometimes a cultural trend becomes dominant across Europe and beyond. Changing pop cultures represent the most convincing example of such a trend during the post-1945 period. But not all kinds of culture acquire a similar social, political, and economic importance. The works of an intellectual, writer, or artist are not representative of society as a whole. However, they stand for a certain debate which subsequently might have had an impact on the social and political development of Europe. It is characteristic of the cultural transformation of twentieth-century Europe that at least in some areas the division between so-called high culture and popular culture and the social distinction with regard to cultural attitudes diminished or even disappeared. This is true to a great extent for fashion, for some aspects of musical culture, and for the consumption of the mass media, and to some extent for film. All over Europe literacy became the rule, but there are still different levels of literacy. Visits to museums, access to higher education, reading practices are no longer an indicator of social distinction in the same way as in the first half of the century. This trend suggests that in an assessment of culture in Europe since 1945 an exclusive and narrow focus on culture in its most abstract form of expression—e.g. literature, theatre, so-called 'serious' music, or the arts—becomes obsolete. Because of its specific social and cultural transformation, a cultural history of post-war European society must at least try to take a broader approach. Unlike earlier traditions of intellectual history and *Geistesgeschichte*, a cultural history of Europe since 1945 has to include the cultural practices of everyday life within a broad social framework. However, this does not mean that opera, literature, and intellectual debate can be excluded.

An analysis of cultural developments in post-1945 Europe provides an understanding of certain conflicts about social change, but similarly of attitudes which the existing political order, in the West or the East, took towards society as a whole. In the West the wearing of unisex jeans provoked debates about gender; and when jeans, as a class-transcending fashion, entered universities, parliaments, and wedding ceremonies some people complained about the disintegration of social distinction. In the East a different kind of ideological concern prevailed about jeans. Here it was an issue of the state fearing the American way of life. The new Western youth culture was seen as undermining socialist values—as the attraction of the younger generation to a lifestyle that was opposed to the ideas of a socialist society. From the appearance of the Beatles in Liverpool, Hamburg, and London it took the communist part of Europe about fifteen years to allow for a compromise between socialist values and Western youth culture. Only in the late 1970s was Alexej Batachov allowed to organize his jazz concerts in Moscow, and groups such as the Puhdys could officially become icons of GDR youth culture. In particular, where freedom of expression was restricted, the writer, composer, or artist, independent of the kind of culture he represented, assumed the role of expressing discontent and hopes for society. This allows us, retrospectively and through records of cultural activities, to analyse the relationship between political order and society. The philosopher Kopriva, in Václav Havel's drama *Largo desolato* (1984), represents all those people who, unwillingly, through their quest for truth, became dissidents, but still tried to keep an identity beyond political protest. It is difficult to find a 'conventional' source for this kind of socio-political process if not on the level of cultural communications.

Changing social and political frameworks of cultural development

Social cleavages of cultural practice

Changes in the structure of social cleavages had an impact on the cultural development of Europe from 1945. During the second half of the twentieth century Europeans experienced both a disintegration and a multiplication of identities. Interest in and exposure to a specific type of culture became less class-specific. Regionalization, transnational integration, and globalization also had a disintegrating impact on formerly perceived identities. Moreover, cultural life, particularly in the big urban agglomerations, has increasingly been marked by new social divisions. New identities—generational, ethnic, or sexual—appeared, based on shared experiences and ideals. Conflicts based on experience and cultural identity emerged in East and West with the end of the war, with the return of soldiers, partisans, and prisoners of war from the front, as illustrated in the work of Vasco Pratolini and Marguerite Duras, and the radio plays of Wolfgang Borchert. Similarly problematic was the encounter of German refugees from the East with the population of West Germany; and later the integration of the Pieds Noirs into French society. Since then, labour and post-colonial migration, and subsequently the formation of multicultural communities, have been at the origin of a major transformation of European society. Changing definitions of gender encouraged a more liberal attitude to sexual identities, in particular to gay culture. The discovery of new social groups (defined by age, ethnicity, or other factors) as a potential target of the market has contributed to this process. Not only has the materialism of the post-war consumer society made an impact on the development of new identities; it is also one of the roots for the decline of traditional identities in Europe, in particular of religious practices. Despite the efforts of the church to accommodate Christian faith in modern society—at the Second Vatican Council (1962–5) Pope John XXIII finally declared the 'end of the Counter-Reformation'—Christianity has become a minority belief in Western Europe. However, in Eastern Europe since the end of the communist regimes Catholic, Orthodox, and evangelical religion, as well as new religious sects, have witnessed a remarkable revival.

The result of these shifts of identities is a multicultural society which is nevertheless characterized by a very small amount of inter-action between these cultures. Most European countries are unprepared to meet the cultural needs of their multicultural inhabit-ants and taxpayers, e.g. in terms of linguistic politics, civil law, or religious education. At the basis of new social conflicts we often find ignorance about the different cultures that mark contemporary European society. A central issue for any cultural history is therefore to assess the relationship between social experience and cultural—and in particular aesthetic—expression. Although it remains difficult to explain specific aesthetic forms, we can learn about social struc-tures by analysing a society's culture. Social experiences shape collect-ive identities, which are translated into aesthetic forms and enacted as cultural practice. Cultural practice again creates social experience and contributes to the formation of identities.

For the historian of culture the analysis of objective distinctiveness is less interesting than the explanation of subjective perceptions of reality which lead to the cultural construction of the above-mentioned new identities. The continuously changing web of iden-tities defines the cultural world of Europe through fashion, and trends in music, the arts, and literature. This trend has challenged the importance of what was traditionally understood as European culture; and consequently, at least during the last decades of the century, European culture has become less focused on itself. Despite the power of the global market, Indian curry in London and Turkish felafel in Berlin play probably a more important role in food culture than McDonald's. In other fields of culture we can observe a similar trend towards internationalization. During the forty years following the end of the Second World War thirty-five Nobel prizes for literature went to authors of European origin, and only seven to non-European authors (of whom three were residents of the United States). Since then this trend has been reversed. Between 1986 and 1999 there were seven European laureates, and seven from other parts of the world (of whom only one was resident in the United States). While in towns like London and Paris young people dance with dreadlocks to Caribbean music, some of their parents may read novels by Kenzaburō Ōe and the poetry of Derek Walcott, or attend a concert by Vieja Trova Santiaguera.

Since the 1950s rising wages turned the masses into consumers, formulating their material needs according to increasingly aggressive advertising in the media. With the development of a commercialized mass culture, former privileges of cultural practice became accessible for a growing portion of society. As one of the consequences of this process class consciousness declined. A good example of the change in cultural practice is travel. Once a privilege of the middle classes, it has now become a mass phenomenon. In 1939 Blackpool counted 7 million visitors; in 1990 the famous town of piers, gambling halls, and ice cream counted 15 million visitors—and this despite the fact that even people with a smaller income can afford holidays abroad. Among the group with the lowest income in Britain the amount spent on leisure and holidays in 1971 was twice as much as it was in 1954.[1] However, the fact that since the years of the 'golden age' (Hobsbawm) almost everybody can afford a car, a holiday, and a meal in a restaurant does not mean that cultural practice has liberated itself from social connotations. A holiday in Blackpool, driving a Vauxhall, or the CD with the three tenors represent a different

---

[1] Kaspar Maase, *Grenzenloses Vergnügen. Der Aufstieg der Massenkultur 1850–1970* (Frankfurt am Main: Fischer, 1997), 246.

cultural capital than a holiday in Tuscany, a Deux-Chevaux, and a CD of the Borodin Quartet.

Education

The French sociologist Pierre Bourdieu has provided detailed analysis of the traditional educational system in France, much of which can be applied to other national systems too: recruitment of educational elites was and still is based not so much on intellectual capacities but on the handling of a specific mix of cultural and social capital. With regard to the exclusiveness of the educational system we observe interesting parallels between Western and Eastern Europe. Private education or well-resourced schools in the affluent suburbs of Western towns privileged its traditional elites in a similar way as a small number of better-financed schools in well-provided areas did with regard to the new party elites of communist Europe.[2] In Eastern Europe access to secondary schools and higher education depended on political conduct; decisions concerning professional training were largely based on the regime's economic needs and planning, not on individual choice. From an early age military training formed an important part of education. Historical materialism became the dominant theoretical framework of all subjects taught, although the school system itself often remained unchanged: the nineteenth-century dual system of education fitted the new needs of exclusiveness.

The West, too, failed to make a radical new beginning after the Second World War, and a half-hearted reform was delayed for several decades. Society was regarded as necessarily class-structured, and a corresponding educational system would serve the development of an expanding economy. Only the development of the service sector and technological advancement created awareness of a need for more secondary schooling. When François Mitterrand, in response to social tensions and youth unemployment, argued in the early 1980s for a radical increase in numbers of students with the baccalaureate, politicians in France and other parts of Europe still argued against such a model of social mobility. However, in most West European countries secondary schooling with A levels or the equivalent has

[2] James Brown, *A History of Western Education*, 3 vols., iii (London: Methuen, 1981), 522 ff.

been recognized as both an important element of social promotion and a necessity for prosperous economic development.

The expansion of secondary education has led since the mid-1960s to enormous pressure on universities. Protests against poor material conditions in overcrowded lecture theatres met with the rejection of an educational system viewed by students as 'authoritarian capitalist indoctrination'. Part of a post-colonial discourse, the form and the content of Western knowledge and education were largely denounced as a pretentious social construct. Leading to major political conflicts beyond the traditional left–right division, the 1968 uprisings proved, at the university level at least, to be to some extent successful. Since then new universities have been built, teachers with different social backgrounds have managed to enter the system, the canon of traditional education has changed. Among the long-term consequences of this challenge has been the integration of women's and gender studies as an academic discipline since the 1980s.

Rocking youth culture

Generational conflict is not a new phenomenon in European history, but never before had youth culture provoked such an important social cleavage. Originally linked to the process of Americanization in Western Europe during the 1950s and to the political radicalization of the 1960s, youth culture has since then developed into a sometimes uncritical and apolitical industry. In the words of Eric Hobsbawm, this cultural revolution of the later twentieth century represents 'the triumph of the individual over society'.[3] This generational cleavage is most strongly expressed through styles in music, dance, and fashion. The first hit of the British group The Who in the 1960s was a song named 'My Generation'.

During the 1950s it was still difficult to find rock 'n' roll on European radio broadcasts. Nevertheless, the programmes for American soldiers, the distribution of James Dean movies, and the new, youth-specific consumer culture of petticoats and hula hoops gave a taste of the new influences on European culture. Although it was Elvis Presley who introduced the new music into Europe, we find the origins of

---

[3] Eric Hobsbawm, *Age of Extremes: The Short Twentieth Century: 1914–1991* (London: Abacus, 1995), 334.

both the American rock 'n' roll of the 1950s and the British Beat of the 1960s in the Afro-American blues and rhythm and blues of the 1940s. The Rolling Stones were named after a song by Muddy Waters and covered Robert Johnson's 'Love in Vain'; in 1988 the Irish group U2 played together with B. B. King, the idol of rock guitar. But the first European rock 'n' roll by Cliff Richard, Adriano Celentano, and Johnny Hallyday were copies and translations of Elvis's songs.

In the beginning European rock 'n' roll symbolized a devotion to everything American; but from the mid-1960s onwards young people developed a more critical relationship to the 'American way of life'. Similar to the original rhythm and blues, rock music became a critique of consumer society, war, and social injustice. At the start of the 1960s more than 1,000 bands in Liverpool and Manchester played beat songs against the boredom and about the problems of daily life. Beat was an anti-bourgeois culture, played by young people from a working-class background, leaving school, and changing their white shirts for jumpers and jeans (though for their first concerts they were still wearing ties and ironed shirts). The Beatles, the Who, the Animals, and the Rolling Stones provoked a radical change not only in European music, but also in social and cultural attitudes to all aspects of society: sex, youth, politics, authority—in step with the claims of the 1968 movement. From the very beginning this new youth culture crossed national borders. A year after their first English concerts under the name the Beatles, the group played in Hamburg. 'Love Me Do' entered the British hit parade in 1962; a year later 'Twist And Shout' was in the German hit parade. In 1964 they gave their first concert in Paris. Groups like the Rattles in Germany and Sauterelles in Switzerland demonstrated that young rock music could develop outside Britain. Drafi Deutscher's 'Marmor, Stein und Eisen bricht' was later adapted by English and American musicians.

The rock music of the 1960s had been a synthesis between Afro-American rhythm and blues and various European traditions of popular music. On their 1967 LP *Sgt. Pepper's Lonely Hearts Club Band* the Beatles referred to the tradition of the English music hall. Some years later 'Strawberry Fields for Ever' was the start of psychedelic rock, soon picked up by Pink Floyd. From the 1970s and the development of the synthesizer rock musicians started to look for musical inspiration in Asia and Latin America, later developing ethno-beat and world music. Interestingly, just a little earlier the

Italian composer Luciano Berio had also started to work with a variety of traditional styles and examples of folk music, stretching from the United States to the Auvergne, from Sicily to Armenia and Azerbaijan. Immigrants in Britain influenced the success of Jamaican reggae. Similarly, rap and hip hop started as black music and during the 1980s were adopted by young musicians in Britain, France, and Italy. Their speech became the new beat—demonstrating the teenagers' superiority over parents, teachers, and old people—supported by drum-computer and sampler rather than musical instruments.

Hard rock during the 1970s and heavy metal during the 1980s worked mainly with the effects of decibel, light, and pyrotechnics. The name of the British band AC/DC and their album *High Voltage* represented a programme in itself. Kraut rock, with groups like Can, Kraftwerk, and the Scorpians, demonstrated that hard rock existed also beyond the English-speaking world. But although French law obliged radio broadcasts to play a minimum of 40 per cent French titles, most new trends in European rock music still came from Britain and the United States. In Italy and France pop and rock music never completely replaced the *cantautore* or the *chansonnier*. These national traditions resisted the process of Americanization; and while for the Eurovision Song Contest the North European countries started to present their titles in English (the Swedish group Abba winning the competition in 1974 with 'Waterloo'), most singers from Southern Europe continued to sing in their native languages.

Returning to the origins of rock music, punk bands like the British Sex Pistols and the Jam became the symbols of a new subculture: the political critique of existing society. But it was not only socio-economic issues that formed the background for the music of the 1970s and 1980s. Western rock music was one of the big attractions for people in Eastern Europe; and several musicians discovered the arms race and the cold war as important issues for their music. Pink Floyd and others performed highly symbolic concerts in Berlin, in proximity to the Wall. To the tune of Glenn Miller's 'Chattanooga Choo Choo' Udo Lindenberg asked Erich Honecker, general secretary of the East German state's party, for permission to play his songs in the Republikpalast, seat of the GDR parliament. However, cultural exchange on this level remained exceptional. Nina Hagen grew up in the GDR with the dissident poet Wolf Biermann and started her career at the age of 17 in Poland; in the 1970s she became a rock idol in

West Germany. Occasionally East European songwriters appeared at West European peace festivals, and in the 1980s the East German Puhdys and Silly acquired a certain fame in the West. But with the fall of the Iron Curtain most of the established groups in the East lost the support of their traditional fans. For this kind of cultural heritage there was little space on the Western CD market and in free radio broadcasts.

Since the 1950s music has developed into one of the most import-ant means of social distinction, symbolizing the cleavage between young people and adults. It reflects the social condition and the ideas of the young people who produce it. But the sound also represents the young people who consume this music and who might appreciate it for reasons different from the original intentions of the producers. Often teenagers know little about the suburbs of Liverpool or the black ghettos of New York from where their music comes, and the rhythm of black rap music can inspire the music of a Nazi skin band. Through its performance in a specific context the music becomes a metaphor for young people's identity and a means of social and cultural distinctiveness.[4] This search for distinctiveness represents a major issue in the cultural development of post-1945 European culture.

'Hope I die before I get old' sang the Who in the 1960s. Unlike the Beatles, who played for no longer than ten years as a group, the Rolling Stones continue to amaze the masses in the late 1990s with their concerts. But rock music has come of age. At the end of the century the Rolling Stones no longer represent generation cleavage but the memory of the cultural change which was introduced with their music thirty years earlier.

Culture and the state during the cold war

Culture serves not only as an expression of discontent and alternative ideas of society, as was the case with most post-war rock music and youth culture. For state and society culture serves as a producer of ideas and memories (e.g. through festivals, conferences, monuments, and museums); but equally as a means of creating social and political

[4] Simon Frith, 'Music and Identity', in Stuart Hall and Paul du Gay (eds.), *Questions of Cultural Identity* (London: Sage, 1996).

cohesion, of pacifying social and political conflict. In both Western and Eastern Europe culture had this dual role. In order to achieve this cohesion, the state can either leave a great amount of autonomy to the arts, giving the artist almost complete freedom of expression, or, alternatively, the state can adopt an attitude of patronage and thus keep control over certain cultural developments.

With regard to new national, regional, and political identities, culture had to fulfil the role of bridging cleavages in societies between former collaborators and resisters, splits along ideological lines between men and women, rich and poor, immigrants and natives. After the Second World War culture was needed to create a new sense of belonging, to help the transition from Pétain's *État français* back to the tradition of the French nation, to link the idea of national liberation in Central Europe with the new communist ideology. During the immediate post-war period culture represented legitimacy for the new political order. Intellectual debate, first exhibitions, the revival of publishing houses demonstrated a new beginning and were therefore welcomed by the political class. With different political backgrounds, the philosopher Benedetto Croce in Italy, the historian Friedrich Meinecke in West Germany, the writer Louis Aragon in France had been exponents of pre-war cultural activity and stood now for its revival after 1945—for continuity. The cities of Wrocław in 1948, and Paris and Prague in 1949, organized huge cultural conferences with the aim of bringing together intellectuals and artists from all over Europe. In most cases these were an early cultural battlefield of the cold war. Germany, as the centre of the cold war, permits an interesting comparison. While writers like Heinrich Böll and Wolfgang Koeppen expressed their disappointment about the lack of a new beginning in the West, the young GDR attempted to create legitimacy for itself, at home and internationally, by attracting prominent artists and in particular writers, among them Bertolt Brecht, Helene Weigel, and Hanns Eisler. Stefan Heym, who after exile had returned to Germany in the uniform of an American army officer and who had written novels about the liberation of concentration camps, decided to settle not in the West, but in what he described as 'the better Germany'. Similarly, Anna Seghers did not return to her native Rhineland, but became a prominent representative of early cultural life in the GDR. Heinrich Mann was elected president of the East German Academy of Arts, but died before his arrival in Berlin. His brother Thomas, after his return from American exile, decided to stay in Switzerland, but was criticized strongly in West Germany for accepting an invitation to speak in the GDR on the occasion of the one hundred and fiftieth anniversary of the death of Schiller. The East German publisher Aufbau, not his traditional publisher, S. Fischer, in the West, published the first edition of Thomas Mann's collected works.

Unconvincingly, universities in the West claimed after 1945 that they had always been independent of Nazi rule, although in some cases they left it to former Nazis to rebuild their faculties. Historians who had assisted the Nazi regime in its *Lebensraumpolitik* now were among the founders of the new social history. East German universities explicitly invited academics to return from exile, like the philosopher Ernst Bloch, the musicologist Ernst Hermann Meyer, and the Germanist Hans Mayer. They decided to help the GDR in the attempt to construct a new, better, and different Germany which stood for a clear break with Germany's past. However, universities in the GDR also still employed many former members of the Nazi party, and the early optimism of many socialist intellectuals soon faded away. After some years of experience with actually existing socialism and the regime's doctrines of anti-fascism they went to the West, or were forced to do so. The West, too, used culture to promote the underlying ideas of the new political order. However, here artists and intellectuals accepted early on their role of expressing critical ideas of a different and better society; and the West allowed for this critique.

In Eastern Europe the state emphasized with pride the cultural achievements of socialist society. Composers from Poland, musicians from the Soviet Union and the GDR, theatre companies from Hungary and Czechoslovakia, were acclaimed worldwide. In 1979, 62 per cent of East Germans visited a theatre, compared to 23 per cent in the West. Often part of this achievement was an emphasis on the superiority of Russian culture within the Soviet Union and in Central and Eastern Europe. Even during the brief periods of thaw there was little space for innovation, critique, or the avant-garde. For Walter Ulbricht, general secretary of the GDR state's party, socialism meant that the workers too read Faust and listened to Beethoven.[5] Most of

---

[5] Maase, *Grenzenloses Vergnügen*, 261.

Eastern Europe was marked by *zhadanovism*, the regimentation of cultural life. Although not an anti-Soviet novel, *Doctor Zhivago* was not published in the Soviet Union and, attacked as a traitor to his socialist fatherland, Boris Pasternak was forced to reject the Nobel prize in 1958. There was a bit more openness from the 1960s. New subjects like problems of the development of socialist societies were discussed in books, on stage, or on screen. Formerly forbidden novels such as those of Ivan Bunin were published, but Khrushchev still opposed any critique of the official party line. Alexander Solzhenitsyn's depiction of daily life in the Soviet labour camps (*One Day in the Life of Ivan Denisovich*, 1962, and *The Gulag Archipelago*, 1973–4) were described as the 'pathological preoccupation with marginal aspects of Soviet life'. They were less marginal to the rest of Europe, and in 1971 Solzhenitsyn received the Nobel prize for his work. Like Lev Kopelev, he had to leave the country. Other dissidents, like the physicist and father of the Soviet H-bomb Andrei Sakharov, his wife, Jelena Bonner, and the civil rights campaigner Juri Orlov, were sent into exile. Despite the restrictions with regard to publications and performances, cultural life in Eastern Europe often served to compensate for political dissatisfaction with the official regime. On the one hand, reading literature, and going to concerts and to the theatre, expressed a retreat from the political sphere into the private; but, on the other hand, this culture also opened an alternative space for a critical public sphere.[6] If critique of social and political reality was possible in the East, its forum was cultural life. With glasnost under Gorbachev and the crisis of the communist regimes, novelists, playwrights, composers, and film directors assumed a leading role in the construction of a new political sphere.

It would be wrong to assume that the cold war resulted in complete isolation of Central and East European culture. Even countries from the periphery of Eastern Europe, like Bulgaria and Romania, maintained a certain amount of academic exchange with the West. Music is a good example of the dialogue across the Iron Curtain. The Internationale Ferienkurse für Neue Musik in Darmstadt—together with the Institut de Recherche et Coordination Acoustique Musique at the Centre Georges Pompidou in Paris the most important forum for

---

[6] David Bathrick, *The Powers of Speech: The Politics of Culture in the GDR* (Lincoln: University of Nebraska Press, 1995).

contemporary music in Europe—presented in 1962 twenty compositions from Poland, twelve from the USSR (including seven pieces by Stravinsky), seven from Italy, four from the United States, three from the United Kingdom, two from the CSSR, and one each from Argentina, Belgium, Bulgaria, Greece, the Netherlands, Japan, Romania, Sweden, and Switzerland.[7] Bohumil Hrabal and Milan Kundera, the latter living since 1975 in Paris, reminded the West of the Czech tradition of narrators. Thanks to the Italian publisher Inge Feltrinelli Europe rediscovered Boris Pasternak, whom André Malraux had called as early as 1935 'one of the greatest poets of our times'. Krzysztof Kieslovski's *The Double Life of Véronique* and his films inspired by the French *tricolore* are beautiful documents to demonstrate that the cultural division of the continent remained fragmentary.

The impact of the economy

In the post-war period important changes occurred in the economic framework of cultural development. Again, youth culture and its related music appears as the most striking example of this transformation. In the 1950s the music industry still depended largely on radio broadcasts, on selling scores to dance bands, and on organizing concerts. This changed dramatically with the availability of cheap recordplayers. In 1963 the returns for Beatles songs sprung from zero to 6 million pounds. Youth culture had become a major industry. The modern record industry relies for over 70 per cent of its sales on 14- to 25-year-olds.[8] Stars like Michael Jackson have sold up to 40 million copies of a single album. Since the start of the 1990s the worldwide return for records amounts to approximately £5 billion per year. Linked to the music business are commercialized fashions which change on an ever more rapid basis. In the mid 1970s disco emerged as a new style in music, based on a combination of simple music, uncritical text, and new dance formations. With groups like Abba new dance palaces mushroomed all over Europe. In the 1980s and 1990s the most influential medium for pop music became the technically very sophisticated video clip, reproduced all over the world,

---

[7] Reinhard Kannonier, *Bruchlinien in der Geschichte der modernen Kunstmusik* (Vienna: Böhlau, 1987), 243.

[8] Hobsbawm, *Age of Extremes*, 328.

twenty-four hours per day, by private television companies like the London-based MTV. The combination of video clips and advertising produces the dream worlds of the young generation all over the world. The house music of the 1980s and 1990s techno were originally critical of the commercial aspects of music. Producing new sounds through the sampling of already existing music was an innovative challenge recognized by such authorities in the field of electronic music as the composer Karlheinz Stockhausen. The idea was to produce music ad hoc and for the moment, rejecting the big business of rock stars and the record industry. The music was meant to be fun, emerging from beat, light, colours, an imaginative DJ, and a new generation of synthetic drugs. Nevertheless, through the impact of video, the cult of the DJs, and international raves, the new scene became just another example of commercialized youth culture. Today, for any kind of youth culture spending money seems to be a condition of their social distinctiveness.

In the work of Walter Benjamin, or in the critical theory of Adorno, Horkheimer, and Marcuse, the capitalist economy has often been held responsible not only for the change in but also for the decline of 'culture'. Critics point to the impact of market criteria on theatre and concert life and to the commercialization of leisure activities. In most cases such judgement starts from a rather narrow definition of culture. Thanks to the market orientation of public museums, a completely new public has been introduced to the arts; it is easier to make a larger opera public familiar with Puccini than with Aribert Reimann. However, this trend reduces space and funding for a more specialized culture and for avant-garde. Similarly, television has been criticized for replacing the local cinema and for reducing the number of visitors to bingo and music halls, theatres and football stadiums. After early experiments during the 1930s, television was introduced in France in 1944, followed by the United Kingdom in 1946 and the Federal Republic of Germany in 1952. But despite the start of television, public theatres in Germany sold twice as many tickets in 1960 as in 1949–50;[9] and writers of modern theatre plays such as Tom Stoppard and Harold Pinter have also produced for television. The percentage of people following the news on television since the 1970s is higher than the number of people who read newspapers in the

---

[9] Maase, *Grenzenloses Vergnügen*, 247.

1950s. Furthermore, the decline of cinema cannot be attributed exclusively to the rise of television; other factors have also left an impact. A growing number of consumers have preferred to invest their money in goods such as private cars and domestic equipment rather than traditional leisure activities. For various reasons cinemas had to be modernized in the 1960s, which resulted in higher prices for tickets and a smaller but socially distinctive public. Cultural preferences differ from country to country: in its peak year of 1946, before the wide diffusion of television, Britain counted 5,000 cinemas. In Italy the peak was ten years later, in 1956, but here there were 10,000 cinemas. In 1960 the number of private television sets in Britain exceeded 10 million, whereas in France only 1 million had been sold.[10] Five years later 80 per cent of homes in Britain had a television; West Germany reached this level in 1970, France in 1975. At the end of the century 97 per cent of homes in Britain owned a television set.

Television had a major impact on traditional leisure activities, and one example of this transformation is the way Europeans engaged with their most favourite sport: football. Again some critiques argue that the decline of visits to stadiums was a consequence of football on television: in 1989 Britain counted only 23 million spectator visits, half as many as fifty years earlier.[11] But again, such an interpretation would be short-sighted. Going to a football match had to compete with innumerable new leisure activities unknown before the war, and attendance became more expensive with the development of all-seat stadiums in the 1980s. In compensation, football on television is today a major occupation for large and socially differentiated sections of society. The game is still a major factor in social, local, and national identity—a process which was even strengthened through television. For some people football became an intellectual fashion, featured also in the quality press. However, since the 1960s fans have witnessed the radicalization of hooligans and disasters such as those in Bradford, Heysel (Belgium), and Sheffield, the latter costing the lives of ninety-five spectators in the Hillsborough stadium in April 1989.[12]

With the abolition of maximum wages for players (in Britain in

[10] Pierre Sorlin, *European Cinemas, European Societies* (London: Routledge, 1991), 81 ff.

[11] John Bale, *Sports, Space and the City* (London: Routledge, 1993), 3.

[12] Ibid. 23.

1961), and the development of football on television, the game's economic role and subsequently its political meaning changed. Top managers of football clubs often play a major economic and political role: Silvio Berlusconi of Milan is a major shareholder in supermarkets, the building sector, publishing and television; as leader of the populist right-wing movement Forza Italia he was for a short period prime minister of Italy in 1994. It was widely suggested in the media that Bernard Tapie, manager of Olympic Marseilles, was involved in certain political scandals. Cecchi Gori, manager of the legendary Fiorentina, invested a large part of his capital in cinema and went into politics. After a long period of public service West European television is now dominated by the market-place. Rupert Murdoch, who has the major shareholding within the British press, competes with Leo Kirch and Silvio Berlusconi for the television rights of the European Champions League. With the help of his exclusive rights to cricket and football, Murdoch's BSkyB channel became one of the most powerful companies in Europe.

To what extent is culture—from football to opera—able to survive on the free market and without the intervention of the state? Britain and the United States have seen film production purely in economic terms. Partially in reaction to the decline of cinema, but also as part of its cultural policy, Germany started to subsidize film production in 1965, along the same lines as France and in accordance with its own public spending on theatre and concerts. Today European film depends increasingly on multinational cooperation and international finance that since the 1980s has made it impossible to give a national label to most productions. 'Percent for Art', 'Kunst am Bau', and 'art in architecture' proposed a legal basis for cultural subvention: a certain percentage of the cost of a public building had to be spent on art, e.g. a sculpture in front of the entrance. The state also subsidized art forms which were originally conceived to express the artist's lack of respect for the state. Among these ventures were public funding for conceptual art, graffiti projects, and installations. The state or private companies offered buildings or industrial sites for the use of artistic projects like presentations in the Paris Métro, various installations in Berlin-Kreuzberg, Damien Hirst's 'Freeze' exhibition in London's Docklands in 1988, or the *band-désigné* façades in Brussels.

Despite public spending on culture, the art market remained an important condition for and influence on cultural development.

During the 1950s a powerful market for pop art developed in the United States, at the time still unknown in Europe. Nevertheless, most of the artists who wanted to sell their works in the United States still needed to legitimize their work through participation in European exhibitions such as the Documenta in Kassel, the Venice Biennale, or the important retrospectives in Paris and London. A market that was independent of the debate between artists, critics, and the public did not emerge until the 1980s. This new market rejected the political art of previous decades which questioned traditional techniques and methods by replacing paint with margarine, canvas with the body, or the museum with outdoor performances. Art had to be 'beautiful' again. This demand of the market led to the resurgence of traditional painting, sometimes misleadingly called 'trans-avant-garde', as a conservative reaction to the liberating modernity of the critical artists. Not public spending for the arts, but rather the taste of consumers who multiplied their private fortunes during the years of Reaganomics and Thatcherite economics, influenced the development of this particular style in the arts.

Changing political meanings in culture and the arts

Experiences and memories of the Second World War

One single topic in post-1945 European culture has had a major impact on literature, music, the arts, and intellectual debate. This is the attempt to come to terms with the experiences and memories of war and occupation, of the Holocaust and of deportation, of victory, liberation, guilt, and defeat. This 'unmasterable past' (Charles Maier) has determined the individual and the collective memories of soldiers and civilians, of collaborators and resisters, of victims and agents of the Holocaust, of survivors, displaced persons, orphans, of men returning from the front, and of women who had been sexually abused by the occupiers. In different ways this past has influenced the lives of the first, second, and third generations of post-war Europeans. Attitudes to these experiences and memories varied in relationship to individual, social, and national histories. They extended from de Gaulle's claim that all French were resisters to the debates about Marcel Ophüls's film *The Sorrow and the Pity* (1969) and Robert Paxton's *Vichy France: Old Guard and New Order* (1972); from the glorious commemorations of the 'great patriotic war' in the Soviet Union to Emir Kusturica's ironic film *Underground*; from the German 'inability to mourn' (Margarete Mitscherlich) to the official doctrine of anti-fascism in the GDR; from political confrontations about the nature of the 'guerra civile' in Italy (Claudio Pavone) to the 'Historikerstreit' and the 'Goldhagen-Debate' in the FRG. It seems impossible to separate post-war European culture from the legacy, the experiences, and the memories of the war.

How were these experiences and memories of war, collaboration, and Auschwitz recorded? With the works of Heinrich Böll, Marguerite Duras, Max Frisch, Günter Grass, Elsa Morante, Harry Mulisch, Ignazio Silone, Claude Simon, and others the topic has been confronted by the most important authors of post-war European literature. The war remains ever present in European film, from Rossellini's neo-realism of the 1940s and countless British war films on public television to Fassbinder's *Maria Braun* (1978), Edgar Reitz's television series *Heimat*, and François Truffaut's *Le Dernier Métro* (1980). Based on more complex forms of expression, Bernd Alois Zimmermann and Siegfried Matthus depicted the horror of war in their operas. And still, all these memories and commemorations are selective and incomplete. Primo Levi, Italian survivor of Auschwitz, has described this dilemma: 'We, the survivors, are not only a tiny but also an anomalous minority. We are those who, through prevarication, skill or luck, never touched the bottom. Those who have, and who have seen the face of the Gorgon, did not return, or returned wordless.' There is no way to come to terms with Auschwitz. Paul Celan, a true European equally at home in Černowice, Tours, Bucharest, Vienna, and Paris, asked how one can write poetry after Auschwitz. In their attempt to explain, the philosophers Max Horkheimer and Theodor W. Adorno questioned one of the most fundamental paradigms of European civilization: they outlined the dangers of modernization by pointing to the 'dialectic of Enlightenment'.

The cultural memory of the war, of resistance and liberation, did not come up with simple answers. In particular West European film has recorded the end of the war as an extremely complex experience.

Roberto Rossellini's *Paisà* (1946) gives a critical account of the role of the British troops in the liberation of Italy; his *Germany, Year Zero* (1947) depicts the moral decline in occupied Berlin; his *Rome, Open City* (1945) treats similar themes. Unlike the patriotic films of Eastern Europe, most of the approximately 200 Western films about the resistance are extremely pessimistic, and work to a large extent with horrifying stories unknown to other genres of European film. They include Helmut Käutner's *Last Bridge* (1954), Robert Bresson's *A Man Escaped* (1956), Louis Malle's *Lacombe Lucien* (1954), and the Taviani brothers' *The Night of the Shooting Stars* (1982). In France and Italy post-war societies were built upon the legacy of the resistance; but even here the memory of liberation was depicted as extremely painful and was confronted with unease.

Primo Levi, Alexander and Margarete Mitscherlich, and Erich Fromm remind us of the difficulty of remembering and mourning. In particular during the 1950s there were few attempts to reflect upon the recent past through music, as Arnold Schönberg had done in his *A survivor from Warsaw* (1947) or Arthur Honegger in his later symphonies. In 1966 Paul Dessau, Boris Blacher, K. A. Hartmann, Rudolf Wagner-Régeny, and Hans Werner Henze composed the *Jewish Chronicle*, directed at its first presentation by Christoph von Dohnányi, himself a son of a prominent resister against Hitler.[13] But events like this were exceptional. At the Internationale Ferienkurse für Neue Musik in Darmstadt the modernity of the Second School of Vienna was further developed into 'serial music', in the 1950s most strongly associated with the names of Olivier Messiaen and Pierre Boulez. This music was meant to be free from ideology, values, and politics. The emotional content of Schönberg and Berg was replaced by mathematical calculations. Music had to be logic—there was no place for a reworking of the past. Cultural memory and politics were closely linked; and there is probably no better example of this complex relationship than in the work of Dmitri Shostakovich. His Seventh Symphony, 'Leningrad' (1941), represented the official memory of the great patriotic war: the German siege of Leningrad, but also the hopes of the Soviet people and the victory over fascism. In later works Shostakovich also remembered aspects of Soviet history that the regime did not appreciate. In his String Quartet No. 8

[13] Kannonier, *Bruchlinien in der Geschichte der modernen Kunstmusik*, 220.

'In Memory of the Victims of Fascism and War' (1960) he quoted many elements of his earlier music which had been rejected as 'bourgeois formalism': the First Symphony of 1926, still representing the avant-garde of the early post-revolutionary years; the Fifth Symphony, written in 1937 and recalling Stalin's terror; motifs from his First Cello Concerto (1959), which was dedicated to the cellist and conductor Mstislav Rostropovich, who with his wife, the soprano Galina Vishnevskaya, had been forced to leave the country; and his opera *Lady Macbeth of Mtsensk* (1934/1958), at the time still banned for its progressive musical language and for symbolizing the terror of the Gulag. Moreover, the Quartet's second movement exposes in the middle of brutal *sforzato* accents a small piece of beautiful Jewish music, at a time when the Holocaust was still neglected by the regime's official memory of the great patriotic war. In his Thirteenth Symphony, 'Babi Yar', from 1962 the composer used a poem by Yevgeni Yevtushenko about the murder of 34,000 Jews by the SS near Kiev, again remembering a neglected aspect of history and denouncing the Soviet Union for its own antisemitism. Rostropovich once called Shostakovich's symphonies a 'history of Russia', but his music can equally be called a 'history of the twentieth century'.

In the arts we observe a variety of responses to the experience of the war. On the one hand, artists chose abstract expressionism: Pierre Soulages opposed the Western idea of education and academic accuracy by 'pure painting', spontaneous action in which the paint and the painting itself forms the centre of interest, not the object shown. The Hungarian Zoltan Kemeny contributed, with his metal works, to a new synthesis between painting and sculpture. Subsequently new materials have been used in the arts—objects of daily life, but also air, light, sound and water, the body. This new synthesis between media, materials, and forms of expression also contributed to a new understanding of scenic music (e.g. Mauricio Kagel) and since the 1970s to modern dance, most strongly associated with choreographers such as Pina Bausch and Anne Teresa de Keersmaeker.

On the other hard, artists turned away from abstract expression in order to communicate feelings and thoughts in a more accessible way. The Florentine sculptor Marino Marini built his horsemen, representing peasants and animals terrorized by air raids. The realistic image is a message in itself, contradicting the traditional theme of the horseman representing soldiers, statesmen, or emperors. The same language was later explored in a different context by Giacometti. From the 1960s to the 1980s the works of the German artist Joseph Beuys were closely connected to his wartime experiences when he was shot down as a bomber pilot, rescued, and kept alive by being smeared with fat and wrapped in felt. These experiences and the two materials, felt and fat, have become the essence of his work; his political activity for the pacifist Green Party was also part of his artistic statement. Klaus vom Bruch constructed for the 1987 *documenta* a video sculpture entitled 'Coventry—War Requiem', playing Benjamin Britten's famous music from 1962 in the background. Anselm Kiefer reflected on Paul Celan's dilemma of arts after Auschwitz with a series of work on his *Todesfuge* (1952): 'Your golden hair Margarete/ Your ashen hair Sulamith'.

The contemporaneity of different styles and movements, even within the work of a single artist, is one of the characteristics of post-war developments in the arts. This also applies to developments in music. The response and reaction to the early dogma of serial music came partly from the United States, with John Cage's 'aleatoric music', based on hazard, but also from the other side of the Iron Curtain. In Poland, Witold Lutoslawski, Henryk Górecki, and Krzysztof Penderecki continued to work in the tradition of Béla Bartók or used the new techniques of cluster and glissando. The Hungarian György Ligeti went his own independent way. Heribert Eimert and Karlheinz Stockhausen started working in a new studio for electronic music in Cologne; French composers experimented with 'musique concrète' used by the choreographer Maurice Béjart for his 'spectacle total'; Iannis Xenakis wrote music with the help of computers. Nevertheless, the end of tonality in the so-called 'classical' or serious music of the twentieth century never overcame the break with the larger audience, unlike modernity in the arts, in painting, and sculpture, which has been broadly accepted by the public.

The variety of trends and directions in modern art and music reflects both the uncertainty about the meaning and the dialectic nature of responses to the experiences and memories of the war.

Existentialism

Existentialism developed out of the experience of fascism, occupation, and resistance during the Second World War into a major position in European thought. It has its origins in the search for motives for the individual's social and political action. Jean-Paul Sartre's *L'Être et le néant*, published in 1943, reflects the breakdown of ideals and ideologies, the desperation and anger about an order which had shown itself incapable of resisting the enemy. On these grounds Sartre develops a consciousness for the need to act, reflected in his literary work *Les Chemins de la liberté* (1949) and critically discussed in Simone de Beauvoir's *Les Mandarins* (1954). Sartre's 'projet fondamental' has been similarly discussed by Albert Camus, arguing for a philosophy which unites negative attitude with positive action, beautifully illustrated in his biographical fragment *Le Premier Homme*, published posthumously in 1994. Conservative critics have denounced existentialism for its atheism and as a mode of futility. However, Camus's writings in particular appeared to his readers as messages of hope, will, and positive attitude towards life: even within a collective drama as described in *La Peste* (1947) man is free to act. In order to exist man has to create himself and has to fight against the continuous danger of falling back into 'being without existing'. Rejecting the moral justification of existence as a pure consequence of social condition, Sartre's work stands in a certain tension to some principles of Marxist thought. During the years of the war this caused misunderstandings in the communist resistance, but led to prolific debate among the left during the first decades after the war. Existentialism also served as a philosophical framework when the first postwar generation started to question their parents' passive attitudes during war and occupation. Still in 1968 Sartre's existentialism appealed to many students as an escape from both the uncritical and conservative views of their parents and teachers and the dogmatic views of communist parties. In a similar way existentialism also influenced dissidents in Eastern Europe, despite the difficulties of getting hold of Sartre's or Camus's writings. Here, existentialism belied the positivist socio-political attitudes of the official regimes and motivated political opposition.

Although existentialism has left important tracks in post-war European literature and philosophy, the same experiences of fascism and war have influenced such different approaches as Benedetto Croce's philosophy of praxis, critical theory in the Frankfurt school tradition, and later the ideas of Michel Foucault. Although based on completely different political grounds, Sartre's work has developed in close relationship with Martin Heidegger's consideration of the 'Seinsfrage'. (He worked on *La Nausée* during his time in Berlin before the war.) A similar question motivated the *Existenzphilosophie* of Karl Jaspers, who influenced political debate in the FRG through his works on the question of collective guilt and on the atomic bomb. For both Sartre and Jaspers human psychology played a major role in their work. Apart from literature it is difficult to find much direct impact of existentialism on the arts. The best example might be European film. Since the 1950s various directors have tried to move away from the classical narrative of objective reality, focusing more on symbiosis with the subconscious, with dream, with removed experiences. Ingmar Bergman's *Wild Strawberries* (1957) received first prizes at the festivals in Berlin, Venice, and the National Board of Review in the United States, an Oscar, the Golden Gate at Hollywood, the Danish Bodil, and further prizes in Norway, the United Kingdom, Argentina, and Italy. How do we understand the complex structure of this film? It is Professor Borg's nightmares and his Proustian 'search for times lost' which create, by the end of the journey from Stockholm to Lund, a new person. While during the 1950s and 1960s the social sciences, based on positivist approaches, emerged as the leading academic discipline, existentialism led to a complete reconsideration of the nature of the individual in the humanities.

Modernism and Americanism

The experience of war and dictatorship shed a critical light on the idea of human progress, but the response to this experience was not to withdraw from the project of modernity. Most cultural actors took a rational approach to the adjustment of modernity, critical of their social surroundings, but based on a largely positivist attitude to human knowledge and the mastering of the world through scientific progress.

In many parts of Europe the end of war and Nazi occupation permitted the rediscovery of the modernity of the pre-war years, the arts and the music which the Nazis had labelled *entartet* ('degenerate'). The works of the composers Karl Amadeus Hartmann and Ernst Krenek were already discussed in the 1950s; others, like Erich Wolfgang Korngold and Berthold Goldschmidt, had to wait until the second or third post-war generation took an interest in their works. The renaissance of Gustav Mahler's music in the 1960s played an important role in this process. Brecht got his theatre in East Berlin and was introduced to post-fascist Italy by Giorgio Strehler. The modernism of the 1950s and the tradition of the 1920s formed an eclipse around the dark years of dictatorship and war. In the early post-war years the modern world was strongly associated with Americanization in the West and Sovietization in the East. In economic terms Sovietization stood for a certain idea of an industrialized society, culturally reflected in the works of socialist realism. In the West the American dream was most strongly associated with Coca-Cola, nylon stockings, the zip, and Hollywood. In the 1950s Hollywood produced about 500 movies per year, more than the whole of Western Europe together. With national variations, between 40 and 75 per cent of the films in European cinemas came from the United States—a percentage which becomes significant if one considers that in 1955 the average citizen of Western Europe went to the pictures sixteen times (3,000 million tickets were sold).[14] European film was unable to take over the continental market. Hollywood spoke an international language, whereas European film was largely related to the cultural, political, and social context of its individual countries: the experiences of the war in the 1940s, the German *Heimatfilm* of the 1950s, national problems relating to terrorism in the 1970s, and Nanni Moretti's political diaries in the 1990s. A striking example of the transnational television success of American soap in the 1980s was *Dallas*. Across Europe viewers enjoyed *Dallas* as escape and entertainment. How do we explain the success of the American series? In line with Richard Hoggart's analysis of working-class readings and music,[15] we can say that people appreciated in *Dallas* the unrealistic beauty of a fairy tale. In most cases it is not blind admiration of the Ewings' wealth. It is the narrative form, not the content, of the story that the consumer enjoys—the artificial illusion of reality and the reinterpretation of the episodes and characters in terms of the viewers' own life experience.[16] In the comment of a middle-aged Dutch worker: 'I too know, in real life, a monster like JR. Except that he is an ordinary builder.' *Dallas* may be defined as 'emotional realism'.[17]

[14] Sorlin, *European Cinemas, European Societies*, 1, 81.

[15] Richard Hoggart, *The Uses of Literacy* (Harmondsworth: Penguin, 1965), 157.

[16] Alessandro Silj *et al.*, *East of Dallas: The European Challenge to American Television* (London: British Film Institute, 1988), 61–70.

[17] Ibid. 71 et sq.

Jack Lang, French minister of culture under Mitterrand, once called *Dallas* a 'symbol of American imperialism'.[18] Most of the imported material on national television is shown between 8 and 11 p.m., and in the 1990s there was a significant rise in transnational television both in terms of global ownership and in the use of the distribution technologies. The transnationalization of television has been described as a profit-oriented and ideological strategy of big countries and multinational corporations, imposing cultural and political values, business norms, consumption orientation, and lifestyles on the rest of the world. However, the statements quoted above show that viewers do not always read the supposedly positive American message in *Dallas*; and statistics provide a much less dramatic picture of Americanization through television. In 1988 the supply of television programmes from the United States varied from 28 per cent in Ireland and 22 per cent in France, to 13 per cent in Britain and 6 per cent in Italy. The smaller countries import more foreign television than the bigger, but the supply is at the same time more diversified with regard to national background. On average Western Europe was 68 per cent self-sufficient: 14 per cent of national network television was supplied by other West European productions, 15 per cent by the United States.[19] *Dallas* reached up to 7 million people in Italy, where home productions sometimes had up to 16 million spectators. In Ireland the series never outperformed *Glenroe*. In Britain it reached its peak with the episode 'Who shot JR?' in November 1980 with 20 million viewers or 39 per cent in share. In Germany *Dallas* was watched by up to 22 million people, but the audience for the Austro-German production *Schwarzwaldklinik* ('Black Forest Clinic') rose to over 28 million, well above a 60 per cent share of the audience, and was later sold to the United States, Italy, Britain, France, Belgium, Switzerland, Finland, and South Africa.[20] In recent years the trend has been less in the direction of Americanization of television but rather towards geocultural markets defined by language, history, religion, ethnicity, shared identity, gestures, and non-verbal communications; these 'geocultural markets' include 'what is considered funny or serious or even sacred, clothing styles, living patterns; climate influences

---

[18] Ibid. 26.
[19] Preben Sepstrup, *Transnationalisation of TV in Western Europe* (London: Libbey, 1990), 37, 78, 93.
[20] Silj *et al.*, *East of Dallas*, 78, 145, 148.

and other relationships with the environment'.[21] Broadcasting develops here into 'narrowcasting'.[22] This helps to explain why most popular national television series are so difficult to sell abroad: the success of the Irish series *Glenroe,* the British *East Enders,* and the German *Lindenstrasse* depend on their specific national environment. After more than a quarter of a century *Coronation Street* was still in the top three programmes in Britain; but the series remained unknown to Germans, French, and Italians. At the same time transnational television need not always be mass culture. Channels like the Franco-German Arte or programmes like *Odéon* and *Artissima* on Euronews mainly reach a well-educated, culturally interested élite.[23] In short, the impact of transnationalization in television—and in particular the process of cultural Americanization through television—should not be exaggerated.

Critique of the process of Americanization was also a central issue in the arts. Although it is most strongly associated with the works of the Americans Lichtenstein and Warhol, pop art was invented in Britain by artists like Richard Hamilton, Eduardo Paolozzi, Nigel Henderson, and Peter Blake, many of them having later developed in different directions. Exploring the banal techniques of mass visual culture and thus forming a distance from the emotional expressionism of abstract painting, their work described and analysed the commercialization and Americanization of Europe in the years following the war. Its idea was not to please the public with familiar images. The exploitation of the techniques of advertising served to criticize a consumer society which lived with the illusion that material progress could replace the overcoming of war and dictatorship. The best examples of this critique are the 'consumer's dream-house interiors' by the British artist Richard Hamilton. *Just What Is It That Makes Today's Homes So Different, So Appealing?* is the name of one of his famous collages. Breaking with the traditional canon of styles in the arts, pop art is as experimental as the expressionist or primitive arts.

The 1960s witnessed in the arts a radical search for new ways of

[21] Straubhaar, quoted in Kay Richardson and Ulrike H. Meinhof, *Worlds in Common? Television Discourse in a Changing Europe* (London: Routledge, 1999), 4.

[22] Ibid. 87.

[23] Ibid. 143 ff.

reflecting upon society. Forming a synthesis between abstract expressionism and pop art, a group around Richard Smith, Allen Jones, Derek Boshier, and Peter Phillips at the London Royal College of Art started to use objects from everyday life in combination with abstract painting. Similar to the new minimalist trend in sculpture, now defined as 'three-dimensional art', these developments recall in some respects the experiments of early Soviet art before the Stalinist era. In Paris, Amsterdam, and Düsseldorf galleries regrouped artists working with motored and moving constructions. Artists from Britain, France, and Hungary exploited visual illusions of movement in op (i.e. optical) art. With the help of light and mirrors luminism integrated the viewer into the object of art; some conceptual artists used the viewers' or their own language. Christo and Jean-Claude started with the wrapping of objects, monuments, and landscapes, moving away the border between the creation and the exposition of art. Environmental art and installations followed similar aims. Minimalist art developed into *arte povera*. The artist and his body were in the centre of conceptual art, brought to an extreme in Vito Acconci's public masturbations or the self-destructive performances of the Yugoslav Marina Abramovic. These trends point to a more complex reality than nineteenth-century realism, US pop art, or socialist realism in the East. The critical analysis of social reality in the arts, understood as a modernist statement, was made explicit in René Block's Berlin gallery, demonstrating in 1963 Konrad Lueg's and Gerhard Richter's *A Demonstration of Capitalist Realism*, showing the artist in a living room in front of the television. Still, most artists saw themselves in the tradition of European art, aiming for an analytical view of society and questioning, in the words of Joseph Beuys, 'the basic premisses of the prevailing culture'.[24] But some artists rejected this rational approach and limited their objective to the definition of the world as colours, space, and proportion. It can be seen as part of this programme when many of them called their works 'Untitled'.

Hence, continuous critique of social reality was inherently part of the modernist project. Apart from rock music it was film that translated the intellectual critique of contemporary society into a more widespread language. In his *Dolce Vita* (1960) Federico Fellini depicts the dirtiness and boredom of the beautiful contemporary lifestyle.

[24] Michael Archer, *Art Since 1960* (London: Thames & Hudson, 1997), 110.

This critical content is packed into a modern form: his language is one of modernity. He does not need the classical narrative to communicate his message; instead he speaks through episodes, with the help of pictures, accessible even without words.

Under the conditions of capitalist consumer society the narrowness of the idea of progress and the alienation of the human being were most visible in an urban context. The critical analysis of this context became one of the major themes in post-war European cinema, from the above-mentioned works of Italian neo-realism, to Pier Paolo Pasolini's *Accatone* (1961), from the works of Godard to the early films of Wim Wenders (*Alice in the City*, 1973). This new genre of European film, largely unknown in the United States, accounts for social and cultural changes in urban society, often speaking about a world we do not know, although it exists next to us (Pierre Sorlin).

Although West and East to some extent shared their respective ideas of progress and utopia, the modernism of the East appeared less convincing. The revolutionary romanticism of socialist realism, decreed by Stalin as 'national in form and socialist in content', relied too much on its own achievements and lacked the critique of social reality as a means of progress: *Look, Great Things have been Achieved* (1972) by GDR artist Werner Petzhold shows smiling building workers and engineers on a petrol refinery. However, it would be short-sighted to put the whole of East European culture under this label. Nonconformist art existed also in the East. Described by the cultural authorities as products of Western decadence, it was more difficult, if not impossible, to get permission for public performance or publication. This often underlined the political meaning of the work of art: body art and performance art were centred around the artist as individual; hence, when it first appeared in the East, it had a political dimension that reached far beyond the political dimension of conceptual art in the West.

Undoubtedly, democracy had a liberating influence on cultural development. Democratic consolidation in Spain, Portugal, and Greece, and their reintegration into the community of Europe after years of fascist isolation, was accompanied by an explosion of artistic activity during the 1980s. The modernist emphasis behind this development was visible in the success of events such as the art fair ARCO in Madrid, the architectural development of Barcelona on the occasion of the Olympic Games in 1992, the new museum in Bilbao, the cultural events around the international exhibitions in Seville (1992) and Lisbon (1996), the rediscovery of the Portuguese writer Fernando Pessoa in the context of European literature, or the nomination of the composer Mikis Theodorakis as minister of culture in Greece. The sculptures of Susana Solano synthesized the experience of minimalism and expressionism. Camilo José Cela's contribution to European literature, standing for realism and avant-garde, was recognized with the Nobel prize in 1989. Interestingly enough, most of the cultural accents in these countries during the 1980s and 1990s were refreshingly independent of the post-modern developments in other parts of Europe.

Marxist debate and radical culture

Marxist debate in the West and 'real existing socialism' in the East were both understood as part of a modernist project. However, after the 1960s it became more and more difficult to reconcile the different fractions of Marxism. The post-war consensus of the left which in particular had dominated intellectual debate in France and Italy had broken apart. Intellectuals felt a new uneasiness about traditional understandings of Marxism in the established parties of the left. Across Europe intellectuals and social scientists rediscovered the work of Antonio Gramsci and started a critical debate about the relationship of the communist movement to one of their principal theorists and martyrs. The works of Lukács, Althusser, and Bloch played a similar role in the debate. Parts of the left rediscovered the works of Trotsky, others looked for alternative roads to socialism in Maoist China. What they all shared was the conviction that the revolution was soon to come. Bertolucci's *Before the Revolution* (1964) represents an early example of this idea, which dominated the political debate of the left up to the mid-1970s. The search for new ideas expressed, on the one hand, dissatisfaction with the kind of progress described as the economic miracle in the capitalist societies of the West; on the other hand, it stood for scepticism towards the authoritarian approach of communist parties, comparable to the hopes for a 'socialism with a human face' in Czechoslovakia.

The political activism of the 1960s was part of a major social and cultural transformation which again was anticipated and documented in the arts. The sexual revolution found in film an important communicator. Musicians and artists, motivated by reading Franz Fanon, looked for new inspiration among 'the wretched of the earth' (the French publication with the famous preface by Jean-Paul Sartre dates from 1961; the first English translation was published in 1967). Others experimented with traditional or new drugs. Luigi Nono worked with sounds from East Asia against the Eurocentric perspective in music. For the anarchist artist Jean-Jacques Lebel the student revolt of May 1968 in Paris was art put into practice; former members of the Cobra group went out on the streets. Art became revolt; as in the 'happening' of the Dutch 'Provos' during the wedding of Princess Beatrix, or the 'Puddingattentat' of the Berlin Kommune I against the American vice-president Hubert Humphrey. Hans Werner Henze wrote an *Oratore volgare a militare per Che Guevara* in 1968, and a year later he presented his Sixth Symphony in Havana, using Vietnamese, Greek, and Cuban songs in his scores. Neo-Marxist debate played a major role in the teaching of Joseph Beuys. Luigi Nono, together with Maurizio Pollini and Claudio Abbado, performed concerts in factories, including the workers in performances. Gerhard Richter and Rainer Werner Fassbinder documented in their works the prison suicides of the members of the Baader–Meinhof Group. Rock music played an important role in the European peace and green movements, and since the 1980s in AIDS campaigns, the Irish U2 being among the most famous examples.

To a large extent 1968 was a generational conflict about values, ideas, and memories. But 1968 was also a conflict about the access of the first post-war generation of Europeans to cultural and political institutions. Cinema witnessed an extremely fruitful conflict between different generations of directors about the artistic value of film, about economic independence, about access to one of the most powerful means of cultural communication. Since the 1960s the new wave in European film had challenged the classical language of the United States, using cinema for more than just realistic narratives. In France Chabrol, Godard, and Truffaut preferred free, direct shooting to the studio. They understood film as art, not as product for the market. The *neue deutsche Film* followed a similar logic against the market. Not in Munich or Berlin, but in the industrial Ruhr town of Oberhausen young directors such as Alexander Kluge, Volker Schlöndorff, and Wim Wenders rebelled against the establishment of an older and all too powerful generation of directors. Working with a low budget (small casts and few locations) while claiming public funding, they emphasized the artistic aspect of cinema. In Britain generational change was represented by Karel Reisz and Lindsay Anderson, in Italy by Bertolucci, Antonioni, and Fellini. Similar conflicts about economic and institutional power took place in journalism, resulting in a new generation of left-wing newspapers: *Libération* in France, *Il Manifesto* in Italy, *Die Tageszeitung* in Germany. But also less radical papers, such as *El País, La Repubblica,* and *The Independent* made use of the new political and cultural skills of a generation which had been formed in the demonstrations against the Vietnam War and on the barricades of 1968.

Thirty-five years later there is again a generational conflict about access to cultural and political institutions. Now the generation of 1968 defends its position in academia and politics against a younger generation, often misleadingly labelled as post-modern rebels. However, especially in the field of music this younger generation, represented by conductors such as Antonio Pappano, Welser-Möst, and Pekka Salonen, have done rather well in occupying leading positions in European concert and opera life.

The feminist challenge

The radicalism of 1968 had only an indirect impact on gender relations. The politics of the student movement were for many women a disillusioning experience.

Feminism developed simultaneously as a political movement and as a philosophical position reflecting the limits of Marxist and related theories. We recognize the impact of feminism on the cultural development of post-war Europe on three different levels. First, literature, music, and the arts discussed the feminist movement and the situation of women in post-war European society. Secondly, culture has played an important role in the creation and diffusion of a feminist consciousness. Lastly, the arts and their history have themselves been the object of feminist critique.

Simone de Beauvoir had claimed that women have to assimilate to men, that femininity is only oppression and has to be abolished. Since then there have been two main directions in post-war feminist thought. First, liberal feminism, maintaining the division of private and public, and seeking affirmative action which improves the female condition in both spheres. Secondly, radical feminism, which insists on the political meaning of gender, which is held responsible for the patriarchal, authoritarian, and individualistic structure of social organization inside and outside the family. Through its psychological approach to subjectivity certain currents within feminist thought played an important role in promoting the issue of identity in political and intellectual debate, thus challenging the objectivity of the traditional and male-dominated social sciences and contributing to the critique of the modernist project.

On a superficial level it seems easy to demonstrate the cultural emancipation of women during the second half of the century. Women have access to higher education and finish their degrees often with better results than men. Eastern Europe in particular was quick to provide university places for women, including in the faculties of engineering and medicine. In 1989, 55.5 per cent of Soviet students were female. Women in the West managed to attain top positions in some culturally influential areas like libraries, archives, museums, and the media. Publishing houses from the 1960s initiated series of feminist literature; female artists were successful in exposing and selling their works. Marguerite Yourcenar was the first woman to be elected to the Académie Française. The Austrian Ingeborg Bachmann has been acknowledged as the most important German-speaking poet of the twentieth century. However, women still make up only 25 per cent of published writers in France.[25] In most European countries the number of female professors is still disproportionately low. Women have established themselves as theatre and film directors, but the position of internationally recognized female conductors is still negligible; only very few works by female composers are presented in public concerts.

Since the 1960s feminist issues and feminist theory have challenged the arts. A first objective was to point to the fact that the meaning of art does not lie in the art work itself but arises out of the political and social context. Historically, this context was most often defined by men. Feminist artists started to question the male character of art history—and of artistic performance. Minimalism was analysed as cool and impersonally masculine. The body performances of

---

[25] Marini, in Georges Duby and Michelle Perrot (eds.), *A History of Women* 5 (ed. F. Thébaud) (London: Harvard UP 1994).

conceptual artists appeared to be phallocentric, different from the eroticism of, for example, Louise Bourgeois. In theatre women started to interpret the traditional roles of masculine characters—from Faust to Hamlet. More than any other cultural medium, film had presented women as sexual objects; objects for the spectator as for the main characters in the films themselves. Some directors gave a critical view of women's position in a male-dominated society (Visconti's *Rocco and his Brothers*, 1960). In the new cinema of the 1960s actresses such as Monica Vitti, Hanna Schygulla, and Catherine Deneuve started to present a more natural character, using the language of face and body, instead of performing a pre-defined role. However, even at the end of the century most women in film perform still a passive role, depending on men to fulfil their hopes and ideas.[26]

Developments in the East were in many respects different. Socialist women were 'free' by definition, but feminist discourse never played the same role as in the West. Women's organizations were represented in parliament but hardly built a forum of critique. More women than in the West had permanent employment (50.6 per cent of Soviet workers were female in 1989) and the state provided the necessary child care (although in France and Italy the state looked after a higher percentage of children than in the Soviet Union).[27] The female factory worker or 'die rote Traktoristin' have been romantic topics of socialist realist art, comparable to the paintings in which Stalin decorates 'heroic mothers' for giving birth. However, this art was propaganda for an idea and did not reflect reality. Up to 80 per cent of the workers in the less qualified professional categories of the Soviet Union were female; women held only between 5 and 10 per cent of highest categories.[28] Even the percentage of women in the various bodies of political representation decreased during the postwar era. The Soviet composer Sofia Gubaidulina was respected by radical fellow artists, but until the years of Gorbachev's glasnost her music was officially banned. However, female writers in the GDR in particular expressed their dissatisfaction with important aspects of the political system in feminist terms. Helga Königsdorf called her novel about the situation of professional women in the GDR *Respektloser Umgang* ('Irreverent Manners', 1980). Monika Maron

---

[26] Sorlin, *European Cinemas, European Societies*, 201.
[27] Navailh, in Duby and Perrot (eds.), *A History of Women*, 5.
[28] Ibid.

told the story of a female historian who falls ill, but nobody at work notices her absence (*Die Überläuferin*, 1986). Helga Schubert, Helga Schütz, and Christa Wolf gave similarly frustrated accounts of the situation of women in 'real existing socialism'.

Through their 'power of speech'[29] women in the East were successful in constructing a sphere of critical public debate. This was much less the case in the fascist dictatorships of Spain and Portugal, where female issues were too closely linked to republican memory. Only the revolutions of the 1970s led to the spread of feminist discussion groups, feminist literature, and a new position of women in public.[30]

A post-modern crisis?

The project of modernity relied on the idea of infinite material and intellectual resources: the foundation of Euratom in 1957 started from the principle that humanity had discovered never-ending sources of energy. The experience of the oil crises, Chernobyl, and new critical approaches to the objectivity of knowledge damaged these beliefs.

The philosophical responses to the experience of war and dictatorship in the 1940s were the first to criticize the dialectic nature of the Enlightenment. In his writings Karl Popper questioned the positivism and teleological historicism of the modern age. After Einstein knowledge would be neither permanent nor absolute. Against the theories of the social scientists—until the late 1970s the leading academic discipline in societal debate—he projected an 'open society' of liberal democracies triumphing all over Europe. During the period of decolonization intellectuals and artists influenced by Franz Fanon pointed to the Eurocentric character of the concept of 'modernity'. Despite its claims, Western philosophy was not 'universalist'. At the end of the 1960s Joseph Kosuth started to use Wittgenstein's *Tractatus* to explore the relation between concept, reality, and representation in the arts. In conceptual and performance art the interpretation of the work by the viewer became as important as the intention of the artist. The performance and the public creation of the work of art privileged the context for the definition of meaning. In the aftermath of

[29] Bathrick, *The Powers of Speech*.
[30] Marini, in Duby and Perrot (eds.), *A History of Women*.

Michel Foucault, supposed knowledge was increasingly seen as serving political aims and social suppression. Discourse forms the object of which we speak. Jean-François Lyotard published *The Postmodern Condition*, and Jacques Derrida threatened social scientists with the deconstruction of their textual sources. To a growing number of political activists the traditional analysis of social reality no longer represented an objective image; they started making claims for the recognition of subjective difference, based on new social, ethnic, and sexual identities. The Western idea of progress was further questioned when from the 1970s people realized the high price which humanity as a whole had to pay for the technological advancement of the West. By the mid-1980s the project of modernity was in crisis.

A broad concept of 'recycling' appeared as the only answer: the recycling of material resources in the process of industrial production; the recycling of ideas in philosophy and humanities; the recycling of styles in the arts. This was the new age of postmodernism. The big outlines for a better human society disappeared; the end of the cold war was interpreted as the end of ideology or even as the end of history. Already in the 1970s Ernst Gombrich had argued that the reason for openness towards modern experiments in the West was to provide a contrast to the restriction of artistic expression in the East: 'Official sponsorship of extremist rebels in the Western camp might not have been so eager had it not been for the opportunity to drive home this very real contrast between free society and a dictatorship.[31] The breakdown of the Iron Curtain was used as justification and as explanation for a less 'ideological' post-modern way in the arts. Before, skyscrapers could demonstrate progress and superiority in the mastering of the future; now their aim would be to please the market through the recycling of decorative evergreens. Walter Benjamin had already seen the victory of the engineer over the architect in the design of urban centres as a consequence of bourgeois capitalism. Post-modern art, music, and architecture no longer aimed for the amelioration of existing society. If modernism was based on the critique of social reality in view of a better utopia, post-modernism wanted to please, without the illusion of a 'better'. Art became quotation and pastiche, easy to appreciate, uncritical in principle.

[31] Ernst H. Gombrich, *The Story of Art* (London: Phaidon, 1972).

However, by the end of the 1990s one had to pose the question whether this crisis was really the end of modernity or if it was not rather a coherent part of the modernist project itself: the radical critique of social and cultural reality in order to build a new utopia for the twenty-first century. Noberto Bobbio demonstrated that 'right and left' were still distinguishable, even at the end of the century. Instead of rejecting modernity, Jürgen Habermas called it an 'uncompleted project'. The label 'post-modern' appears to be in itself easily deconstructed, and certain cultural trends at the end of the century illustrate this. Rap, being based on the recycling and sampling of existing sounds and styles, has been discussed as an example of post-modernism. However, the new sound represents both a universal and a political language; and the appropriation of pre-existing sounds has been used in European music since the times of Bach. Rap exploits the most advanced technology, thus forming a fruitful tension between tradition and innovation. Luciano Berio anticipated the idea of sampling in his *Recital for Cathy* (1971), a collage of scraps from Monteverdi, Bach, Rossini, Verdi, Mahler, Milhaud, Poulenc, Bernstein, Marlene Dietrich, and many others, including his own compositions. Recalling certain ideas of Samuel Beckett's theatre, Berio depicts here the recital of a soprano waiting frustratedly for her pianist—all this with an effect not dissimilar to certain techniques in popular music at the end of the century. There was nothing new about the techniques of post-modernism. From this perspective it becomes difficult to see post-modernism as a concept describing a historical epoch; as a philosophical position it rather appears as a critical category of analysis, questioning—often with a certain amount of irony—some serious characteristics of the modernist project.

Despite the impact which cheap post-modern engineering has left on cities like Brussels over the last two decades of the century, it appears difficult to see European architecture as a whole dominated by post-modernism. Critics, the market, and the public have demonstrated openness towards the experiment, and the search for new means of artistic expression is broadly appreciated. Most contemporary architecture is still meaningful, as demonstrated in Mitterrand's 'grands projects', the British Library in London, the government buildings of the Berlin Republic, or the new university buildings in Graz. Similar trends in the urban planning of post-Francoist Spain have been discussed above.

This leads to the question of whether the public appreciation of modernism still leaves space for avant-garde. An action painter who receives public funding and is given an exhibition hall by an industrial Maecenas cannot be called avant-garde; he rather represents consensus. In this light the graffiti-sprayer might appear as the last avant-gardist in contemporary European art. This situation is completely different from the condition of cubist or futurist artists during the first half of the century. Public and private funding for non-conformist art has become the rule. It has become widely accepted that the artist looks for new responses to the contemporary challenges of post-industrial society.

New systems of communication and globalization

One of the ways of confronting the post-modern crisis in Europe was a new focus on non-European and post-colonial culture, and more specifically the overcoming of the arts' traditional Eurocentrism. 'Magiciens de la Terre', an exhibition of 100 artists from all over the globe at the Centre Georges Pompidou in 1989, tried to signal such cultural globalization. The exhibition pointed critically to the limitations of Western progress, searching at the same time for a new, global answer to the crises. However, the East Asian and in particular Japanese interest in the European cultural heritage is still confronted by most Europeans with arrogant if not racist superiority, regardless of our own ignorance in matters of non-European culture.

One of the most powerful issues in the debates of the *fin de siècle* has been the communications revolution, and in particular the possibilities of the Internet, with its 147 million users worldwide (in 1998). Different versions of the origins of the Internet have been discussed: military and FBI, radical students during the 1970s, cranks. Towards the end of the century an end-of-the-world mood was disseminated caused by conspiracy theories about the breakdown of the computer network during the night of the millennium.

Consciousness of the end of one epoch and the start of another, since the Middle Ages associated with the turn of centuries, relies on the constructed semantics of time, based on specific memories of the past and certain expectations of the future. The communications revolution served such aims, and over the last decade of the twentieth century was the object of powerful mystification. Some people argued that electronic records would completely replace books. However, during the 1990s the publication of books and journals on paper increased further, and the market still offers new daily and weekly newspapers. People still prefer to spend their time in bookshops instead of ordering their books on the Net. Ironically, information about new websites and Internet services is often communicated through traditional newspapers, demonstrating the limits of the new medium. The nature of information provided through the Internet is in many cases not different from or better than written and visual communication in printed media—books, newspapers, or leaflets. As television courses in the 1970s were unable to replace professional training and university teachers, distance learning and news and discussion groups on the Net are still unlikely to challenge the traditional structures of academic life on a large scale. The new medium has provoked some debate in the arts, but even highly specialized centres such as the Arts Electronica in Linz still resemble a gigantic play station inspired by *Star Wars* rather than a real challenge to the means and ends of abstract cultural communication. The bridge between painting and sculpture of the 1960s, and the video installations at the 1992 Documenta IX or the 1996 survey at the Louisiana Arts Centre near Copenhagen, have so far had more impact on the development of post-war arts than cyberspace.

It cannot be denied that the Internet allows for cheap global communication, only restricted through access to the computer (63 per cent of the population in Finland, but less than 1 per cent in most parts of the world). During the eighteenth and nineteenth centuries people shared their newspapers in coffee-houses; today only a few cities such as Vienna still offer this opportunity. However, where access to personal computers is still difficult, Internet cafés have provided a comparable service since the 1990s. Email has replaced an important part of correspondence, which historians one day will regret. Discussion groups on the Net bring people into contact and add an interesting aspect to what Robert Darnton called, in a different context, 'the low life of literature'. However, there is little evidence that this debate influences the public sphere in the same powerful way as the articles and letters published during the Gulf and the Kosovo Wars in newspapers such as *La Repubblica*, *Die Zeit*, *Le Monde*, or *El País* by intellectuals and politicians.

European culture, culture and Europe

If a history of Europe aims for more than a selective overview of political, social, economic, and cultural developments, but seeks a definition of Europe, then culture deserves a very prominent place in this undertaking; and culture represents not only the means, but also the end of the definition. Culture appears as the glue which holds the loose concept of Europe together and draws the lines between the political, social, and economic concepts of Europe.

Geographical definitions of Europe have changed over time and are of secondary importance for questions of social development. The Urals, the Bosporous, and the Straits of Gibraltar form less of a geographical border than the Alps or the Pyrenees. Despite the claims of some European politicians, a Christian notion of Europe does not correspond to the social reality of an increasingly secularized society in which Christians, Jews, Muslims, and Atheists have lived together for generations. Concepts of Europe based on political and legal considerations first emerged in the eighteenth century; in response to the experience of nationalism and war they inspired the fathers of European integration, but at the end of the twentieth century this ideal still represented more a hope—and for some Europeans a fear—than a reality. Only a cultural definition of Europe was able to bridge the changing concepts of Europe over the centuries and even survived the cold war.

Inherent in a cultural definition of Europe is its internal cultural diversity, which through reciprocal inspiration and competition created Europe's strength and too often provoked its sense of superiority in confrontation with other cultures. Nevertheless, European culture is not better than but different from other cultures. Be it the Russian Alfred Schnittke or the British Roger Waters, European music is still based on its own harmonic system, which is different from traditional Japanese music. When during the twentieth century cubist artists in Europe got interested in African art, they did so specifically because this art was different from European styles.

Without question Pasternak and Bunin represent European culture; the history of twentieth-century European music cannot be written without Shostakovich; Andrei Tarkovsky's films are among the most important documents of contemporary European culture. The examples build a semantic bridge between West and East

European culture. The question whether Russia should be regarded as European appears obsolete if one considers the works of Tchaikovsky, Dostoyevsky, Gorky. The culture of the Soviet Union built a bridge between Europe and Asia: Shostakovich clearly represents the European aspect of Soviet culture, while most of Chingiz Aitmatov's writings, whose novel *Djamila* has been described as the most beautiful European love story, stand for its Asian aspects. A similar scheme can probably be developed for the place of British culture in Europe. Through its linguistic and economic ties British culture has been under stronger influence from the United States than other European cultures. However, Benjamin Britten is just as important to post-war European culture as Shostakovich.

It is in cultural terms that Europe is most clearly defined. This definition is based not only on Europe's cultural heritage, but on its contemporary culture, by the means of everyday culture, by literature, film, music, and the arts. In cultural terms Europe is more than its own museum.

6

International and security relations within Europe

Klaus Larres

Until 1989–90 the history of Europe since 1945 was characterized by the division of the continent into two competing blocs dominated by the United States of America on the one hand and the Soviet Union on the other. Very few European countries managed to remain truly neutral. During these four and a half decades the history of Western Europe was dominated by four separate but closely intertwined strands: the cold war, the European integration movement, the transatlantic relationship between the West Europeans and the United States, and the USSR's authoritarian rule in Eastern Europe. Until the end of the cold war and the dissolution of the Soviet Union in December 1991 the nations of Eastern Europe were not able to become involved in European integration and transatlantic relations. Moreover, as far as the cold war was concerned most of the time they had no choice but to remain passive bystanders and loyal supporters of the USSR. A degree of unswerving loyalty also characterized the relationship between the countries of Western Europe and the powerful United States of America. But Washington's hegemonic position in Western Europe was of a qualitatively very different nature from Moscow's coercively obtained empire in the East of the continent.

The European continent had in common that all of its countries were involuntarily exposed to the vast economic, financial, and political–cultural sacrifices imposed upon the world by the cold war in general and the superpower conflict in particular. Undoubtedly the most severe sacrifices were shouldered by the nations of Eastern Europe. Throughout the cold war the quality and quantity of industrial production and thus living standards remained appallingly low in such nations as Bulgaria, Romania, and Albania, the poorest of them all, but also in Poland, Czechoslovakia,[1] and Hungary. These countries were in no position to compete with the economic miracles that characterized the developments throughout the 1950s and 1960s in West Germany, the Benelux countries, France, Britain, Scandinavia, and Italy. Moreover, in the 1970s and 1980s Spain, Portugal, and Greece, and eventually Ireland in the 1990s, enjoyed a kind of 'economic miracle'. In particular, the West Germans prospered throughout the post-war era and were able to enjoy their full integration with the Western world. The East Germans had to pay for the temporary solution to the German question. This was the country's division as it emerged between 1945 and 1949. Only since the fall of the Berlin Wall in November 1989 has a certain convergence taken place on the European continent. The countries of Eastern and Western Europe have gradually begun to reconnect with each other and discover their common European heritage.

This chapter will deal with the West and East European experience during the cold war before analysing the development of an ever more integrated Europe in the years since 1990 which, paradoxically, appears to be characterized by both lively multilateralism and the desire for unity. The chapter has been organized along several thematic sections. It will commence with a brief look at the role of ideology in European history. Then the concept of the year zero and the importance of the German question in post-1945 Europe will be considered. This is followed by several parts which analyse developments in Western and Eastern Europe during the cold war. A separate section is devoted to the development of European integration and common European institutions from the early 1950s to the late 1990s.

---

[1] On 1 Jan. 1993 the CSSR was dissolved and replaced by two sovereign states (connected by a customs and trade union): the Slovak Republic and the more prosperous Czech Republic with former playwright and dissident Vàclav Havel as president.

Ideological factors in post-war European history

All of the four strands which have been identified as having dominated a large part of the European continent between 1945 and 1990 (the cold war, European integration, transatlantic relations, Soviet rule in Eastern Europe) had political, military, and economic as well as ideological dimensions. At times all of these gave rise to severe disputes among the countries concerned and, owing to various unique developments and events (usually economic or military ones), caused numerous political crises, albeit at very differing levels of intensity. The often overlooked ideological aspect of developments in post-war Europe has perhaps been most contentious.

Throughout the second half of the twentieth century fundamentally differing world-views for example were greatly influential regarding the controversies over the purposes and aims of European integration. The West European countries were extremely divided between the federalists (largely present in Germany, the Benelux countries, Italy, and to some degree in France), who advocated the development of an ever more integrated Europe in both economic and political–military terms, and the more Euro-sceptic and pragmatic functionalists, who were dominant in Britain and the Scandinavian countries. The former favoured the development of supranational institutions and the gradual loss of sovereignty of the individual nation states. The functionalists tended to believe that the creation of a single economic market without any common political, security, and monetary dimensions ought to be the limited goal of European integration. Thus, integration was only seen as desirable with regard to a limited number of clearly defined areas (e.g. the coal and steel industries in the 1950s, and agriculture in later decades). It was argued that the maintenance of national sovereignty and independence was essential for the well-being of the individual European nation states.

Ideological issues also played an important role with respect to the economic (free trade) dimension of transatlantic relations. During much of the post-1945 period strong Christian-democratic and social-democratic beliefs in the values of a regulated social market economy, Keynesian economics, and the welfare state dominated politics in many Western European states, in particular Italy, France, and West Germany. They were pitched against a very different American philosophy. In the United States the doctrine of free trade, including the removal of protectionist tariffs and currency restrictions and the development of an uninhibited free market economy with a strong emphasis on supply-side economics, dominated economic thinking for much of the post-war period.

Another major semi-ideological factor of disagreement between Washington and many West European countries throughout the post-1945 era took place within NATO. It referred to the Atlantic community's military strategy and European exclusion from nuclear decision-making. NATO's strategies were dominated by American thinking in terms of 'massive retaliation' and subsequently by the not much more subtle 'flexible response' policy. In Europe it was perceived that underlying these strategies were two tiresome American preoccupations: Washington's temptation to embark on isolationism by frequently considering whether or not to withdraw or substantially reduce its troop strength on the European continent; and apparent American readiness to resort to the first use of nuclear weapons in a war with the Soviet Union without consulting its European allies. Thus, it appeared that any minor conflict might quickly escalate into a nuclear contest and lead to the destruction of much of Europe in the process. Yet, this ideological tension in transatlantic relations was interspersed with pragmatic political–economic concerns. The Europeans relied heavily on the American nuclear security umbrella. Moreover, for budgetary reasons and with respect to domestic public opinion, they were seldom able to agree on spending as much money on conventional forces as Western military experts deemed necessary to repulse any Soviet attack on Western Europe without resort to nuclear warfare.

The cold war was often depicted by both policy-makers and writers on the subject as merely a power-political contest and a test of will between East and West. This has largely characterized the heated debate over the origins of and the responsibility for the cold war between the orthodox, revisionist, and post-revisionist accounts of the cold war which have dominated academic writing on these issues.[2] The importance of ideology was generally downplayed in favour of the primacy of political power and security as promulgated by realist and neo-realist theories of international relations.[3] Moreover, in the Western world sinister ideological cold war motives were only attributed to Soviet-inspired Marxism–Leninism and its expansionist doctrine and ambition to export international communism to the rest of the world.

However, not only the Soviet Union but also the United States had a strong missionary drive; indeed, both countries worked to spread their mutually exclusive domestic systems. Yet, the United States only exercised its hegemonic leadership in Western Europe with the agreement of the West Europeans themselves. This so-called 'empire by invitation' was largely based on democratic participatory principles.[4] Frequent violations of these principles, West European demand for greater co-determination, American 'arrogance of power', overblown rhetoric for public consumption, and many other problems did not lead to any long-lasting serious questioning of America's presence in Western Europe. Almost the only notable politician who took exception to American hegemonic leadership in Western Europe was French president Charles de Gaulle. On the whole the West Europeans never had to forgo a say in their own affairs, although as far as security issues were concerned some countries (Italy, West Germany) came very close. Instead, it appears that during the entire post-1945 period, West Europeans were able to influence American policy-making in political, economic, and sometimes even military affairs to a considerable degree.[5] Moreover, at a very early stage and based on the model of its own national experience, the United States became an enthusiastic supporter of the creation of a

[2] See G. Lundestad, 'Moralism, Presentism, Exceptionalism, Provincialism, and Other Extravagances in American Writings on the Early Cold War Years', *Diplomatic History*, 13 (1989), 527–45; M. P. Leffler, 'New Approaches, Old Interpretations, and Prospective Reconfigurations', *Diplomatic History*, 19 (1995), 173–96.

[3] See H. J. Morgenthau, *Politics among Nations: The Struggle for Power and Peace*, 6th edn. (New York: Knopf, 1985); R. O. Keohane (ed.), *Neorealism and its Critics* (New York: 1986); R. O. Keohane and J. S. Nye, *Power and Interdependence*, 2nd edn. (Glenview, Ill., 1989).

[4] G. Lundestad, 'Empire by Invitation? The United States and Western Europe, 1945–1952', *Journal of Peace Research*, 23 (1986), 263–77.

[5] J. G. Ikenberry, 'Rethinking the Origins of American Hegemony', *Political Science Quarterly*, 104 (1989), 375–400; T. Risse-Kappen, *Cooperation among Democracies: The European Influence on US Foreign Policy* (Princeton: Princeton University Press, 1995).

United States of Europe characterized by political stability, the build-up of sound military forces, and a huge single market ready to absorb American goods.[6] While not an altogether altruistic enterprise, the informal American empire over much of Western Europe was a qualitatively very different affair from the much more directly controlled empire of the Soviet Union in Eastern Europe. The latter appeared to be driven by strong anti-Western motives of both an ideological and a power-political nature.

Year zero and the importance of the German question

Despite the important turning-point in world politics which the end of the Second World War and the dropping of the nuclear bombs on Hiroshima and Nagasaki in August 1945 represent, it appears to be unwise to consider 1945 as the year zero. Although the cold war, the Soviet Union's rule in Eastern Europe, European integration, and transatlantic relations largely commenced in the years after the end of Second World War, all these interdependent strands of European post-war history were also deeply rooted in Europe's past. The cold war had its roots in the East–West conflict which began with the Bolshevik Revolution in 1917 and the Allied intervention in the Russian civil war. Despite the NATO–Russian rapprochement in the 1990s (for example, the 1995 'Partnership for Peace' agreement and the 1997 political cooperation agreement), serious disagreements with Russia and indeed with China during the 1999 Kosovo War (and in its aftermath) indicated that the East–West conflict may not yet be over for good. Moreover, the Russians are hugely disappointed by the failure of Western style *laissez-faire* capitalism to reform dramatically the economy of their country, and largely blame the West for it. NATO's eastern enlargement in April 1999, with the admission of the former Warsaw Pact members Poland, Hungary, and the Czech Republic, was also greatly resented in Moscow. The intention to admit former parts of the Soviet Union to NATO like the Baltic states,

---

[6] G. Lundestad, *'Empire' by Integration: The United States and European Integration, 1945–1997* (Oxford: Oxford University Press, 1998).

Russia's so-called 'near abroad', is perceived as even more humiliating. It is also regarded as a severe potential threat to Russia's national security.

The post-1945 movement for European integration is above all rooted in the attempts made after the First World War by French prime minister Aristide Briand to unify Europe in order to downgrade any potential danger from Germany and avoid another major war. It was intellectually underpinned by Count Coudenhove-Kalergi's Pan-European Union and, during the war, by Altiero Spinelli's vision of European federation. After the end of the Second World War these ideas were greatly influential, in conjunction with the urgings of French economist Jean Monnet and Belgian politician Paul-Henri Spaak, in setting up a federal European unity. This was also the aim of the work of such organizations as the Belgian Paul van Zealand's European Liga, the French-based Union of European Federalists, and the United Europe Movement, founded with the help of Winston Churchill in 1947.

Similarly, the roots of transatlantic relations were laid in America's economic involvement with European affairs in the inter-war years. While all three American governments of that decade displayed strong isolationist convictions with regard to their involvement in international politics and security, this was not the case as far as the international economy was concerned. For example, American banks provided many much needed credits and loans to European countries (not least to Germany) to help them rebuild their economies. Moreover, on behalf of the central government in Washington, American bankers were most influential in mediating between the Weimar Republic and the Allies of the First World War to arrive at mutually acceptable plans for German reparation payments (e.g. the Dawes and Young Plans). The so-called Anglo-American 'special relationship', an integral part of contemporary transatlantic relations, was brought about by America's decisive involvement in the First and, above all, in the Second World War and by the good, though not always very harmonious, working relationship between Franklin D. Roosevelt and Winston Churchill.

Thus, there were plenty of images and memories of the past that heavily influenced policy-making in post-1945 Europe. To some extent subjective perceptions and preferred interpretations of the past were responsible for prescribing a certain framework for the future of the European continent and the bilateral and multilateral relationships within Europe. For example, it was only in the 1980s and 1990s that the strong general belief in the importance of upholding the full sovereignty of the nation state showed signs of decline in Western Europe, albeit not in Eastern Europe and the Slavic world. In particular during the immediate aftermath of the Second World War decision-makers often found it very difficult to extricate themselves from travelling along well-trodden paths of thought.

This applied above all to the many problems which needed to be resolved with respect to the future of Germany. After all, the Western Allies always remained aware of the perceived failure of the Versailles peace treaty for peacefully reintegrating Germany into the community of nations following the First World War. After 1945 the questions of the administration, governing, and economic rebuilding of this country in the middle of Europe as well as the de-Nazification and re-education of the German people were only some of the most pressing tasks following the collapse of Hitler's Reich and Germany's unconditional surrender on 8 May 1945. Furthermore, the traditional enmity between France and Germany, fuelled by three humiliating German invasions of France in the course of seventy years, needed to be addressed. The influence of communism on the unstable and economically devastated states of continental Europe (above all on Germany, France, Italy, Greece) as well as the so-called Rapallo complex also worried the Western Allies. The latter was rooted in the entirely unexpected 1922 Treaty of Rapallo and the beginning of anti-Western German–Soviet cooperation which culminated in the Hitler–Stalin Pact of 1939.[7]

Underlying all these concerns lay the mere size of Germany's territory and population as well as its economic and industrial potential with its traditional centres of coal and steel production in the Ruhr and Saar Valleys. The question had to be addressed whether or not it was advisable (as strongly advocated by the French until 1947–8) to reduce the country to a more manageable size or even turn it into a largely agricultural state (as advocated by the Morgenthau Plan signed by Roosevelt and Churchill in 1944). However, soon the potentially

[7] K. Larres, 'Germany and the West: The 'Rapallo Factor' in German Foreign Policy from the 1950s to the 1990s', in K. Larres and P. Panayi (eds.), *The Federal Republic of Germany since 1949: Politics, Society and Economy before and after Unification* (London: Longman, 1996).

negative economic consequences of such policies for Germany's neighbours were recognized. There was also the very real danger that economic chaos and national dissatisfaction with the separate administration of Germany by initially four very differently organized occupation zones would have disastrous results. It could clearly not be ruled out that the country might easily fall victim to yet another extremist political movement from either the right or, as was generally thought more likely in view of Moscow's activities, from the left. After all, by 1945 the Red Army had occupied Germany, including its capital, Berlin, up to the Elbe, and the Soviet occupation authorities displayed no inclination to establish democratic institutions in Eastern Germany and leave their zone of occupation in due course.

Germany's central role on the European continent meant it was the only nation that came to play an important role in all four strands that shaped the future of post-war Europe: the cold war, European integration, transatlantic relations, and the Kremlin's sphere of influence in Eastern Europe, which of course included its rule over East Germany. In contrast, the United Kingdom was largely confined to an influential role in the cold war (particularly during the first ten to fifteen years) and transatlantic relations. France primarily played an important part in transatlantic relations (particularly in the 1960s) and European integration. France and West Germany, together with Italy and the Benelux countries, were the core six countries that established the European Economic Community (EEC) in 1957–8. The latter four nations have remained largely only of international importance as far as European integration is concerned.

The same applies to a great extent to the South and Northern European countries. However, Portugal and Spain still had (and have) a certain influence in Latin America and their former colonies. Greece, with its troubled economic and political post-war history (1967–74 military regime) and its involvement in the Cyprus conflict with Turkey, was mostly also outside mainstream West European politics until 1974. While Turkey (and Greece) became a member of NATO in 1952, due to its serious human rights violations (especially with respect to the Kurdish question in the north), the country's long-standing European Community application (since 1964) has been put on hold.

The cold war and European security

It may be justified to some extent to characterize the cold war and the largely bilateral world between 1945 and 1990 as a period of 'long peace'.[8] Yet, this does appear to ignore the numerous wars that did take place (Korea, Vietnam, and the many conflicts by proxy in the developing world). It also seems to downplay the immense human, economic, and sociocultural sacrifices that were made by the entire international community but in particularly by the communist and developing world. To speak of a 'long peace' may be most appropriate when referring to the cold war in Europe. After all, it was only with the long conflicts in Bosnia (1992–5) and Kosovo (1999) in the former Yugoslavia that war returned to the European continent. Still, even during the cold war years peace in Europe was seriously disturbed by the Kremlin's ruthless military interventions to terminate anti-Soviet uprisings in East Germany (1953), Hungary (1956), and Czechoslovakia (1968). Moreover, the imposition of martial law in Poland in December 1981 (until July 1983) may well have prevented yet another application of Moscow's Brezhnev Doctrine as announced in 1968: the Red Army's invasion of a country regarded as part of the USSR's East European sphere of influence. Instead of a 'long peace' it might therefore be more appropriate to speak of an enforced uneasy stability on the European continent during the cold war.

The cold war in Europe is most conveniently divided into three phases: first, the period of transition, occupation, and early cold war years between 1945 and 1953; secondly, attempts at peaceful cooperation and renewed cold war between 1953, the year of Stalin's death, and the late 1960s; and, finally, the gradual beginning of détente in the early 1970s, a further period of high tension in the early 1980s, and the end of the cold war in 1990–1.

---

[8] J. L. Gaddis, *The Long Peace: Inquiries into the History of the Cold War* (New York: Oxford University Press, 1987).

The years of transition, occupation, and reconstruction, 1945–1953

In the immediate aftermath of the Second World War the reconstruction of the European continent and the hope of continued cooperation between the West and the Soviet Union dominated European politics. There were also strong grass-roots movements (particularly in Italy, Belgium, and the Netherlands) which aimed at bringing about a united federal Europe in order to prevent the recurrence of the horrors of the past; it was believed that if Europe continued to be dominated by hostile and competing states it would be prone to slide again into a major conflict. However, initially neither East–West cooperation nor European integration were particularly successful.

In the immediate aftermath of the Second World War the dream of the creation of a united Europe led only to the realization of the long-envisaged customs union (since 1944) among Belgium, the Netherlands, and Luxembourg which took effect in January 1948 (Benelux). The Scandinavian countries set up a consultative Nordic Council in 1951, and considered a joint customs union in 1954. Other activities were of only a symbolic nature. For example, the grand convention in The Hague in 1948 which saw the participation of Churchill and other major statesmen did not achieve anything, although it aroused much attention as it called for the creation of the United States of Europe, including the reintegration of defeated Germany in the community of nations. The establishment of the Council of Europe in Strasbourg in May 1949 did not result in any meaningful economic or political integration of Europe either. The Organization for European Economic Cooperation (OEEC, renamed OECD in 1960) was also unable to contribute to the unity of the European continent.[9]

The OEEC was established in 1948 in response to American secretary of state George Marshall's announcement of the European Recovery Programme in his address at Harvard University in June 1947. While greatly beneficial to the economic reconstruction of

[9] Members were Austria, Benelux countries, Denmark, France, Greece, Iceland, Ireland, Italy, Norway, Portugal, Sweden, Switzerland, Turkey, the United Kingdom, West Germany since Oct. 1949; the United States and Canada became associate members in 1950.

Western Europe, it was also crucial for undermining the temptation in Italy, Greece, and in the unstable Fourth Republic in France to move ever closer to communist rule. Yet, the Marshall Plan and the OEEC resulted in the further political polarization of the European continent. After all, not entirely unexpectedly, at a foreign ministers' conference in Paris in late June and early July 1947 Soviet foreign minister Molotov angrily rejected the liberal-capitalist economic conditions imposed by the United States under which all European countries would be able to participate in the Marshall Plan. Stalin strictly forbade Poland and Czechoslovakia to pursue their great interest in attending the sixteen-nation conference in Paris from July to September of 1947 which was convened to organize the European Recovery Programme generously financed by the United States.[10]

In Eastern Europe plans for a Yugoslav–Bulgarian and a Yugoslav–Albanian union were ventilated in 1947–8 but did not find favour with Stalin. Instead, the Soviet dictator concentrated on consolidating the whole of Eastern Europe under Soviet tutelage by means of the renewal or establishment of mutual assistance treaties between Moscow and the East European states. In January 1949 this development culminated in the creation of the Council for Mutual Economic Assistance (Comecon) among the USSR, Poland, the CSSR, Hungary, Bulgaria, and Romania. Stalin's conflict with Yugoslavia's independent-minded leader, Tito, led to the country's economic boycott and non-inclusion in Comecon. Bilateral treaties among the East Europeans themselves were also concluded. Although Stalin had insisted on annexing the Baltic states and eastern Poland in the course of the Second World War, after 1945 he did not annex any other neighbouring states like Finland, which was able to retain a finely balanced independent status.

On the whole, economic cooperation in Eastern Europe was heavily tilted towards the needs of the Soviet Union for land reform and Moscow's concentration on heavy industry and machinery and a centrally planned economy. This often disadvantaged the individual East European nations. Very little heed was paid to the demand for consumer goods and more liberal ways of life to satisfy the

---

[10] M. Hogan, *The Marshall Plan: America, Britain, and the Reconstruction of Europe* (Cambridge: Cambridge University Press, 1987); A. Milward, *The Reconstruction of Western Europe, 1945–1951* (Berkeley: University of California Press, 1984); also A. Milward, 'Was the Marshall Plan Necessary?', *Diplomatic History*, 13 (1989), 231–53.

populations in these relatively developed and industrialized countries. The ruthless use of force was necessary to suppress these desires
as, for example, during the first sudden and entirely unexpected erup-
tion of discontent in East Germany and also in Bulgaria in 1953. The
various communist parties, which soon dominated the governments
across the Soviet half of the continent, were Moscow's most effective
instruments for its ruthless exercise of power. This was clearly
demonstrated by their role in the purges, show trials, and executions
of critical and democratic spirits in many East European countries as
well as in the USSR itself in the course of the first post-war years.

The cold war begins

Already in the closing stages of the Second World War tension and
differing ideas about Europe's new post-war order had become apparent among the four Allies of the anti-Hitler coalition. However, as long
as Hitler had not been properly defeated and was still holding out in
his bunker in Berlin, these disagreements were mostly successfully
contained. Once the war in Europe (May 1945) and then also the war
in Asia (August 1945) had been terminated, the ever more profound
disagreements between the Western Allies (United States, United
Kingdom, and France) and the Soviet Union became increasingly
obvious. While the cold war first erupted over disagreements with
respect to the Soviet Union's unnecessarily prolonged occupation of
oilfields in Iran and Moscow's attempts to put pressure on Turkey to
give the USSR access to the Mediterranean, the developing East–West
conflict soon concentrated on events on the European continent.

In Europe disagreements became particularly manifest during the
various foreign ministers' conferences established by the four Allied
powers in the course of the Potsdam Conference in July–August 1945.
They were meant to settle any outstanding territorial and financial
questions arising from the Second World War. In particular, relations
among the former Allies severely deteriorated with respect to the
bitter clashes over reparations from Germany. Relations also suffered
in view of strenuous Soviet activities to establish a loyal communist
regime under the leadership of Walter Ulbricht and the suppression
of all democratic parties in its German zone of occupation. Equally,
the Soviet Union's successful endeavours to set up communist
governments in Poland and the other East European states were most

controversial. However, it was above all the February 1948 coup in Czechoslovakia, a country with an established democratic tradition, which greatly disillusioned the Western world. The replacement of most of the democratic government ministers in Prague with communist ones, the subsequent purges in the country, and the erection of a centrally planned economy contributed decisively to the growing conviction in the Western world that Stalin was not interested in peaceful cooperation and the maintenance of a united European continent.

By 1947–8 it was becoming increasingly clear that two opposing spheres of influence in Europe and two very different philosophical and political conceptions about the future of Europe were being realized. Moreover, the establishment of the Cominform in September 1947, in the course of a conference in Poland, with the participation of East European, French, and Italian communists, was interpreted as the beginning of Stalin's intention to export his dictatorial model to Western Europe. It was assumed that he would not shrink from using force. Alternatively, he might concentrate on skilfully undermining the weak Western economies and democracies. After all, the Cominform appeared to be an imitation of Lenin's Communist International (abolished in 1943). It clearly aimed at centrally organizing all East and West European communist parties to spread world revolution. Yet, the weak coalition governments in France and Italy survived. The strenuous efforts by the communist parties in both countries, by means of widespread strikes, to prevent these countries from accepting Marshall aid and thus American leadership were unsuccessful. For once, the CIA's clandestine and well-financed efforts had triumphed over Moscow's support for the communists.

Moreover, Yugoslavia remained a thorn in Stalin's side. In 1948 Tito was expelled from the Cominform, and henceforth his country and its semi-neutral status was courted by the Western world. Mistakenly it was believed that Tito's ability to insist on his independence was the beginning of the unravelling of the Soviet bloc. In the 1970s and 1980s the West had a similarly mistaken perception of the importance of Romanian dictator Nicolae Ceauşescu's conflict with the Soviet Union. Despite the impoverishment of his country and the numerous human rights violations throughout his long period in power (1965–89), Ceauşescu's attempt to pursue a fairly independent foreign policy was feted among anti-communists in the West.

Initially it had been the post-1945 Labour government in Britain, and particularly Foreign Secretary Ernest Bevin, who had become convinced that it would be impossible to cooperate with the Soviet Union in post-war Europe. The views of the American Truman administration towards Moscow fluctuated considerably between a placid belief in Soviet goodwill and firm condemnation of Stalin's activities in Eastern Europe. Not least Churchill's dramatic speech in Fulton, Missouri, in March 1946 gradually changed this when he drew world attention to the Iron Curtain which had 'descended across the continent' stretching 'from Stettin in the Baltic to Trieste in the Adriatic'.[11] Yet, only in March 1947, during a joint session of Congress, did Truman clarify American foreign policy. The president used the occasion of British withdrawal from the support of the anti-communist forces in Greece and Turkey for financial reasons to announce the global Truman Doctrine. He declared that the United States would support any peace-loving country which was threatened by international communism. Even then, however, it was still somewhat unclear whether the myth of American isolationism was really a thing of the past and whether there would be moral as well as prolonged practical American commitment to Europe.[12]

Politicians in London remained pessimistic regarding the possibility of persuading the United States to remain committed to Europe. Some politicians on the left of the Labour Party and on the patriotic right of the Conservative party also denied the desirability of convincing the Americans to stay in Europe. Yet, the British government began advocating plans for an economic and military Western union (above all with reference to close Franco-British cooperation). It was also hoped that this would facilitate the build-up of a British-led independent force in world affairs to balance American and Soviet power. However, it soon became apparent that in view of Britain's considerable global commitments from Malaya to India (as well as its expensive zonal responsibilities in Germany) and its depleted economic resources, London would be unable to assume such a role. The rapid deterioration of relations with the Soviet Union and Britain's

[11] See F. Harbutt, *The Iron Curtain: Churchill, America and the Origins of the Cold War* (New York: Oxford University Press, 1986).

[12] J. L. Gaddis, 'Was the Truman Doctrine a Real Turning Point?', *Foreign Affairs*, 52 (1973–4), 386–402; M. P. Leffler, *Preponderance of Power: National Security, the Truman Administration, and the Cold War* (Stanford, Calif.: Stanford University Press, 1992).

increasing awareness of its own weaknesses ensured that the further economic, political, and military involvement of the United States in the European continent was seen as absolutely essential. Thus, the United Kingdom immediately took the initiative to establish the Brussels Treaty Organization (BTO) with France and the Benelux countries in 1948 when the United States indicated that, in view of the perceived Soviet threat, Washington might be interested in cooperating with the West Europeans in security affairs. However, the United States expected some prior initiative by the Europeans to provide for their own security.[13] Once the BTO had been created in early 1948, negotiations for the establishment of the North Atlantic Treaty Organization were entered into.

In view of Stalin's activities in the East, by 1948 the Western occupation powers also decided to finalize plans to set up a liberal-democratic West German state and to reform the economy of West Germany and West Berlin by means of the introduction of a new currency. The British and American zones in Germany had already been merged in January 1947. However, Stalin still appeared to hope that at some time in the future the western part of Germany and West Berlin might escape from the influence of the Western Allies and turn neutralist; he does not seem to have expected that West Germany would go communist. Stalin therefore opposed the formal division of Germany. In June 1948 Moscow embarked on the Berlin blockade to force the Western world to rescind its separatist plans. But this backfired. The West countered by introducing a major airlift to prevent the starvation of the West Berlin population. Western solidarity for the population in the divided city at the front line of the cold war was a major factor in tying the Germans and the West closer to each other. Only a mere three years after Hitler's suicide the airlift provided the West Germans with the feeling of 'belonging' to the Western world. The Berlin blockade also strengthened Washington's resolve to become part of NATO and thereby, for the first time ever, commit itself to the lasting deployment of ground troops on the European continent in times of peace.

As soon as it became clear that the United States would remain committed to supporting the European continent militarily, the British government lost all interest in the Western European Union

[13] The 1947 Dunkirk Treaty between Britain and France had still been a traditional bilateral military treaty directed against renewed German aggression.

concept. London clearly favoured Atlantic cooperation. Thus the BTO was merely the means of obtaining the North Atlantic Pact which was signed in April 1949 by the BTO members and the United States, Canada, Italy, Iceland, Norway, Denmark, and Portugal. Much to Britain's delight, NATO was an alliance among sovereign countries, albeit firmly and clearly led by the United States, but it was not a supranational organization. Ever since, policy-makers in Britain have believed that it would be best for the United Kingdom's national interest in economic, political, and strategic nuclear affairs if the country concentrated on strengthening and expanding its bilateral 'special relationship' with the United States. London began to display a distinct lack of interest in the integration of the European continent. Yet, paradoxically, this ran counter to American policy.

In the late 1940s and early 1950s American policy-makers recognized that only a united Western Europe at peace with itself would be able to create a concerted front against the military and ideological threat from the Soviet Union. Moreover, only such a Europe would ensure the reconciliation of the Federal Republic of Germany (FRG) with the countries of the Western world and thereby generate lasting Franco-German friendship while avoiding tendencies towards neutralism and defeatism. Underlying the American vision was above all the assumption that only a fully integrated, stable, and economically viable Europe would develop into a peaceful and democratic continent. Achieving prosperity in Western Europe appeared to depend on the creation of a unified single market. In due course this strategy would have the advantage of making unnecessary the continuation of American economic aid to Western Europe. Thus, throughout the post-war period Britain and other European countries were frequently admonished to assume a more pro-integrationist attitude. After all, in Washington active American governmental support for and interference in European affairs were always regarded as limited and temporary. Moreover, it was expected that an economically healthy Europe would be able to build up strong military forces and abide by a policy of strength towards the Soviet Union. On occasion it was even contemplated that in due course it might be possible to liberate the 'captive peoples' of Eastern Europe by means of force.

The Western policy of preventing the Soviet Union from making further encroachments in Europe beyond the River Elbe, which divided the Eastern and Western sphere of influence on the European continent, became known as the 'strategy of containment'. Its principal author was American diplomat and historian George F. Kennan. While Kennan strongly believed in his original economic–political conception of containment, the Truman administration paid increasingly greater attention to the military dimension of containment. After all, the Berlin blockade crisis had made it clear that there was a looming threat of a military clash with the Soviet Union in the divided city of Berlin in the middle of Germany. Washington's belief in the necessity of rearming the countries of Western Europe (including most controversially the new West German state) and of expanding and modernizing America's conventional and nuclear forces was above all strengthened by the outbreak of war in Korea. In June 1950 communist North Korean forces invaded South Korea, the American protectorate. Parallels were drawn with the precarious position of divided Germany in Europe.

Moreover, in March 1950 it was announced that the Soviet Union had already exploded its first atomic bomb in August 1949—much earlier than had been expected in Washington and London. Britain would only be able to embark on its first atomic test explosion in 1952, and it would take France until 1960 (China exploded such a device in 1962). Thus, under the impact of the Korean War the huge rearmament programme called for in the American document NSC-68 was signed into law by President Truman. In September 1950 NATO created an integrated command structure under a Paris-based American supreme allied commander. The 1952 NATO conference in Lisbon confirmed the willingness of West Europeans to make huge rearmament efforts in the conventional field. However, economic and financial realities in Western Europe would prevent these ambitious and quite unrealistic military goals from ever being achieved.

Furthermore, Stalin's death in March 1953 and the rise to power of a collective leadership in Moscow with *primus inter pares* Georgi Malenkov led to a certain thaw in East–West relations. The perception developed in most West European countries (but not so much in the United States) that the military threat posed by the East was diminishing. Yet, by 1953 the cold war had led to the firm division of the European continent. Only a handful of neutral or semi-neutral countries (Switzerland, Liechtenstein, Austria, Sweden, Spain, Andorra, Ireland, perhaps Yugoslavia) had not been forced into taking sides.

East–West cooperation, nuclear brinkmanship, and crises over Berlin and Cuba, 1953–1963

In the course of the 1950s it gradually became clear that both Western and Eastern Europe were hardly more than passive bystanders in the conflict between the superpowers. This led to desperate British and French efforts to maintain their great power roles. But by the early 1960s the multipolar cold war had developed into a bipolar conflict. In the wake of the Cuban missile crisis of October 1962, which brought the world close to nuclear war, cautious cooperation between East and West began, with important repercussions for the European continent. The Vietnam War and French president de Gaulle's anti-American policies also caused major reverberations in European politics. How-ever, within each part of Europe the respective superpower was able to consolidate its hegemonic position. This resulted in numerous stra-tegic and economic–monetary conflicts between Washington and its West European allies, most of which could be resolved by prolonged consultative procedures. Despite the achievement of a certain degree of economic prosperity throughout Eastern Europe in the 1960s, there was increasing unhappiness with Moscow's ever more oppressive rule; Moscow had to resort to force to maintain its influence.

As far as the European continent was concerned, the 1950s were still largely preoccupied with the German problem. For the Soviet Union initially it was still a question of how to separate the FRG from the West and establish a reunited and neutral Germany. For the West it was a question of how best to integrate West Germany irreversibly with the Western world and bring about a rapprochement between Bonn and Paris. The latter was attempted by means of European integration and, in view of Moscow's overwhelming conventional strength, through the rearmament of West Germany.

However, the French categorically refused to agree to German rearmament and the integration of a German army into NATO, as the Americans had insisted upon during a Western foreign ministers' conference in Washington in September 1950. Instead of setting up a separate German army, French prime minister Pleven suggested a German contribution to a European army within a European Defence Community (EDC) led by a European minister of defence. But the Pleven Plan discriminated against the West Germans. The Bonn government was not allowed to set up a general staff and the

European army would consist of mixed divisions; there would be no purely German units. Moreover, the EDC member states intended only to integrate part of their army into the EDC while retaining a substantial number of forces as separate national armies for fighting the rising number of nationalist uprisings in their colonies, as for example in French Indo-China and the Belgian Congo. Furthermore, the United Kingdom refused to participate in the supranational EDC. In London it was argued that an army's quality was defined by the individual soldier's nationalist enthusiasm for defending his country of origin; it was unlikely that he would be willing to risk his life on behalf of a vaguely defined Europe. Moreover, the genuine fear existed that NATO and the American commitment to Europe might be weakened by the establishment of the EDC. Initially, the American government was also very sceptical about the military value of the EDC, but due to the persuasive skills of Jean Monnet, Washington changed its mind.

In May 1952 the EDC treaty was concluded by France, the FRG, Italy, and the Benelux countries. At the same time the so-called contractual agreements were signed which would turn West Germany into an almost sovereign state. The latter was Chancellor Adenauer's reward for West German participation in the EDC. In the course of 1953–4 the United Kingdom effectively entered into associate status with the EDC and agreed to close military cooperation. These gestures did not convince French public opinion. The sacrifice of the French army's national identity appeared unacceptable. In addition, before signing the treaty the German chancellor had achieved some notable changes to the EDC treaty. It provided for the more equal treatment of West Germany, but it seemed to weaken any potential French dominance of the EDC. The French feared increasingly that the Germans would soon dominate the EDC in military as well as in economic terms. After all, there was strong Italian and Dutch pressure to expand the EDC into a political and economic organization.[14]

In August 1954 the EDC was rejected by the French parliament. The entire project of anchoring the West Germans with the West and of stabilizing the European continent seemed to have received a decisive setback. It was Britain's Foreign minister, Anthony Eden, who

[14] The Italians and the Dutch even managed to commit the EDC's assembly to draft a federal constitution which contained a clause envisaging the political and economic unity of the member states.

received the credit for the proposal to realize the original American plan of integrating West German forces with NATO. However, prior to joining NATO on an equal footing with all other member states, the FRG would join (together with Italy) the revived and reformed BTO, renamed the Western European Union (WEU). The WEU would be used to organize the defence procurement of its member states and thus give each member state a veto over the purchase of arms of any of the member states. Thus, by means of West German membership of the WEU it would be possible to keep a watchful eye on the rearmament efforts of the Germans. Moreover, Adenauer 'voluntarily' promised that his country was not interested in obtaining ABC weapons (atomic, biological, and chemical arms). To reassure the French further, Eden also promised that Britain would not withdraw its NATO forces on the continent without the consent of the WEU countries.

Thus, Britain's traditional nation state approach to the problems of European integration, European security, and the German question had won the day. In May 1955 West Germany joined NATO and, in return, became a fully sovereign state within the Western concert of nations (except for Allied provisions for Berlin and Germany as a whole, including reunification). The Soviet Union was not as hostile to this development as had been gloomily anticipated. The Kremlin's answer to West German admission to NATO was the setting up of the Warsaw Pact on 14 May 1955. This was the Soviet-dominated military organization that loosely integrated Moscow's satellite states in Eastern Europe; the GDR became a full member in January 1956.

The United States and the West Europeans were immensely relieved about the successful integration of the FRG with the West. After all, just before the original EDC treaty was signed in May 1952, Stalin had done his utmost to tempt the West Germans away from the West. By way of his famous note of March 1952 Stalin had offered reunification to the Germans. Effectively, he appeared to offer the release of the East Germans from his sphere of influence if the West Germans left the Western camp and became a neutral country. Whether or not his note was meant seriously is still a matter of great controversy in the scholarly literature.[15] Despite strong pressure from

---

[15] For two opposing views: R. Steininger, *The German Question: The Stalin Note of 1952 and the Problem of Reunification* (New York: Columbia University Press, 1990); G. Wettig, 'Stalin and German Reunification: Archival Evidence on Soviet Foreign Policy in Spring 1952', *Historical Journal*, 37 (1994), 411–19.

the opposition parties in the West German parliament to 'check out' Stalin's offer, the Bonn government immediately encouraged the Western Allies to refuse the offer, which they gladly did.

However, much to the horror of politicians in Washington, Bonn, and elsewhere, only a year later, a few months after Stalin's sudden death in March 1953, British prime minister Churchill (who had returned to office in late 1951) made a very similar proposal. Inspired by the apparently more liberal course of the new collective leadership in Moscow, he advocated a neutral reunited Germany as well as the conclusion of a German–Soviet friendship treaty (a Western Locarno) which would be supervised by Great Britain. Churchill hoped that this position and an early end to the cold war would enable the United Kingdom to concentrate on economic reconstruction and thus remain one of the world's leading countries. He was also convinced that the continued division of Germany would lead to disturbances, if not to a nuclear war, in Europe. Stability on the continent could only be achieved if the Germans were satisfied as far as their national ambitions were concerned. The uprising in East Germany in June 1953 appeared to confirm his view. However, even in London there was little support for the prime minister's ideas. Most other European states were equally unenthusiastic about the prospect of having to deal again with a united Germany. Only Sweden appears to have had some sympathies for Churchill's vision. The hesitation of the new Soviet leadership to give their agreement to a four-power summit meeting, as well as secret American–West German collaboration in the summer of 1953, prevented the realization of Churchill's vision of how to solve the German question.[16]

The Soviet Union's sudden agreement to the Austrian state treaty during negotiations in Moscow in April 1955, after years of disagreement with the West over the future of the country, provided for the termination of occupation status and the establishment of a fully independent Austria within its 1938 borders. However, Austria was obliged to renounce all future intention of merging with Germany and to adopt the status of a neutral country independent of the two competing alliance systems. Moscow's agreement to the Austrian

---

[16] K. Larres, 'Integrating Europe or Ending the Cold War? Churchill's Post-War Foreign Policy', *Journal of European Integration History*, 2 (1996), 15–49; K. Larres, 'Preserving Law and Order: Britain, the United States and the East German Uprising of 1953', *Twentieth Century British History*, 5 (1994), 320–50.

state treaty and the expectation that the FRG would desire to emulate the Austrian solution must probably be regarded as the Soviet Union's last attempt to drive the FRG away from the Western side. But Moscow did not succeed. Once West Germany had been fully integrated with the Western Alliance in May 1955, the USSR lost interest in any neutrality and reunification plans. New Soviet leader Nikita Khrushchev began advocating his 'two-state theory' and thus the permanent division of Germany. Having been unable to prevent the incorporation of West Germany into the West, Moscow accepted the new realities. The Soviet Union now began advocating the international recognition of its German state. The time when Moscow was prepared to sacrifice the existence of the GDR was over. By 1955 Europe had definitely been divided into a western and eastern half.

This was above all symbolized by the Soviet invitation to the West German chancellor to travel to Moscow, which was viewed with great distrust in Washington as well as in most European capitals. During his visit in September 1955 Adenauer agreed to enter into diplomatic relations with the USSR and exchange ambassadors in return for the release of the remaining 10,000 German prisoners of war in the Soviet Union. However, embarking upon official relations with the Kremlin threatened to undermine West Germany's and the entire Western world's non-recognition of the GDR, as Bonn had now taken up diplomatic relations with a state which recognized the legitimacy of the GDR and the Oder–Neisse line as Germany's eastern border with Poland. Thus, the Adenauer government announced that the Soviet Union, as one of the four occupation powers, was a special case. The recognition of the East Berlin regime by any other country would have been regarded as an unfriendly act to be followed by appropriate action. This was the so-called Hallstein Doctrine, which was strongly supported by the United States and the West European states. As events would show, in the late 1950s and in particular during the 1960s it would prove ever more difficult to insist on the international non-recognition of the GDR. The official recognition of East Germany in 1957 by Yugoslavia and in 1963 by Cuba led to the rupture of diplomatic relations between the FRG and these countries. Observing the Hallstein Doctrine was also to become an important bone of contention between the West Germans and its West European partners, who increasingly wished to exploit trade opportunities with the GDR. In particular, France, Britain, the

Scandinavian countries and initially Switzerland, were tempted to intensify trade relations with East Germany. Indeed, with the exception of the strategic items placed on the so-called COCOM list of forbidden goods for trade with the Eastern bloc, trade links between Eastern and Western Europe steadily intensified after the mid-1950s.

By the time Adenauer visited Moscow the first four-power summit meeting since Postsdam had taken place in Geneva in July 1955. It was followed by a four-power foreign ministers' meeting in October. Although neither conference managed to solve any of the many outstanding cold war problems, they led to a more relaxed international climate. The first signs appeared that it might be possible to contain the cold war in Europe peacefully and agree to disagree; a policy which became known as 'peaceful coexistence.'

Khrushchev also attempted to open a new chapter with respect to Soviet domestic affairs. But his policy of de-Stalinization backfired. During a secret speech in February 1956 (which was almost immediately leaked to the Western media) he condemned the policies of the hitherto much admired Stalin and accused him of hideous crimes. His speech led to widespread hopes throughout Eastern Europe that Moscow was embarking on a more liberal course. This did not prove to be the case. Instead, Moscow ruthlessly suppressed the 1956 uprising in Hungary (and the somewhat less dramatic protests in Poland) which led to the killing of thousands of people including the execution of reformist prime minister Imre Nágy. The Kremlin forced Budapest to rescind its decision to leave the Warsaw Pact and to halt the build up of a multi-party system.

Still, until the late 1950s European international relations were characterized by an uneasy spirit of détente. This (temporary) de-escalation of East–West tension, however, had little to do with the various disengagement proposals and the creation of neutral demilitarized zones in the middle of Europe along the East–West German border which were suggested by, among others, Anthony Eden, George Kennan, and (in the shape of an even more ambitious scheme) by the Polish foreign minister Adam Rapacki.[17] As far as Moscow was concerned, the increasingly obvious Sino-Soviet split contributed to the Kremlin's desire to preserve peaceful relations on

---

[17] E. Hinterhoff, *Disengagement* (London: Stevens, 1959); M. Howard, *Disengagement in Europe* (Harmondsworth: Penguin, 1958).

its Western front. Moreover, the 1956 uprisings in Eastern Europe took place at a time when, in the course of the controversial Suez crisis, two Western democracies were also busy bombing a country that had acted contrary to their wishes (see below). Thus, Western attention was focused on the Middle East. No one in the West seriously advocated offering military support to the Hungarians as this inevitably would have led to a dangerous clash with Moscow.

To some extent the East–West rapprochement in the mid-1950s was disrupted by the so-called sputnik shock of 1957, which shook the Western world and particularly the United States, whose superiority in missile technology seemed to have disappeared overnight. After all, Moscow had succeeded in sending the first ever satellite into space and managed to launch the first ever intercontinental ballistic missile. American cities, and not merely European ones, could now be reached by Soviet nuclear bombs. Soon politicians talked about a 'missile gap' to the detriment of the West. A frantic well-resourced programme was launched by Washington to catch up with Moscow. Sputnik contributed to the fact that the American government was more than ever interested in relying on nuclear containment while expecting the West Europeans to provide for the cost-intensive conventional means of defending the European continent from any Soviet encroachments. Much to the irritation of the United States, the Europeans were both unwilling and unable to dedicate the expected resources to defence. This would have severely affected their economic reconstruction.

Between 1958 and 1963 Europe was overwhelmed by the sudden unexpected escalation of the cold war. The Berlin crisis and, above all, the October 1962 Cuban missile crisis brought the world close to nuclear war. The August 1963 Test Ban Treaty between the United States, the United Kingdom, the USSR, and any other state who wished to join this international agreement which made nuclear test explosions in the atmosphere illegal was one of the lessons drawn from the missile crisis. Another one was the installation of a 'hot' telephone line between Washington and Moscow. Moreover, after Cuba East–West détente was widely seen as the only option to ensure the world's long-term survival.

As far as the European continent was concerned, it was the second major Berlin crisis (1958–62) which caused particular tension. In his ultimatum of November 1958 Soviet leader Khrushchev demanded the western recognition of the GDR as an independent and sovereign state, the removal of the Western powers from Berlin, and the creation of an independent free city of West Berlin. This crisis not only led to a serious East–West conflict with Soviet and Allied tanks confronting each other in the middle of Berlin; it also caused much friction within the Western Alliance. British prime minister Macmillan appeared to be opposed to Washington's strict refusal to enter into a compromise solution with Khrushchev. Macmillan was inclined to extend recognition to the GDR and agree to the withdrawal of Western forces from West Berlin in return for a peaceful solution to the crisis. Not least on the occasion of the prime minister's 1959 visit to Moscow Britain seriously clashed with West Germany, France, and the United States, and had to give up its compromise formula.[18] The Berlin crisis was eventually resolved by the building of the Berlin Wall in August 1961. It much upset the Germans, but was tacitly accepted by the two superpowers and also by most Europeans in East and West as an unpleasant but necessary device for overcoming the German question and de-escalating the potential of an East–West military clash in Berlin.

By this time both Britain and France had effectively been eliminated from the world's great power club. Above all, this was symbolized by the Suez crisis of 1956, when Britain and France (in collusion with Israel) attacked Nasser's Egypt as they wished to reverse the Egyptian president's nationalization of the Suez Canal. American anger at not having been consulted and Washington's fear that the British–French action would open the doors of the Middle East to the Soviet Union (as indeed it did) led to the first occasion when the United States and the Soviet Union sided against two European countries. The Soviet Union even threatened to employ nuclear weapons against London and Paris. However, Washington's activities were more effective. An American-inspired run on the pound sterling and the effective imposition of an oil embargo on Britain by President Eisenhower had the desired result. Much to the anger of France, which caused a great deal of anti-British resentment in Paris, Britain gave notice to the French that they would have to withdraw from Egypt.

Suez made clear that if even former world powers like Britain and

---

[18] J. P. S. Gearson, *Harold Macmillan and the Berlin Wall Crisis, 1958–1962: The Limits of Interests and Force* (Basingstoke: Macmillan, 1998).

France, who still retained a good deal of global influence, could not embark on independent international action without the approval and support of the United States and the Soviet Union, other West and East European countries would certainly be unable to do so. The Suez crisis symbolized the decline of Eastern and Western Europe to the status of mere satellite states of the two superpowers. London's strenuous efforts to obtain American technological support for its so-called 'independent' nuclear weapons programme in the following years confirmed this further. It became apparent that without the provision of American Skybolt and Polaris missiles which would be fitted with British nuclear warheads, London would be unable to maintain its status as the third nuclear power. Moreover, in the course of another adventure in the Middle East, during the British and American invasion of Lebanon and Syria in 1957, it was apparent that the grand ambitions of the Macmillan government in the region were firmly restrained and controlled by Washington.

With the exception of the quadripartite Berlin agreement in 1971–2, the abortive four-power conference in Paris in 1960 was the last major summit conference until the two-plus-four conferences in 1990 (which led to German unification) where Britain and France were represented. After 1960 the cold war had largely become a superpower affair. This was gradually also realized in Britain and France. In London it led to Prime Minister Macmillan's ever closer relationship with the United States and to his half-hearted application to join the EEC. In Paris President de Gaulle desperately attempted to carve out a great power role for his country in opposition to the United States.[19]

De Gaulle's European vision, 1963–1969

While in the 1950s politicians in East and West had largely concentrated on attempts to find a solution to the German question, the 1960s were dominated by French president Charles de Gaulle's anti-American policies, as well as by growing European discontent with American involvement in Vietnam. Washington's growing inclination to base its foreign policy on the existence of a European continent permanently divided into spheres of influence also faced much

[19] R. O. Paxton and N. Wahl (eds.), *De Gaulle and the United States: A Centennial Reappraisal* (Oxford: Berg, 1994).

opposition in Europe. In particular, the increasingly confident West Germans, who wished to participate in NATO's nuclear decision-making,[20] feared quite rightly that the aim of obtaining German unification had been given up by Washington. De Gaulle also resented the tendency on the part of the Anglo-Saxon powers to stabilize the status quo of the cold war and maintain American domination of the European continent for the indefinite future. After all, his proposal in 1958, shortly after he had regained power, to set up a US–British–French directorate to oversee the Western world's cold war strategy had been politely rebuffed. In response de Gaulle withdrew his Mediterranean fleet from NATO.

Furthermore, de Gaulle began to develop his own ideas for the future of Europe. On the whole, his foreign policy was characterized by his intense anti-Americanism and his attempts to revitalize France's 'natural' role as a global power by making it the leader of a 'European Europe'. In 1962–3, once de Gaulle had managed to settle France's bloody war in North Africa by withdrawing and granting independence to Algeria, and had developed a French nuclear capacity, he actively began to advocate his own plans for Europe: a French-led Europe that was independent of the United States and based on a bilateral understanding with West Germany. De Gaulle was convinced that if continental Europe managed to organize itself and its economic resources properly, it might well be able to challenge American and Soviet hegemony of the European continent and eventually overcome the East–West conflict. This explains why in January 1963 de Gaulle vetoed Britain's application for membership of the EEC. He was not prepared to allow London to undermine his European strategy by means of its 'special relationship' with the United States. He regarded Britain as America's Trojan horse and therefore objected to Britain joining the EEC.

De Gaulle viewed the Franco-German bilateral treaty of 1963 as a step towards a French-led European third way in world politics.

---

[20] This led to Washington's proposal to create a multilateral nuclear force (MLF) which would give the Europeans the opportunity to participate in NATO's nuclear decision-making while the United States would still retain its finger on the nuclear trigger. However, although the West Germans were interested, the MLF came to nothing as the United Kingdom and France preferred to retain real control over their nuclear forces instead of obtaining the illusion of control over the American-controlled MLF.

However, he was soon disillusioned. Not only did the West German parliament insist on adding a preamble to the treaty emphasizing the FRG's close links with the United States and the Atlantic Alliance, but Adenauer's successor, Ludwig Erhard, was a convinced Atlanticist. Bonn could not be moved to choose between Washington and Paris in favour of the latter. Moreover, de Gaulle was increasingly irritated by America's ever more obvious preference for dealing with the Soviet Union bilaterally and ignoring the Europeans—including the two European countries with nuclear arms. The Cuban missile crisis, the test ban negotiations, the evolving new 'strategy of flexible response' imposed on NATO by the United States,[21] as well as Washington's ill-advised Vietnam policy, were all conducted without any consultation with the Europeans and thus contributed to de Gaulle's resentment. In the mid-1960s, when he largely realized the futility of attempting to draw Bonn away from Washington, de Gaulle began to develop a new strategy for increasing France's independence in world politics.

Already, between 1960 and 1965, he had started to withdraw French military units from participating in NATO exercises, and eventually, in mid-1966, the French president decided to withdraw his country entirely from the integrated military command of NATO, thereby deliberately isolating it to some extent. Most importantly and closely connected with his NATO strategy was de Gaulle's decision to embark upon *Ostpolitik à la française*. He hoped that in the long run this policy would succeed in creating a less bipolar world, that it would strengthen France economically and give his country a mediating role between East and West. In early 1964 France recognized China diplomatically. In 1965 Soviet foreign minister Gromyko visited Paris. In 1966 de Gaulle himself paid a highly successful state visit to Moscow, which was reciprocated the following year, when Soviet head of state Kosygin came to Paris. The Six Day War in the Middle East in June 1967 found France on the side of the East Europeans, Moscow, and the Arab states, while most other West European countries (including the FRG) and the United States supported Israel.

---

[21] This meant in essence that NATO would first use conventional weapons, then short-range nuclear weapons (so-called battlefield nuclear weapons), before embarking on full-scale nuclear war to rebuff any Soviet attack of Western Europe. For a solid overview, see B. Heuser, 'The Development of NATO's Nuclear Strategy', *Contemporary European History*, 4 (1995), 37–66.

By this time de Gaulle had also begun to conclude trade treaties with all East European countries except the GDR.

In view of West German sensitivities de Gaulle refused to recognize the GDR. He continued to woo West Germany when the Grand Coalition (1966–9) ruled in Bonn. At times the French president still hoped that he could weaken West Germany's close partnership with the United States. He clearly underestimated the extent to which Bonn perceived itself to be entirely dependent on Washington as far as its external security, its economic well-being, and the status of Berlin was concerned. The French president even repeatedly emphasized that his concept of a 'common European home' included the reunification of Germany on the condition that Bonn accepted the Oder–Neisse line and promised never to obtain nuclear weapons.[22]

This strategy seemed to have two advantages to de Gaulle. It indicated to the West Germans that if they did not defer to de Gaulle's all-European policy he might well recognize the GDR and thereby decisively undermine Bonn's unification ambitions and its claim to speak for the whole German nation. It also kept Bonn's own Eastern policy under French control as it would prevent any action not previously agreed with France. After all, if Bonn should embark on its own *Ostpolitik* it could be expected that it would lead to an increase in West Germany's political and economic influence in Eastern Europe. Moreover, de Gaulle's frequent public declarations regarding the right of the Germans to reunify focused the East Europeans (especially Poland) on the potential revanchist ambitions in Bonn. They would thus look to France to counterbalance the West German ambitions. Paris hoped that this would prevent the emergence of any independent relations between West Germany and the East European nations and therefore any policy that would challenge the French claim to the leadership of Europe.

However, in 1968, when both the American administration as well as the Grand Coalition in Bonn had begun to embark on a more active Eastern policy, France's *Ostpolitik* came to a standstill. There were several reasons for this. Both the United States and West Germany were economically as well as politically and strategically more

---

[22] De Gaulle did not exclude the possibility that Bonn might be able to participate in the decision over the use of nuclear arms by the great powers, including France.

interesting partners for Moscow than Paris. Moreover, the almost revolutionary events in Paris in May 1968 fundamentally undermined de Gaulle's reputation as well as his political strategies. The Brezhnev Doctrine and Moscow's invasion of the CSSR in August 1968 and the deposition of the liberal communist regime led by Alexander Dubček abruptly ended any hope that the Soviet Union might be willing to tolerate a degree of independence in Eastern Europe. It provoked de Gaulle to the painful questioning of his own *Ostpolitik*. After all, it had been the main aim of his Eastern policy to overcome the rigid East–West divide and create a French-led Europe largely free from the interference of both superpowers. Instead, the invasion had revealed that in Moscow France and de Gaulle's political strategies had not really been considered as all that important.

Moreover, since the Soviet invasion of Prague in 1968, the USSR had become more intent than ever to 'secure an agreement with the West that would recognise the legitimacy of Soviet influence in Eastern Europe and thereby lessen the prospect of another Czechoslovakia'.[23] This, however, meant not so much an agreement with France but above all one with Washington and Bonn.

In the last months of his presidency de Gaulle began indicating that he might be prepared to consider a certain coordination of French and NATO nuclear forces as well as Britain's entry into the EEC. This policy of rapprochement with Britain in order to use the United Kingdom as a counterweight to an increasingly self-confident and economically strong West Germany would be continued by de Gaulle's successor, Georges Pompidou, but to a much lesser degree.

Ostpolitik and the end of the cold war

Although on the whole de Gaulle's *Ostpolitik* must be regarded as a failure, it appears that his example had a stimulating effect on the politicians in Bonn, who were moving much more cautiously than the 'Grand Nation'. By the mid- to late 1960s West Germany seemed to be leaning towards the elimination of the increasingly outdated Hallstein Doctrine. It was gradually realized in Bonn that the rigid political and legal aspects of Adenauer's traditional 'policy of

---

[23] A. Stent, *From Embargo to Ostpolitik: The Political Economy of West German–Soviet Relations, 1955–1980* (Cambridge: Cambridge University Press, 1981), 155.

strength' strategy towards the East was self-defeating. But Bonn was not yet ready to follow the declaration by the Warsaw Pact countries in 1967 that West Germany should recognize the GDR to bring about an East–West rapprochement. However, some of the leading West German politicians realized that unification could only be achieved in the framework of a larger European settlement. In this context France as well as the United States were essential partners for West Germany's opening to Eastern Europe. Therefore, West German politicians were not in a position to choose between Paris and Washington as de Gaulle urged them to do. They always realized that they had to remain on good terms with both crucial partners as well as with the other European countries. The problem was that West German politics had to become more flexible and independent in its approach without, however, provoking the suspicion of the United States and the West Europeans that Bonn was siding with Moscow and the East Europeans. In this respect, the West Germans were fortunate (as well as inspired by it) that their *Ostpolitik* corresponded with the beginning of a general period of gradual superpower détente since the advent of the Nixon administration in Washington in early 1969.

Ostpolitik was vigorously pursued under Chancellor Willy Brandt's social-democratic-liberal government (1969–74). It led to friendship treaties with the USSR (August 1970) and Poland (December 1970). His policy also contributed to the Berlin Agreement between the Allied four powers (December 1971–June 1972) which resolved the permanent crisis situation surrounding Berlin. It clarified the position that the Western powers were entitled to retain their military forces in West Berlin and that West Berlin was closely linked to West Germany, although constitutionally it would remain a separate entity. Above all, *Ostpolitik* resulted in the Basic Treaty between the two German states (December 1972).[24]

The importance of the treaties with Moscow, Warsaw, and East Berlin consisted of the fact that the West Germans now accepted the post-war frontiers in Europe, including the border between East and West Germany as well as the Oder–Neisse line as the border between Germany and Poland. Thus *de facto* (though not *de jure*, this would have to wait until 1990) the West Germans gave up any claims to the

---

[24] W. Brandt, *My Life in Politics* (New York: Viking, 1992), 154–241.

territory lost as a result of the Second World War. They also accepted the GDR as the legitimate second German state and thus recognized the division of Germany but retained the ambition to obtain peaceful unification some time in the future.[25]

With these dramatic policy changes the Bonn government followed the necessities of the changed international situation as well as the wishes of its partners in the Western Alliance and the East European countries. It was believed that the settling of the German question and the acceptance of the post-war European borders would commence a much greater level of intensive political and economic cooperation between Eastern and Western Europe. And indeed trade links as well as cultural exchanges in Europe greatly expanded from the early 1970s. *Ostpolitik*'s series of bilateral treaties was concluded when Bonn signed a treaty of reconciliation with Czechoslovakia in December 1973.

After that *Ostpolitik* became fully integrated into the general process of superpower détente and East–West disarmament negotiations which had slowly begun in the course of 1970. Its first achievement was the signing of the first Strategic Arms Limitation Treaty (SALT I) on 26 May 1972 during President Nixon's visit to Moscow. In November 1972 discussions about a conference on security and cooperation in Europe (CSCE) began in earnest; they resulted in a series of meetings between 1973 and 1975 which concluded with the important Helsinki conference in July–August 1975.[26] The Helsinki Agreements were signed on 1 August 1975 by thirty-five European countries and the United States and Canada. Only Albania's hard-line communist and pro-Maoist leader, Enver Hoxha, refused his signature. Owing to Albania's impoverished and pro-Chinese leanings Hoxha had also managed to leave Comecon in 1961 and the Warsaw Pact in 1968. The establishment of the CSCE was a major breakthrough. Until the end of the cold war it was the only forum at which all European states,

---

[25] However, the FRG did not recognize the sovereignty of the East German state with respect to such issues as the GDR's borders, citizenship, reunification, and membership in international organizations. Bonn wished to preserve the notion of a 'special relationship' between Bonn and East Berlin and the existence of 'one German nation' but two German states. Thus, not ambassadors but permanent representatives were exchanged between Bonn and East Berlin.

[26] See A. Heraclides, *Security and Co-operation in Europe: The Human Dimension, 1972–1992* (London: Frank Cass, 1993).

both communist and capitalist, as well as the United States and Canada met at regular intervals.[27]

On the whole, the Helsinki Accords led to a dramatic decrease of tension between East and West. They were therefore much criticized by many ardently anti-communist forces in both the United States and Western Europe. After all, Moscow had obtained what it had fought for since the 1950s: the recognition of the post-war borders in Europe as brought about by the Second World War and thus the legitimization of its East European sphere of influence. In return, the Soviet Union and all its satellite countries promised to intensify East–West cooperation. By way of signing Basket III of the Helsinki Accords, they also agreed to pay greater attention to the realization of human rights in Eastern Europe (including the rights to travel and to freedom of political and religious expression).

In the course of the 1970s and 1980s the Helsinki Accords stimulated the rise of an ever greater number of dissident movements in the USSR and many East European countries (particularly in the GDR, Poland, Hungary, and CSSR). Together with the stagnating economic situation in Eastern Europe, *Ostpolitik* and the CSCE contributed to the general mood of discontent and dissatisfaction with the status quo within the Eastern world. It is controversial in the scholarly literature whether Helsinki and *Ostpolitik* played a role in bringing about the so-called peaceful 'velvet revolutions' in Eastern Europe in 1989–90 or whether they helped to consolidate and thus prolong the Soviet Union's empire in Eastern Europe. However, it does appear that in the long run both *Ostpolitik* and Helsinki had a considerable indirect impact on the self-liberation of the East European countries; at the very least this helped to speed up the developments that culminated in the events of 1989–90. However, in the short run the results were disappointing. For example, humanitarian groups like the Czechoslovakian Charter 77 attempted to make the government in Prague pay more than just lip-service to the Helsinki Agreements, but its members were often prosecuted and gaoled for their activities. Similar developments occurred in Poland and the GDR. In reply to Western protestations, the Soviet Union insisted

---

[27] Belgrade 1977–8, Madrid 1980–3, Vienna 1986–9, and Helsinki 1992, when the CSCE with its fifty-three members was reformed and became an agency of the United Nations.

that it was illegal for the West to interfere in the internal affairs of Eastern Europe.

Washington's readiness in the early 1970s to embark upon détente with the Soviet Union and to give in to European calls for a relaxation of the cold war was strongly influenced by American economic and financial problems. Some commentators began speaking of relative American decline and the end of the American century. This was symbolized by Nixon's termination in 1971 of the 1944 Bretton Woods economic system by the sudden suspension of the dollar's convertibility into gold, which resulted in the free floating of international currencies and in an effective devaluation of the dollar. Simultaneously, the president imposed a 10 per cent protective tariff on imported goods. These measures were solely dictated by American domestic-economic requirements and disregarded any negative economic consequences for its European allies.

America's problems were largely due to the costs of the Vietnam War, the lingering burden of financing the domestic 'great society' programmes of the 1960s, and the relative overvaluation of the dollar, which helped European and Japanese exports. The EC's imposition of quotas, exchange controls, and import licences on other than EC goods, as well as the Community's protectionist common agricultural policy (CAP), inaugurated in 1966, contributed to America's ever larger budget deficit. The United States not only had accumulated a considerable balance-of-payments deficit, but from 1971, for the first time since 1883, it also had a considerable trade deficit as well as inflationary problems, rising unemployment, and almost stagnant wages, and the position of the dollar, the world's leading reserve currency, was weakening. The situation was soon made worse by the dire international economic climate in the wake of the Arab–Israeli War in October 1973, which led to the imposition of an Arab oil embargo on most Western countries and resulted in much higher global oil prices. Thus, Washington and the Europeans needed to adjust to the new situation, which had to include a much greater degree of mutual cooperation on a more equal basis. Despite all economic competition and the anger which, for example, erupted when American secretary of state Henry Kissinger unilaterally designated 1973 as the Year of Europe without having consulted the Europeans, on the whole, though not without great difficulties, Washington and the West Europeans were able to work out their differences. In the last resort the United States had no choice but to accept West European emancipation from American tutelage.

However, from the mid- to late 1970s it could be noticed that the West and East Europeans gradually and cautiously began to diverge from the policies pursued by their masters in Moscow and Washington. With hindsight it seems that the European nations became gradually aware again of their common European identity and their shared interests in world affairs. In fact, the greater the respective difficulties with Washington and Moscow appeared, the more united the European countries became.

Serious problems in superpower cooperation could be observed in the mid-1970s. For example, the prolonged MBFR (Mutual and Balanced Forces Reduction) arms control talks in Geneva and Vienna after 1973 and the SALT II negotiations during the Carter administration led to great difficulties in East–West relations. Moreover, the strengthening of the American neo-conservative movement in the 1970s appeared to foreshadow a new, hostile phase in the cold war. European public opinion and many West European politicians refused to go along with this.

Yet, the growing consensus in the United States that the Soviet Union was in fact attempting to obtain military and nuclear superiority under the guise of arms control agreements gradually also began to worry a number of European NATO countries such as West Germany and Britain. It eventually led to NATO's 'dual track' rearmament decision of December 1979. This was the attempt to negotiate with Moscow to achieve the reduction or even elimination of the Kremlin's intermediate-range SS-20 missiles which were targeted at Western Europe. If this should prove impossible, as was in fact the case, equivalent American weapons, the cruise missiles and pershing missiles, would be deployed in West European countries, most of them in West Germany. But among the European peoples this decision was much criticized. In Bonn it contributed to the downfall of the Schmidt government and its replacement by the centre-right government of Helmut Kohl in 1982. It also caused many domestic upheavals in France and Italy and led to the rapid development of a European-wide peace movement. The latter largely benefited the new left-leaning, pacifist, and environmental green parties across Western Europe, which were particularly strong in the FRG, France, and the Benelux countries.

The rising tide of Eurocommunism in southern Europe (particularly in Italy, France, and Spain) since the mid-1970s also worried the United States much more than the Europeans. Despite the Eurocommunists' independence from Moscow and their ambition to democratize their party structures, Washington feared that NATO might not survive the international developments in the 1970s. After all, Greece withdrew from NATO in August 1974 in view of the West's ambiguous attitude towards the Turkish invasion of the island of Cyprus after the Greek-inspired coup. The ruling military regime in Athens had hoped to unite Cyprus with Greece and thus improve their plummeting domestic popularity. Moreover, there was the possibility of communists being appointed to cabinet posts in such countries as Italy, France, post-Franco Spain, and revolutionary and politically unstable Portugal. Until 1974 and 1975 the last two states had still been fascist-dominated autocratic states.

Important disagreements could also be observed between Washington and its allies about the Western Europeans' much more relaxed attitude towards American–Soviet differences over the civil wars by proxy in Angola and Ethiopia–Somalia in the mid-1970s. The same applied to the Soviet Union's invasion of Afghanistan in December 1979, which worried the Europeans much less than the United States. America's political elite was increasingly dominated by an ever stronger anti-communism, which eventually culminated in the election of President Reagan in late 1980. Reagan, as already before him Jimmy Carter during the last two years of his presidency, did not hesitate to return to the intensive cold war attitudes of the 1950s and early 1960s, though Washington habitually overlooked consulting or even informing its European allies.

The Western Europeans felt that they had most to lose from returning to the cold war. Thus, they intended to continue with détente in Europe. Much to Washington's dismay, French president Giscard d'Estaing even paid a visit to the ageing Brezhnev in Moscow in May 1980 to de-escalate the crisis over Afghanistan. Yet, there were increasingly heavy-handed Soviet-guided attempts by the Polish government in the course of 1980–1 to suppress strikes and demonstrations organized by the Solidarity trade union movement over food shortages. Ever more forceful action was also taken by the East German government against the multiplying dissident movements in the GDR. However, West German chancellors Schmidt and Kohl were greatly interested in the continuation of the development of close political and trade relationships with the ruling elites in East Berlin and Warsaw. With the exception of British prime minister Margaret Thatcher, many West European governments also refused to follow American advice to criticize openly the Eastern bloc's violation of human rights, terminate economic deals such as aid for the Soviet oil and gas pipeline from Siberia to Western Europe, and embark on rearmament programmes.

These differences of opinion between most West European countries and the United States were largely based on very different political world-views. Many American politicians believed in a more or less crude 'carrot and stick' approach. In Europe it was felt that, despite all the reprehensible activities of the governments in Moscow and Eastern Europe, there was no alternative but to continue talking to these administrations in order to improve the lot of the East European peoples in the long run. The American boycott of the 1980 Olympic Games in Moscow was therefore only hesitatingly followed by a few Western countries like West Germany who felt particularly vulnerable to gestures of American displeasure. In fact, serious tension between the West Europeans and the United States with respect to the economic and political sacrifices Washington expected in order to punish the Soviet Union for its deviation from détente and Helsinki contributed to the development of a European identity. It certainly led to the rejuvenation of efforts to embark on an ever more closely integrated and increasingly independent Western Europe. In 1984 there were attempts to revive the languishing WEU as the military arm of a united Europe.

By the mid-1980s it looked as if the West Europeans had second thoughts about the invitation they had extended to the United States after the Second World War to assume the leadership of the Western half of the European continent. A somewhat more independent policy also emerged in Eastern Europe in the course of the 1980s. The governments in, above all, East Germany, Hungary, and Romania showed an ever greater desire to intensify their economic and trade links with Western Europe. This not only seemed necessary in order to rescue the deeply troubled economies of these countries. It was also intended, particularly in the case of the GDR, to pacify the ever more outspoken political dissidents with a greater degree of cultural links between East and West. Yet, more often than not, dissenting citizens were gaoled or, in the East German case, 'encouraged' to emigrate to West Germany.

The icy East–West atmosphere gradually changed during Reagan's second term in office when Mikhail Gorbachev, the Soviet Union's last leader, came to power in 1985. However, events such as the various summit negotiations between Reagan and Gorbachev in 1986–8 which led to dramatic arms reduction treaties were superpower affairs. The European governments in both East and West were largely passive bystanders. Moreover, not only Moscow but also Washington still showed a conspicuous lack of consultation with its European allies. Indeed, until mid- to late 1989 West European politicians like Margaret Thatcher in London and Helmut Kohl in Bonn were deeply worried about the American–Soviet agreements for the reduction of nuclear arms (like, for example, the INF (Intermediate Range Nuclear Forces) Agreement of December 1987). These appeared only to enhance the security of the American continent while offering much fewer advantages to Europe. Moreover, it made the effectiveness of NATO's 'flexible response' strategy even more questionable than hitherto. Despite Gorbachev's voluntary withdrawal of some Soviet troops from Hungary and other East European states in the spring and summer of 1989, the Europeans were left facing the Soviet Union's still overwhelming strength in conventional warfare.

There was also plenty of suspicion in Eastern Europe. For example, during a meeting of the leaders of the Warsaw Pact countries in Bucharest in July 1989 Gorbachev was faced with strong criticism for not intervening against the reformist regimes in Poland and Hungary. Above all East Germany's Erich Honecker, Czechoslovakian president Gustav Husak, Romania's Nicolae Ceauşescu, and Bulgarian president Todor Zhivkov were not prepared to adopt a more liberal and reform-oriented course. In Hungary such a course had begun with the development of a democratically orientated multi-party system in January 1989. In early May the country even began dismantling its border controls with Austria, thus allowing an ever greater number of East Germans to escape to the FRG via Hungary, which severely undermined Honecker's rule. The Polish Jaruzelski government had entered into round-table talks with Solidarity leader Lech Wałęsa and the Catholic Church in February 1989. By April important political and economic reforms including the build-up of a multi-party system had been agreed. In August 1989 the free elections which had taken place in June led to the instalment of a Solidarity leader, Tadeusz Mazowiecki, as the first non-communist prime minister in the Soviet Union's sphere of influence in Eastern Europe.

Gorbachev's emphasis on a 'common European house' and his frequent remarks that he viewed Europe as a continent with a united cultural and historical identity were attempts to reassure the Europeans about the peacefulness of his policy. However, these ideas and his immensely popular visits to Bonn, East Berlin, London, and Paris in mid-1989, during which he advocated his European vision, could not dissolve the suspicion prevalent in much of Western Europe about the Soviet Union's intentions. The situation was only clarified by Moscow's acceptance of the popular revolutions all over Eastern Europe in the course of 1989 and early 1990. As Gorbachev had promised when he publicly rescinded the Brezhnev Doctrine in his speech to the United Nations in December 1988, he did not intervene militarily to prevent the downfall of the communist regimes in Poland, Hungary, the CSSR, Bulgaria, Romania, and Albania. Yet, the states within the USSR were a different matter. Gorbachev sent troops into Lithuania in March 1990 (though he soon withdrew them again) to prevent the country's secession from the USSR after the first ever free elections in the Soviet Union had taken place there and led to the election of non-communist president Vytautas Landsbergis.

In early 1990, after some initial opposition, the Kremlin even agreed to give up the country which had been one of its most flourishing and cherished possessions during the cold war: East Germany. The decisive event, not least for symbolic reasons, was the sudden and entirely unexpected opening of the Berlin Wall on 9 November 1989. Shortly afterwards Gorbachev and new American president Bush declared the end of the cold war during their bilateral summit meeting off the coast of Malta in December 1989. The year 1990 saw the establishment of democratically elected governments in most of Eastern Europe. In October 1990 Germany was reunited, and by December 1991 the Soviet Union had been dissolved. In the Kremlin Gorbachev was replaced by Boris Yeltsin as President of Russia. Yeltsin also headed the loosely organized Commonwealth of Independent States (CIS) of former Soviet states, most of which had become sovereign nations, including the Ukraine, Azerbaijan,

Armenia, Moldova, and Belarus. Georgia and the three Baltic states (Estonia, Latvia, Lithuania) became fully sovereign and independent states and did not join the CIS. It was, however, apparent that it had not been the European governments but in fact the European peoples who had brought about all these dramatic developments. Only in the course of 1990–1 were the elected European governments able to reassert a degree of control over European politics.

Integrating Europe: from the Schuman plan to the 1990s

The desire to integrate Western Europe after the Second World War was primarily motivated by the need to prevent another war in Europe. This required bringing about a lasting and irreversible rapprochement between France and Germany, the two largest and economically strongest states on the continent. A secondary motive was to realize the speedy economic recovery of Europe from the devastating consequences of the Second World War. Moreover, in the 1970s and 1980s the rapid globalization of world production and trade made the ever closer coordination of economic, financial, and trade policies imperative if the European nations wished to remain internationally competitive. In particular, this applied to the smaller or economically less strong European states, i.e. almost all of them, with the exception of Germany, the European Community's economic driving force. For most of the post-war period the FRG was the world's third-largest trading nation after the United States and Japan. Although the country was soon by far the EC's largest net contributor, the West Germans also received considerable economic benefits from EC membership. Moreover, Germany's governments and people remained attached to the EC for political reasons. The country's Nazi legacy encouraged its governments to show German reliability and trustworthiness by demonstrating its loyalty to the EC (and to NATO). Only in the early to mid-1990s could the rise of a certain Euro-scepticism be noticed in united Germany. However, this more critical attitude towards European integration was shared by most other European countries in the 1990s. It led, for example, to the very low turnout to the European elections in June 1999. Yet, during most of the history of European integration there had always been much scepticism regarding its inherent value and the likely prospects for the economic and political success of such a policy.

The first common European organization was the European Coal and Steel Community (ECSC) which, as the name suggests, created a common market for coal and steel among the Benelux countries, Italy, France, and West Germany. The ambitious policy was announced by French foreign minister Robert Schuman in early May 1950. According to Schuman the ECSC ought to be a supranational organization governed by a high authority whose members were to be independent both from their national governments and from the coal and steel industries in the individual countries. On the insistence of the Benelux countries (especially the Dutch) there would also be a court of appeal, a (fairly weak) parliamentary assembly, and a council of ministers with a strong authority to control the decision-making of the high authority.

One of the motives underlying the ECSC was the French expectation that there would soon be an immense expansion in German coal and steel production which would threaten the revival of the French coal and steel industries. Thus the ECSC was founded for reasons of industrial competition but, even more importantly, also for controlling any potential German warfaring capabilities. The German coal and steel industry—the industries regarded as essential for waging war—needed to be integrated in order to prevent any sudden increase of German coal and steel output for rearmament purposes. In addition, the ECSC was also meant to coordinate prices, productivity, investments, and industrial relations, and decide on the Community's external tariff and on general competition and cartel policies. All these questions were initially most contentious, and in the end it was pressure by the United States which helped to solve the serious conflicts among the ECSC members. Thus, after acrimonious negotiations, the Schuman Plan was signed in April 1951 and Jean Monnet became its first president (until 1955). With hindsight the ECSC was the first step towards a federal Europe and was decisive for the development of good Franco-German relations.

The British did not participate in the ECSC. Britain, with its flourishing and at this stage very productive coal and steel industry, felt not able to join in a scheme with the much weaker industries of the continental European countries. Issues of national sovereignty, the importance of the Commonwealth, and scepticism regarding the potential success of the Schuman Plan were other important factors. London was particularly incensed that the French expected Britain to sign up to the principle of a supranational high authority prior to the negotiations and not at the conclusion of the talks. London concluded that the French had no desire to see British participation in the ECSC. However, in December 1954 Britain became an associate member of the ECSC.

Despite the setback to European integration due to the failure of the EDC in August 1954 (see above), only a few months later two competing schemes emerged which both intended to stimulate the integration process. Dutch foreign minister Beyen's proposal concentrated on a customs union, including the substantial lowering of external tariffs; he wished to avoid mere bilateral trade agreements within Europe. Belgian foreign minister Spaak's suggestion was based on making sectoral progress with European integration by concentrating on atomic energy. In view of the expected exhaustion of the non-renewable energy source oil in the near future, atomic energy was regarded as vital for the future well-being of the industrialized world. Secretly France also hoped to be able to develop atomic weapons and thereby substantially increase its global influence. Both competing proposals were submitted to the ECSC's council of ministers' meeting in Messina in June 1955. However, the ministers were utterly divided. Moreover, even within the respective national governments severe disagreements existed regarding which road to take. Thus, the ministers referred the issues to a study group which was chaired by Spaak and soon characterized by acrimonious discussions among the delegates. The British participated in the negotiations of the study group, but they were only represented by a lowly official. Once again the United Kingdom was not willing to offer a firm commitment to the results of the negotiations. Moreover, Britain was unsuccessful in arguing for the alternative of a free trade area of all OEEC member states. Thus, London soon terminated its participation in the talks for largely the same reasons it had felt unable to take part in the Schuman Plan: a mixture of anti-federalist sentiments and a belief in British sovereignty and continued global importance.

In April 1956 the Spaak Report was released. It proposed both the conclusion of a Euratom treaty for research into the peaceful use of nuclear energy, and, with reference to the example of the United States, a customs union. Spaak's report 'was animated by a vision of growth and integration through competition'.[28] It was the German government which insisted on tying the two treaties together. Bonn feared that France might lose all interest in the common market treaty, if the Euratom treaty was signed first. In late June 1956 official negotiations commenced. It soon became clear that atomic energy with its limited economic role in Europe was not the important issue but rather the common market treaty. Problems were encountered regarding the harmonization of all aspects of social welfare provision, including its costs and work conditions, which the French regarded as highly important in order to prevent any disadvantages to France within the common market. It was also necessary to find compromise solutions regarding the new organization's decision-making structure with regard to French and Belgian overseas territories. The Germans agreed to contribute considerably to the investments needed to modernize these territories.[29] The pattern of Germany paying substantially more than other member states in order to obtain political concessions and international respectability was thereby established.

On 25 March 1957 the treaties were signed in Rome by France, West Germany, Italy, and the Benelux countries. The Rome Treaties and thus Euratom and the European Economic Community (EEC) came into effect on 1 January 1958. Now three separate European institutions existed: the ECSC, Euratom, and the EEC. They were advised (and then also overseen to some extent) by a joint European parliament with its seat in both Brussels and Strasbourg. A council of ministers consisting of ministers of national states who had to agree to any proposed integrationist steps and a Brussels-based European Commission were also installed. The latter's main tasks were to initiate and then oversee the implementation of legislation. In addition, a European court was set up. After 1958 rapid progress towards the creation of a customs union, a common external tariff, and a common trade policy was made. Although it was the Commission's

---

[28] P. M. R. Stirk, *A History of European Integration since 1914* (London: 1996), 141.

[29] This policy was developed by means of the 1963 Yaoundé Convention and the 1975 Lomé Convention, which included Britain's former colonies and was renegotiated in 1980 and 1985. It provided European aid to the developing world, though owing to CAP their trade opportunities with Europe in agricultural goods were severely limited.

responsibility to propose legislation to replace national provisions with common European policies, the Commission needed the approval of the council of ministers and thus of the individual member states to be able to proceed with integration. In due course the European court ruled that common European laws were to take precedence over national laws. This ruling substantially increased the EEC's supranationalism and was decisive for the further development of the Community.

Already in February 1957 Britain had proposed a European Free Trade Area and the elimination of all tariffs on industrial goods (tariffs on food products were to be maintained in view of the United Kingdom's imperial preference agreements with the Commonwealth countries). Negotiations were entered into, but when in September 1958 France publicly declared that the British scheme was unacceptable, London suspended the talks. It realized that Paris was unlikely to change its mind for fear that economic competition would endanger the viability of the common market. However, soon London entered into negotiations with the Scandinavian countries, whose talks regarding a Nordic customs union had also stalled. In July 1959 this led to agreement on a free trade area which developed into the European Free Trade Association (EFTA). EFTA was established in May 1960 and included Austria, Britain, Denmark, Norway, Sweden, Portugal, and Switzerland. They were later joined by Iceland (1970), Finland (1985), and Liechtenstein (1991), which is tied to Switzerland by a customs and monetary union. The organization was dominated by its council of ministers, which tended to decide with unanimity and thus symbolized the intergovernmental nature of EFTA. Above all, unlike the Rome Treaties, EFTA contained no commitment to develop an ever closer political union among its member states.

Thus, in the late 1950s Western Europe had economically been divided into two parts: the six EEC member states and the seven EFTA countries. Moreover, with Charles de Gaulle's return to power in late May 1958 the French had begun pursuing an increasingly nationalist political course intent on re-emphasizing their global importance in competition with Washington and London (and later with Bonn). This also had important repercussions on the development of the European Community. For example, de Gaulle refused Britain's membership application twice (in 1963 and 1967). The very expensive, far-reaching, and, despite all attempts at reform,

increasingly unwieldy common agricultural policy (CAP) as established in 1966 was also largely maintained because of French pressure
to preserve the economic base of France's large agricultural
community.

Moreover, de Gaulle did not hesitate to cause a major crisis by
boycotting all EEC proceedings for six months in 1965 (the 'empty
chair' strategy) as he was opposed to the Hallstein Plan for the financing of CAP. He believed this plan would make the European Commission more independent as the EEC would gain its own resources
from customs duties and agricultural levies and it would also increase
the budgetary powers of the European parliament. And de Gaulle was
deeply opposed to any diluting of the influence of the individual
nation states and the extension of greater supranational powers to the
EEC. He aspired to a 'Europe of Fatherlands', not to a United States
of Europe. Eventually the French president agreed to a compromise
which saw the withdrawal of the Hallstein Plan, the limitation of the
powers of the Commission, a new framework for the envisaged CAP,
and the confirmation that on important principles unanimous
decision-making should be maintained (the 'Luxembourg compromise'). The latter has remained most controversial and has hampered
decision-making within the EC–EU until the present.

On 1 July 1967 the separate administrations of the ECSC, Euratom,
and the EEC were merged and became known as the European
Community (EC). After de Gaulle's resignation in 1969 negotiations
for the first enlargement of the EC commenced in the early 1970s.
Under the government of Edward Heath the United Kingdom was
eventually able to join the EC on 1 January 1973. This was confirmed
by a referendum in June 1975 conducted by Harold Wilson's Labour
administration. Norway withdrew its application after a referendum
made it clear that the Norwegian people were not in favour of joining. However, Denmark and the Republic of Ireland also became EC
members with effect from January 1973.

By the early 1970s Franco-German relations, the core relationship
within the EEC, began to tilt more into West Germany's favour. However, before the West German general election on 19 November 1972
and the signing of the Basic Treaty with the GDR in December 1972,
Bonn largely attempted to appease France's European demands
in order to obtain French endorsement of *Ostpolitik*. Thus until
late 1972, when Chancellor Brandt's parliamentary majority was

extremely slim and when *Ostpolitik* was still in the negotiating phase, the West German government's domestic and external needs for an active *Westpolitik* gave France certain advantages as far as bilateral Franco-German relations and politics within the EC were concerned.

Both Brandt and French President Pompidou were strongly interested in developing the EC. Pompidou's catchwords were 'completion', 'deepening', and 'enlargement'. They referred to the EC's agricultural policy, the reform of EC institutions including greater monetary coordination, and Pompidou's strong support for British membership of the EC to balance the growing economic and political influence of a resurgent West Germany. During the important EC summit in The Hague in December 1969 both politicians succeeded in regenerating the European Community after the constant crisis atmosphere created by de Gaulle's policies.[30] A compromise in agricultural matters was achieved and there was also agreement on the gradual introduction of new economic and monetary policies which culminated in the decision for the development of European monetary union (EMU), which, as the subsequent Werner Report detailed, it was hoped could be achieved by 1980. However, much to Pompidou's anger, the Werner Report favoured a considerable transfer of sovereignty to the EC.

Moreover, there was agreement on the introduction of European political cooperation (EPC), the first step towards turning the EC from a purely economic to a more political organization by persuading the member states to coordinate their foreign policy in the council of ministers. Details for political cooperation were later spelled out in the Davignon Report. The French in particular were strongly interested in political cooperation as the development of a distinct European identity in the political field would reassert European independence in world politics and might give France itself a greater importance on the global stage. After all, like de Gaulle, Pompidou harboured hopes for French leadership of Europe. His policy was similarly characterized by an intense dislike of and rivalry with the United States. Moreover, Pompidou gradually became worried about the independence of West German *Ostpolitik.* This explains the increasingly close relations between Pompidou and British prime minister Heath which could be observed in the early 1970s. Pompidou

[30] H. Simonian, *The Privileged Partnership: Franco-German Relations in the European Community* (Oxford: Clarendon Press, 1985).

hoped that a new London–Paris axis would counterbalance the strength of a rising West Germany.

Despite the strong opposition of both de Gaulle and Pompidou to West Germany dominating the EC and taking the lead in Europe's Eastern policy, by 1973 exactly this had happened—paradoxically 1973 was the tenth anniversary of Adenauer's and de Gaulle's Franco-German treaty. Events would show that Britain's EC membership was not able to reverse this trend and strengthen French leadership claims. Moreover, French attempts to exclude the Americans gradually from any substantial role in European affairs were also rather unsuccessful. The 1973 Declaration on European Identity encouraged EC members to use the instrument of EPC for the coordination of foreign policy positions among all EC countries. However, this was seldom achieved.[31]

Despite the successful management of Europe's economic and monetary crises in the mid- to late 1970s by, above all, German chancellor Helmut Schmidt and French president Giscard d'Estaing, both former finance ministers, most authors view the 1970s largely as a 'dark age' or a 'stagnant decade' for European integration.[32] The two oil crises and the accompanying economic recession with high inflation (best characterized by the phrase 'stagflation') which plagued Italy and Britain in particular, as well as the expansion of the EC from six to nine countries in 1973, caused a severe, long-lasting crisis of adaptation within the Community.[33] On the whole, 'the disarray of Europe' worked to the benefit of the United States. Washington was able to insist on the importance of the Atlantic framework and regain 'its position as the leading power among the partners who were unified only when under its direction'.[34] But the United States continued its tendency to neglect consulting the Europeans on important East–West questions.

As a reaction to this development, in the course of the 1980s

[31] See D. Dinan, *Ever Closer Union? An Introduction to the European Community* (Basingstoke: Macmillan, 1994), 75–87.

[32] J. Peterson, *Europe and America in the 1990s: The Prospects for Partnership* (Aldershot: Edward Elgar, 1993), 42; Keith Middlemas, quoted in Lundestad, *'Empire' by Integration*, 109.

[33] See D. W. Urwin, *The Community of Europe: A History of European Integration since 1945*, 2nd edn. (London: Longman, 1995), 157 ff.

[34] A. Grosser, *The Western Alliance: European–American Relations since 1945* (London: Macmillan, 1980), 281.

there was a strong tendency towards closer European economic and political cooperation. It was above all driven by French president François Mitterrand and West German chancellor Helmut Kohl, and most strongly opposed by Britain's Margaret Thatcher. In 1987 Kohl's and Mitterrand's efforts led to the implementation of the 1986 Single European Act (SEA), which fundamentally reformed the 1957 Rome Treaty. The SEA aimed at the creation of a genuine Single Market and the removal of all trade and customs barriers by January 1993. Moreover, the EC's decision-making procedures were reformed. In order to enable further EC enlargement after Greece and Spain and Portugal had joined respectively in 1981 and 1986, unanimous decision-making in the council of ministers was replaced by majority decision-making and thus by more supranationality as far as Single Market issues were concerned (these were above all, the free movement of labour, capital, services, and products within Europe). It also gave the European parliament greater legislative powers. In addition, foreign policy cooperation among member states was reorganized, though until the Maastricht Treaty foreign policy was not part of the EC's legal framework.

After the cold war: the reuniting of Europe in the 1990s

The EC's intergovernmental conference in Maastricht in December 1991 was a major stage in the development of European integration. An intergovernmental conference is a formal negotiation concerned with treaty revision among the governments (and not between the governments and the Commission or the parliament) of the EU member states. After the enlargements of the 1970s and 1980s, the agreements reached in Maastricht led to a decisive 'deepening' of European integration in economic and monetary policies but also in areas such as home and justice affairs, and regional and social policies. The Maastricht Treaty came into effect on 1 November 1993. The EC was now replaced by the European Union (EU). The treaty laid down regulations and deadlines for EMU which built on the European monetary system (EMS) established in the late 1970s. Once the Single Market had been introduced in 1993 and the EU had been enlarged again in 1994 by admitting Austria, Finland, and Sweden,[35] the realization of EMU was eventually achieved, though somewhat later than anticipated. Thus, the Maastricht Treaty led to a decisive breakthrough in the creation of European monetary and currency union, including the establishment of a European central bank. Although most EU countries had agreed to sacrifice their financial sovereignty in Maastricht, member states retained the right to opt out of the common currency if they so desired. The Conservative government in the United Kingdom, led by Prime Minister John Major, signed the Maastricht Treaty, but it decided to refuse participation in the common currency. A referendum in France and even two referendums in Denmark were necessary in 1992 to obtain a very narrow popular majority in favour of the Maastricht Treaty.

The Amsterdam intergovernmental conference in 1997 (which came into effect in May 1999) confirmed the Maastricht goals and made further progress with the 'deepening' of Europe. It also encouraged the formulation of a common European foreign and security policy (CFSP) as had already been envisaged in the Maastricht Treaty. It had also already designated the WEU as the EU's defence pillar. In addition, the Amsterdam Treaty built on the Maastricht Treaty with respect to handing more rights to the European parliament. For example, in Amsterdam the parliament was given greater control over the Commission. This was meant to overcome the EU's much criticized democratic deficit. Since 1999 the introduction of a new European Commission also needs the confirmation of the European parliament. After the fraud scandals and the unprecedented enforced resignation of the entire European Commission led by Commission president Jacques Santer in the spring of 1999 this appeared to be long overdue. More majority voting in the council of ministers was also agreed. In particular, the Amsterdam Treaty created 'common strategies'. Now the implementation of policies which were already agreed by previous consensus will only require majority voting.

In 1998 the EU's heads of governments decided on the number of EU countries which had demonstrated their ability to fulfil the tough requirements for membership of the currency union (e.g. the achievement of low inflation and a low budget deficit). With the exception of Greece all fifteen EU countries qualified for membership

[35] As this would have only left the small countries Switzerland, Liechtenstein, and Iceland as members of EFTA, the organization was dissolved on 1 Jan. 1995.

of the common currency.[36] There had been some doubts as to whether or not Italy would be able to fulfil the requirements, but Prime Minister Romano Prodi achieved this formidable task. Subsequently, in the summer of 1999, Prodi was appointed to succeed Jacques Santer from Luxembourg as president of the European Commission. For political and economic reasons the United Kingdom and Denmark agreed that they were not ready to join the euro zone. The euro was introduced as an official European payment unit on 1 January 1999. At the same time the European Currency Institute, first established in 1994, became the EU's central bank with its seat in Frankfurt. In January 2002 paper money and coins were to be made available and, after a short transitionary phase, the euro was to be the only legal tender across all the twelve 'euroland' countries.

Another intergovernmental conference was scheduled to take place in 2000. After the successful 'deepening' of the EU in 1993–9, its brief was to prepare the EU for the envisaged enlargement of the EU early in the twenty-first century. Yet, the ever greater economic convergence of Western Europe makes the inclusion of countries such as Poland, Hungary, and the Czech Republic very difficult and expensive. After all, at the turn of the millennium Eastern Europe was still in the middle of a painful process of economic restructuring from a centrally planned economy to a capitalist one. Therefore, the EU drew up a financial framework for the years 2000–6 envisaging far-reaching financial reforms to accommodate Eastern enlargement and the release of substantial financial resources. During the EU summit in Berlin in March 1999 the so-called Agenda 2000 programme was accepted by all EU member states. The realization of Agenda 2000 as well as the agreements to implement modest reforms of CAP and to concentrate the EU's structural funds on the regions most in need of financial assistance appeared essential if the EU was to cope with its difficult Eastern enlargement.

However, the 1999 war in Kosovo in the former Yugoslavia refocused attention within the EU from the often exaggerated differences of opinion over budget costs and other material aspects among the EU countries towards the basic values underlying European integration: the belief in a liberal-democratic continent and the necessity of preserving peace and political stability in Europe. Thus, in many

---

[36] Greece will adopt the euro in late 2000.

EU capitals the war in Europe contributed to a greater understanding of the deeper values of European political cooperation within the framework of European integration. Above all, the war in Kosovo led to greater efforts on the part of France, Britain, Germany, and other EU countries to develop a distinctive European defence structure and identity. An expansion of the Anglo-French St Malo Agreement on a European defence platform of December 1998 had already been considered. Both France and Britain, the only two European countries with a considerable military potential, expressed the intention to develop a European defence capability which was able to act in coordination with NATO but without always involving the United States. After all, European priorities are often very different from American concerns.

Although St Malo was always meant to be the beginning of a wider European defence policy which would include other EU countries (including Germany), the Kosovo War dramatically sped up these plans. Moreover, the French had second thoughts abut the idea of turning the WEU into the main element of a common European defence identity. During the Franco-German summit in Toulouse in late May 1999 both countries made it clear that the EU ought to build up independent means of dealing with serious crisis situations in Europe. This was seen as potentially leading to the build-up of a European rapid reaction force, possibly around the Franco-German brigade established in 1993, which also included Belgium, Luxembourg, and Spain.

The European Council summit meeting in early June 1999 in Cologne largely confirmed these considerations. It was also confirmed that the WEU would be fully incorporated into the EU. This included the so-called 'Petersberg tasks', which give the EU the responsibility for organizing peacekeeping and humanitarian interventions. Moreover, in the course of the Cologne summit it was unanimously decided to appoint Xavier Solana, the outgoing secretary-general of NATO, as the EU's representative for common foreign and security policy. Thus, Solana was made responsible for overseeing the genuine development of a common European foreign policy.

Although the development of an EU foreign policy dimension has been most controversial throughout the existence of the EC–EU, under the impact of the Kosovo War all fifteen EU members, including Britain and France, were in agreement that this was a desirable goal. Dissatisfaction with the Clinton administration's prevarications and domestic constraints throughout the war, as well as European envy of Washington's overwhelming military and therefore also political power, contributed to the feeling that Europe had to make a greater effort to develop its own foreign and security policies. Thus, the 1999 war in Europe gave the EU the incentive to embark on a much greater effort than hitherto to bring about a major departure in European policy. After monetary union, the introduction of a common currency, and the envisaged Eastern enlargement of the EU, foreign and security policy is the area which for reasons of national sovereignty has been most neglected so far. The creation of the CFSP and Eastern enlargement are the two major challenges which the EU will have to tackle early in the twenty-first century.

After all, since 1990 the countries of Eastern Europe have reconnected with their long European tradition and begun to play an increasingly important political, cultural, and also economic role in Europe. Poland, the Czech Republic, and Hungary, as well as Slovenia and Estonia, were given clear indications that they would be considered for EU membership early in the new century. Many other formerly Soviet-controlled East European countries were offered associate status with the EU. Thus, only since 1990 has the 'common European house' developed which Charles de Gaulle envisaged in the 1960s and which Mikhail Gorbachev called for in the late 1980s. While the East European countries were busily extricating themselves from their rather unhappy experiences of their socialist and communist past, the liberal-democratic and capitalist experience of Western Europe became the role model for the whole of Europe in the twenty-first century. In fact, the vast majority of all East European countries were desperate to forget and even ignore their own troubled history during the cold war era and to catch up with the integrationist developments that occurred in Western Europe. After all, viewed over the last five decades of the twentieth century, European integration appeared to have greatly benefited the European continent, both with respect to the preservation of peace and with regard to a substantial increase in living standards.

7

Interaction with the non-European world

David Armstrong and Erik Goldstein

At the risk of oversimplifying a vast topic, Europe's interaction with the world may be considered in the context of three broad themes: the cold war (and its ending), which established both constraints and imperatives for the divided continent; decolonization and its aftermath, which defined Western Europe's relations with half the world and also helped condition the Soviet Union's approach to its adversaries' former colonies; and the processes of globalization and internationalization, which created much of the international political, economic, and cultural environment within which the developments during this period took place.

The cold war

The cold war drew both parts of Europe into two distinct symbiotic relationships with the United States: Western Europe into a sometimes grudging acceptance of dependence on American military and economic power; Eastern Europe into an equally inextricable adversarial structure with ideological, military, political, and economic dimensions. The crucial period during which this pattern was set lasted from 1944, when the Bretton Woods conference gave the US dollar the pivotal role in underpinning the post-war international economy, to 1949 with the signing of the North Atlantic Treaty. Other key dates were 1946, when the United States committed itself to rebuilding Germany (rather than keeping Germany in a state of permanent economic weakness, as once envisaged) and also sent a naval task force to the Mediterranean in a show of strength following a reassertion of traditional Russian claims against Turkey; 1947, when Britain, finding the costs of its involvement in assisting the royalist government of Greece against a communist insurgency increasingly intolerable, announced that it would no longer be able to play its traditional role in Greece and Turkey and the United States responded with the Truman Doctrine, effectively assuming Britain's responsibilities in the area, and the Marshall Plan, under which the United States provided aid worth $13.2 billion to a four-year European recovery programme; and 1948–9, when the Soviet attempt to impose the Berlin blockade was broken by an American-led airlift to the city.

The United States was serving its own security and economic interests during this period and there can be no doubt that its manufacturers benefited greatly from the requirement that Marshall aid had to be spent on American goods, but it is equally beyond dispute that the plan, and the subsequent Korean War boom, rescued the economies of Western Europe from the desperate condition they were in immediately after the war. Nonetheless, the increasingly clear evidence that European states, which had been accustomed to be global top dogs for centuries, were now dependent on their brash partner across the Atlantic inevitably met with a mixed response from the West Europeans. Britain's global interests and undefeated status at the end of the war gave it a somewhat illusory sense that it would be able to resume business as a world power, and its policy rested on what were originally envisaged as three equal foundations: a slightly condescending and semi-detached relationship with Europe, political and commercial links with the Commonwealth, where it assumed it would be able to play a leading role, and a special relationship with the United States. In the event the Commonwealth proved a worthy enough but relatively insignificant enterprise, while European integration was a far more successful and rapid process than Britain had anticipated, necessitating a belated attempt to come to terms with the EU. But a close partnership with the United States remained a central principle of British policy, notwithstanding frequent debate in Britain about the value of the relationship. The United States had shown that it could disregard British interests, for example in its determined exclusion of Britain and other wartime allies from any serious role in occupied Japan, or when it forced Britain and France to bring an end to their intervention in Suez in 1956 by, among other tactics, helping to engineer a sterling crisis, or when President Reagan ordered an invasion of Britain's Commonwealth partner, Grenada, in 1983, without informing the British prime minister, Mrs Thatcher. Nonetheless, British governments have consistently adhered to the view that the advantages of the relationship—including access to nuclear technology and an ability to continue to act on the world, not just the regional, stage—outweighed the disadvantage of being very much the junior partner. This did not mean that Britain was incapable of independent initiatives: it recognized communist China in 1950 and was influential in negotiating an Indo-Chinese settlement in 1954, both in the face of some American disapproval, and also refrained from joining the United States in its Vietnam imbroglio. But elsewhere, in the Korean War (1950–3), the American bombing of Libya (1986), the Gulf War (1990–1), and NATO's Kosovo intervention (1999), Britain was anxious to portray itself as America's most dependable friend. By and large the United States was willing to play along with this, rendering Britain valuable intelligence during the Falklands conflict, for example, although by the 1990s German unification and greater economic power tended to give Germany the pivotal role both in Europe and as an economic ally in the eyes of many Americans. Indeed Germany, it could be argued, has managed to secure the best of both worlds: a near hegemonic role in the European Union while retaining a close relationship with the United States. Certainly Mrs Thatcher was convinced that the United States was in the process of making Germany rather than Britain its principal European ally.

French views of the United States after 1945 were always more ambivalent than Britain's. This was partly because the French, unlike the British, tended to see American culture and its language as deeply subversive, partly because the French could not indulge in the earlier British posture of aloofness from Europe, and so felt uneasy with the way in which America's cold war agenda increasingly drove its European policy (for example, in pushing for German rearmament), and partly because of the influence of the proud and nationalistic General de Gaulle. Under his leadership France massively reduced its commitments to NATO, vetoed the American-supported British application to join the EEC, developed an independent policy towards China and the Soviet Union, and criticized American policy in Vietnam and elsewhere. There were some improvements in Franco-American relations following de Gaulle's resignation in 1969, but French antipathy to the United States outlasted de Gaulle. In 1973 France and other European states took a radically different position on the Middle East War from that of the United States, an early harbinger of an increasingly independent French (and to some extent West European) policy towards that region. In 1974 France refused to join the American-sponsored International Energy Agency. However, such disagreements should not be exaggerated: France retained strong links with the United States and cooperated with it in many areas, notably in Lebanon in 1983 (when Italy too contributed troops) and during the Gulf War. France has essentially been the most vocal and forceful representative of a point of view shared in some measure by many Europeans. The United States has been a necessary and welcome presence in Europe, but such profound imbalances of power and wealth as those between the United States and any individual European state inevitably create tensions. Nonetheless, European public opinion, as measured by polls, has in general been supportive of close ties with the United States. French opinion was a partial exception in the 1950s and 1960s, although not the 1980s and 1990s, with Greece and Spain exhibiting the most hostile views in the later period.

The end of the cold war did not fundamentally change this basic pattern of West European–American relations. Indeed as the relative stability of the cold war years, with its one great threat of global nuclear war, gave way to a more unpredictable scenario with many more, if less dangerous, threats, the American contribution to European security seemed as necessary as ever. Russia seemed unable to make the steady progress towards a well-entrenched democracy within a growing economy that some of its erstwhile Warsaw Pact partners had managed, and remained a potential threat to a general European peace. The Balkans re-emerged as a source of bitter ethnic conflict, which Europe appeared unable or unwilling to deal with in the absence of American military support, particularly in the form of air power. As several Asian economies crashed and the major

European economies faltered in the late 1990s, so the US role as locomotive of the world economy seemed indispensable. At the same time Europe moved ever closer to integration, and the combined resources of the European Union would give it the potential to match American military and economic power—if the will to do so existed.

For the Soviet Union, the United States was no less crucial in determining its post-war foreign policy (and indeed, ultimately, its survival). In essence the cold war obliged the Soviet Union to transform itself from a regional to a world power, and to acquire the military and economic trappings that went with superpower status. There were moments—for example, when it launched the first earth satellite—when the Soviet Union appeared to merit its superpower status, but, as is now clear, Moscow was always struggling to maintain some degree of military parity with Washington, and in the end the cost of doing so virtually beggared its economy.

Moscow enjoyed rather more success, together with some serious problems, in the diplomatic aspect of its quest for global influence. Washington's insistence on the centrality of its relationship with Israel gave Moscow opportunities elsewhere in the Middle East, notably with Egypt, Iraq, and Syria. East Asia was an area of direct Soviet interest for geographical reasons—its long border with China and the important port of Vladivostok—but after the Bolshevik victory in 1917 it became important also as an ideological battleground, with the Soviets able to present themselves as a leading ally against imperialism. After 1945 the region also witnessed two of the major 'hot' confrontations of the cold war, in Korea and Vietnam. Although Soviet troops were not involved in either of these, the Soviet Union provided huge economic and military assistance to its communist allies. But at the start of the 1950s the greatest Soviet success appeared to be the communist victory in the Chinese civil war, followed by a Sino-Soviet alliance treaty in 1950. While Stalin lived, the Chinese leader, Mao Zedong, was content to play a subordinate role, and China proved its worth as a Soviet ally by bearing the brunt of the fighting on the communist side during the Korean War. At this point the West appeared to be confronted with a united communist front covering most of the Eurasian land mass.

Appearances were deceptive, however, and over the ten years following Stalin's death in 1953 a wide range of differences emerged between the two communist giants. Mao and Khrushchev disliked each other, but of more importance were fundamental differences of world-view—the Chinese favouring a far more assertive global posture than the Soviets were willing to contemplate—and, crucially, a Soviet unwillingness to share nuclear technology with China. As the polemics between the two sides developed apace, the Soviets began to resort to more tangible sanctions, notably withdrawing its technical experts from China in 1960 at a time when China was experiencing famine. The signing of the Test Ban Treaty in 1963 between the three nuclear powers—seen by China as an attempt to exclude her from developing nuclear weapons—was followed by intensified polemics but also, more ominously, by China raising the issue of the long border between the two countries. Serious fighting on the border in 1969 led to a veiled Soviet threat of a nuclear attack on China. This produced greater Chinese restraint, as well as a successful attempt to balance its Soviet threat by improving its relationship with the United States. Thereafter, although verbal sniping continued, there was some improvement in the relationship between the two sides. That did not prevent potential conflicts, as in 1979, when China attacked Moscow's ally Vietnam, and during the 1980s both sought to build up their naval power in the region. However, both countries saw themselves as potential losers from the end of the cold war with the emergence of the United States as the sole superpower, and this helped to produce a significant rapprochement after 1989, highlighted by a joint declaration in 1997, although it was not until 1999 that they were able to announce that all border issues had finally been settled.

The Soviets saw the alliance with China partly in terms of the need to prepare against the possibility of a revival of Japanese power. Washington had begun the process of building up Japan as a countervailing force to Soviet power from 1947, a process culminating in the 1951 peace treaty with Japan. The Soviets refused to sign this because they had been unable to secure any of a range of demands, including the demilitarization of Japan and the removal of American bases, as well as Japanese acceptance of Soviet sovereignty over the Kuril Islands, which it had occupied in 1945 (having previously lost them to Japan in 1905). The peace treaty was followed by a US–Japan security treaty, but after much belligerent talk the Soviets pursued a policy of seeking to normalize their relationship with Japan. This paid economic dividends, with trade between the two growing a hundredfold by 1980, although this did not lead to an easier security relationship.

The Sino-Japanese peace and friendship treaty of 1978 was seen by Moscow as anti-Soviet in its intent and implications, a view seemingly confirmed when Japan's 1978 White Paper on defence explicitly named the Soviet Union as Japan's potential enemy for the first time. After 1989 the issue of the Kuril Islands remained unresolved between the two states, although Russian diplomacy has endeavoured to improve their overall relationship.

Elsewhere in Asia the Soviet Union developed a warm relationship with India, particularly after the Sino-Indian War of 1962, but showed it was prepared to use force as well as diplomacy to defend its interests in that region when it invaded Afghanistan in 1979 in support of the pro-Soviet government there, a move that drew it into a long, bitter, and ultimately unwinnable conflict. Indeed it was in part the Afghanistan quagmire that, from the mid-1980s, led the hugely overstretched Soviet Union to seek to break free from the pattern imposed by the cold war. In the period from 1945 to 1990 the Soviet Union had funded two wars against the United States and one against China, built up Sukarno's Indonesia as one of the world's largest naval powers on paper at least in the early 1960s, first provided substantial aid to, then fought against China, built up its naval power north of Japan and then in the larger Pacific region, given economic and military aid to India, and fought its own version of the Vietnam War in Afghanistan: all while retaining a huge arsenal in Europe. Although there can be little doubt that in doing so it helped to tie down the United States, and indeed inflict the greatest defeat of the cold war on its adversary, it is hard to see what other concrete benefits this assertive, if not aggressive, approach brought the Soviet Union in Asia.

Much the same is true of the Soviet Union's attempt to build up influence and confront the United States in areas beyond Asia, notably Latin America and Africa. In both cases the crucial relationship was with Cuba. After nearly achieving the dubious honour of providing the *casus belli* for the Third World War in 1962, Cuba—with the benefit of massive Soviet aid—sent troops to intervene in the Angolan civil war after the end of Portuguese colonial rule there in 1973. At the same time Moscow began to develop a close relationship with another former Portuguese colony, Mozambique. This was part of a larger Soviet policy of increasing its influence in Africa during the 1970s, which also saw, for example, a significant Soviet involvement in conflicts in North Africa. The Soviet objective seems to have been to align itself with the African campaign against South Africa and also foster left-wing regimes that might come under communist influence. Africa, however, defied attempts to slot it into easy categories, and the prospects for revolutionary socialist regimes of the kind hoped for by Moscow were always slender. When Russia ceased giving aid after 1989, much of the Marxist rhetoric of regimes like Angola or Mozambique also stopped.

Although a Russia of any colour—imperial, national, or Soviet— would see Asia and the Pacific as legitimate areas of interest, the size of the Russian involvement there, and the fact that it became significantly interested in Africa and Latin America, derived mainly from its cold-war confrontation with the United States (with a secondary role played by China). After the two superpowers came close to hot war in the 1962 Cuban missile crisis, they sought to develop a range of diplomatic and political ways of coexisting and keeping their ongoing conflict within controllable bounds. These included the 1963 Partial Test Ban Treaty, the 1967 Outer Space Treaty, and the 1968 Nuclear Non-proliferation Treaty. Following Richard Nixon's inauguration as president a more comprehensive approach to reducing tensions between the two, known as détente, was begun, at the heart of which were major arms control initiatives. The first of these, the Strategic Arms Limitation Talks (SALT) produced an agreement in 1972 but the SALT II Agreements, signed in 1979, were never ratified by the United States because of the Soviet invasion of Afghanistan. More extensive arms reduction agreements were reached during the Gorbachev and Yeltsin eras. Most European states, together with the United States, also signed the Helsinki Accords in 1975. These gave the Soviets the recognition of Europe's post-1945 borders that they had long sought, but also gave the West a legitimate right to concern itself with human rights issues in the Warsaw Pact countries. Although Moscow almost certainly saw this latter as a relatively meaningless sop to enable it to achieve its main objective, in practice this commitment was fully exploited by the West and proved to be one of the factors that helped undermine the Soviet Union in the 1980s.

Decolonization

Europe's relationship with the non-European world after 1945 must be considered in two parts: its relations with those parts of the world over which it held sway at the end of the Second World War, and the much smaller portion of the world over which European imperial rule had never extended. From the late fifteenth century until the First World War Europe gradually came to dominate most of the non-European world. Then suddenly in the wake of, and partially as a consequence of, the two world wars that engulfed Europe, most of this territorial control was liquidated within twenty years. For Europe much of its relationship with the non-European world after 1945 consisted of adjusting to this revolution. This developed in three phases: the first was the actual process of decolonization, conducted at varying tempos and with varying degrees of willingness by the different European colonial powers; the second was a sort of shadow period when, having lost the substance of empire, the former imperial powers attempted, with differing degrees of success, to maintain an informal empire, or at least some influence over portions of their former explicit empires; finally, in most cases, once memory and emotion had faded, attempts were made to establish normal international relations with most of the former imperial territories.

In 1945 much of the non-European world was part of the European political and economic order, but this relationship was about to undergo seismic change. Between 1946 and 1975 sixty-five European colonial territories became sovereign states. In 1945, however, decolonization was not the intent of the colonial powers. With the end of the Second World War the European colonial powers once again asserted, or attempted to assert, control over possessions that had come under Axis occupation.

The Dutch were confronted by a movement for independence in the Dutch East Indies (Indonesia). The Netherlands at the war's end was not in a position to reclaim control of this colony immediately, and the occupation of the region fell to Britain. As the war was coming to its end, an independence movement had emerged led by Sukarno, which declared independence as the Indonesian Republic in August 1945. The British forces and Sukarno cooperated to some extent, but when the Dutch replaced the British in November 1946, they proceeded to move against the independence movement, blockading it where it had succeeded in establishing control. Ultimately the Dutch were unable to mount the resources necessary to retain control of Indonesia, and through a UN-negotiated settlement a United States of Indonesia was created, with Sukarno as its first president, theoretically as a partner with the Netherlands in a union modelled on the British Commonwealth. This arrangement lasted until 1956, when Sukarno unilaterally abrogated the arrangement. The following year the extensive Dutch-owned plantations were seized and subsequently nationalized, and most of the remaining Dutch settlers left. The sole remaining Dutch possession in the region, western Papua New Guinea, soon became a target of Indonesian ambitions, and the UN again intervened to assist in a settlement, which resulted in Indonesia gaining this territory in 1969.

The British empire was the largest colonial empire ever created. While the other European states with overseas possessions had strong European interests, Britain's main arena of concern had always lain with its seaborne empire. The process of decolonization for Britain is all the more remarkable, given the centrality of the empire to Britain, when contrasted with the other experiences of decolonization, as it made no serious effort to retain its possessions once it became clear that the local demand for independence was well established. An empire constructed over several centuries of often arduous military conquest was granted independence and dispersed in a matter of years. The process began in earnest with India in 1947 and culminated in 1997 with the return of Hong Kong to China.

Agitation for Indian self-government had begun well before the Second World War, led by Mahatma Gandhi. Various British efforts at a compromise solution during the inter-war period had proved ineffective, and after the Second World War the Labour government of Clement Attlee decided that the only solution was independence. As the last viceroy it chose Lord Mountbatten, a relative of the British royal family and wartime hero. The vast subcontinental British empire in India, the Raj, which had at one point made Britain the greatest land power in Asia, was fracturing along confessional lines, and it was decided that the only solution was partition, with a predominantly Hindu India at the core, flanked by a predominantly Muslim Pakistan, which itself later divided into Pakistan and

Bangladesh. The partition of India unleashed communal violence in which at least 1 million people died. Independence was also granted in 1947 to Burma and Ceylon (Sri Lanka).

Britain was faced almost immediately after the events in India with a deteriorating situation in the Middle East in its Palestine mandate. Assigned to Britain after the First World War, it had been intended, in part, to provide a Jewish homeland. After the Second World War increasing tensions between Jewish and Arab inhabitants, as well as pressure to allow Jewish survivors of Germany's extermination policies to settle in Palestine, finally led Britain to refer the issue to the UN. A UN Special Committee on Palestine recommended partition, which was adopted by the UN and accepted by Britain. Implementation, though, proved difficult. The issue of partition lines and even the creation of a Jewish state provoked violent reactions in the region. The British government reacted by rapid disengagement from the area, terminating its mandate in May 1948. This was the prelude to the establishment of the State of Israel over part of the former mandate, the independence of the Kingdom of Jordan over the other part of the mandate, and an Arab–Israeli war, which continued into 1949.

The last major phase of decolonization for Britain came in Africa. The Gold Coast Colony (Ghana) was the first experiment in the granting of independence in 1958, and by 1965 independence had been granted to almost all of the African colonies. The only serious confrontation Britain faced was in Kenya, which by the 1950s was one of Britain's most valuable remaining colonies with important plantation-owning interests. A rebel movement, the Mau Mau, conducted a terror campaign against British rule, which led to a significant British military intervention. Britain though, in line with its general policy of disengagement, granted independence to Kenya in 1963.

Unlike Britain, France's reluctance to see the loss of its overseas empire led it into a series of debilitating wars, which ultimately threatened the stability of the political order in France. The post-war Fourth French Republic was accompanied by a constitutional innovation, the French Union. This comprised the French republic, its overseas departments, and associated territories, presided over by the French president and a council of representatives. It was not intended to facilitate the devolution of power, but rather, in line with France's bureaucratic traditions, further to consolidate power at the centre.

Despite such imaginative structuring of its constitutional arrangements, France was confronted with the same drive for independence
in its colonies as that faced by the other European powers, and
between the end of the war and 1962 it was continuously engaged in a
series of tough wars waged in a vain attempt to retain its empire.

France was not able fully to reassert its position in the Middle East
in the immediate aftermath of the war and reluctantly recognized the
independence of Lebanon and Syria, which it had controlled as
League of Nations mandates since the First World War. India likewise
pressured France into surrendering its small remaining enclaves
on the subcontinent. The chief struggles, however, occurred over
Vietnam and Algeria.

The French colonial empire in Indo-China consisted of Vietnam,
Laos, and Cambodia, acquired in part through the Franco-Indo-
China Wars of the nineteenth century. During the Second World War
the area was occupied by the Japanese, though a puppet French colonial administration loyal to Vichy France was left nominally in power.
As the war drew to a close, Japan replaced this regime with a Vietnamese emperor, Bao Dai, officially proclaimed independence from
France and appointed a pro-Japanese government. The communists
in Vietnam had formed an effective anti-Japanese resistance movement, the Vietminh, which was strongest in the north, where it had
the advantage of a base in China. When Japan surrendered in August
1945, the Vietminh moved quickly to fill the power vacuum and proclaimed an independent Democratic Republic of Vietnam. Their control spread rapidly and helped to bring about Bao Dai's abdication.
France, however, hoped to reassert control over Indo-China and
reoccupied the main cities. Until early 1946 the French benefited from
the presence of British soldiers, who had originally been dispatched
to assist with the surrender of the Japanese forces.

The first direct confrontation between the Vietminh and the
French occurred when the Vietminh fired on a French warship which
was attempting to block the delivery of arms to the main Vietnamese
port of Haiphong in November 1946. The French retaliated with an
aerial attack in which 6,000 Vietnamese were killed. This was followed by a Vietminh offensive against the French. In an unsuccessful
attempt to assuage the Vietnamese France reorganized its possessions
into the Indo-Chinese Federation, which promised greater local
autonomy. This was later superseded by an agreement to create the

Associated State of Vietnam, which was to have independence in all but foreign and defence matters within the French Union. Most Western powers recognized this government. The Vietminh, however, were determined on full independence and embarked on a guerrilla campaign. Their Democratic Republic of Vietnam was recognized by the Soviet Union and the People's Republic of China.

The initial phase of the conflict was primarily a guerrilla war, 1947–9, which resulted in a stalemate between the combatants. The situation was altered by the communist victory in China in 1949, which provided the Vietminh with a powerful ally to the north. During 1950 the Vietminh forced the French to retreat from most of north Vietnam. Increasingly French control throughout the country was confined to the cities and the maritime fringe. The financial strain of the war was also becoming too great for the French economy, not yet recovered from the Second World War, and from 1952 the United States carried much of the financial burden. In a dramatic attempt to turn the tide of the war the French adopted a plan to entice the Vietminh into an engagement in which they could then be crushed. The site selected was Dien Bien Phu, 220 miles west of Hanoi, near the border with Laos, to which 15,000 soldiers were dispatched. The Vietminh surrounded it, and the siege of Dien Bien Phu lasted from November 1953 until May 1954, culminating in the surrender of the French garrison. This marked the end of French power in Indo-China. The war had become increasingly unpopular within France, and the government opted to extricate itself as best it could, agreeing to a ceasefire in June.

The 1954 Geneva Accords divided Vietnam into two zones. The north would be ruled by the Democratic Republic of Vietnam (i.e. the Vietminh) and the south would be governed by the State of Vietnam. Officially Vietnam remained one country, and the intention was for national elections followed by political reunification. The elections were never held. France's role in the region was slowly replaced by the United States, which became increasingly engaged out of a concern to halt any spread of communist control, which was seen as an extension of Soviet power. The question of the future control of Vietnam thereby became an aspect of the cold war and led to American involvement in the Vietnam War of 1964–73.

Just as the Vietnam conflict was being resolved for France, a new conflict broke out in Algeria. Algeria had long been treated as an integral part of France, and in 1947 French citizenship was granted to Algerians. The local assembly, though, was selected by two electoral colleges, one for the 1.2 million Europeans and the other for the 8.5 million Arabs. In 1959 violent demonstrations accompanied demands for independence, marking the beginning of a protracted and brutal war. At its height a French army of 400,000 was deployed to suppress the rebellion, but without success. The French settlers refused to countenance any compromise, and the ongoing crisis led to the re-emergence into French political life of General de Gaulle. It was hoped that the wartime leader of the Free French would oversee a victory in Algeria. De Gaulle, however, viewed the war as unwinnable and began to prepare for Algerian independence. This brought about a mutiny led by a group of officers based in Algeria. After briefly seizing control of Algiers the mutineers were suppressed, and de Gaulle forced through acceptance of Algerian independence, which was agreed in the Evian Accords of 1962. France retained important oil rights and a naval base at Mers-el-Kebir for fifteen years. In the wake of this decision 900,000 European inhabitants of Algeria moved to France, causing short-term housing and employment pressures. After independence Algeria experienced a period of dangerous political turmoil, but de Gaulle, seeking to maintain some influence in the region, supported the government with substantial aid, which helped stabilize the political situation.

As part of his assumption of power de Gaulle rewrote the French constitution, ushering in the Fifth French Republic, necessitated in large measure by the turbulence caused by France's various colonial imbroglios, which had fatally weakened the fabric of the Fourth Republic. The French Union was now replaced by the French Community, which gave all the components of the French empire the right to self-government and the right to secede. Members would retain a favoured tariff relationship with France. Only Guinea refused to join the new structure. As an object lesson France left the country, stripping it of as much of its infrastructure as could be carried away and cutting all economic aid.

Belgium's colonial empire had been limited to the Congo, a mineral-rich region that was heavily exploited by Belgian interests. Belgium had invested very little in developing the skills of the local population, and even as late as 1960 there were virtually no university graduates or skilled professionals. As France and Britain's neighbouring colonies began to be prepared for and granted independence, a similar movement emerged in the Congo. In the wake of the first violent disturbances in 1959 in support of independence the Belgian government decided upon a precipitate departure, within six months, with virtually no preparation of the local population for self-government. The result was the almost immediate outbreak of civil war. Within days a secessionist movement had seized control of the mineral-rich southern province of Katanga. The Soviet Union, which was seeking a role in the decolonized world as the European powers retreated, began to provide support for the embattled central government, while Belgium supported the secessionists in order to retain control of their most valuable assets in the region. The UN attempted to restore order, in the course of which the UN secretary-general, Dag Hammarskjöld, was killed while on a mission to the Congo. In the chaos which enveloped the Congo one rebel group seized numerous Western hostages at the key city of Stanleyville. This led to a Belgian force of paratroopers being dropped, with American assistance, to rescue the hostages. Some African states condemned this redeployment of the former imperial power as an exercise in neo-imperialism. In the years that followed, in numerous African states, the former colonial powers would continue to intervene occasionally in support of one faction or another.

The last European states to confront the issue of decolonization were Portugal and Spain, which had since the 1930s been ruled by conservative, authoritarian governments which refused to countenance any moves towards colonial independence as a threat to the legitimacy of their regimes. Portugal had inaugurated the European drive to acquire colonies abroad during the age of discovery, and its empire was among the last to be dismantled. The process began when India seized the Portuguese colony of Goa in 1961. In the same year armed uprisings began to occur in Portugal's large African colonial empire, at a time when most of the rest of Africa had just achieved independence from European rule. These revolts started in Angola and spread to Portuguese Guinea and Mozambique. This led Portugal to become involved in a long and debilitating military struggle to retain control of its African empire. The 1974 Carnation Revolution in Portugal was sparked by the proposals of General Antonio de Spinola for a restructuring of the Portuguese empire with the intention of ending the warfare. The revolution in Portugal led to the rapid granting of independence to its African possessions during 1975–6, though East Timor was seized by Indonesia. Portugal's last colony, Macao, which was also the last European colony in Asia, was ceded to China in 1999, marking the end of four centuries of European territorial presence in Asia.

Spain's ageing dictator Francisco Franco had resisted attempts at decolonization by Spain, but during his final illness the last remnants of Spain's once vast colonial empire attracted attention. The states neighbouring the phosphate-rich Spanish Sahara sought to control it, with the Moroccan king organizing a peaceful march by thousands of Moroccans to seize it, while Algeria backed a local independence movement, and Mauritania sought part of the territory. In 1975 Spain left the colony, though its future was still disputed by the states in the region.

The wave of decolonization that followed the Second World War was succeeded by efforts on the part of the former imperial powers to retain links with, and even indirect control of, their former empires. Some of these links were largely symbolic, and served to ease the transition in the relationship. Britain encouraged all its former possessions to join the British Commonwealth, and some even retained for some time the British monarch as their official head of state; France created the French Community; the Netherlands sought a union under a common sovereign; and the Portuguese revolution of 1974 came about as part of an effort to create a Lusitanian Confederation which would retain some connection between Portugal and its colonies.

Britain and France both sought to retain a financial role, and established currency systems that would link some of their former colonies to them, and provide a measure of financial control. Britain's pre-war sterling bloc was transformed after the war into the Overseas Sterling Area (OSA). As part of Britain's attempt to maintain the image of an international role it insisted that sterling be a reserve currency under the Bretton Woods system, evolved towards the end of the war to assure post-war economic equilibrium. As a publicly acknowledged reserve currency it was to be seen as the back-up to the US dollar, thus conferring a reflected prestige upon Britain. Pragmatically it was also an attempt to assure the retention of London as a key international financial centre, with consequent invisible earnings accruing to the country. It was also useful in providing markets for British goods as Britain determined, as the manager of the OSA, the rates of exchange between member currencies. This position also had disadvantages for Britain. Once sterling became fully convertible in 1958, it became an object of speculation, causing several embarrassing runs on the pound. The pound had already been devalued in 1949 from $4.03 to $2.80. In 1967 the government was forced to devalue further to $2.40. Although this devaluation was done for pressing domestic reasons it had the effect of also devaluing all OSA currencies by the same 14 per cent. The result was to cause the member currencies to make other allocations, and to cease to treat the former imperial currency as a reserve currency. In 1987 under the Basle Agreements the OSA was effectively liquidated. Most of France's former sub-Saharan African empire adopted the CFA (Communauté Financière Africaine) franc as their currency, which trades at a fixed rate of exchange with the French franc. Members of the franc zone hold most of their foreign cash reserves in French francs.

Britain retained substantial economic interests in Iran, and in the 1950s the Anglo-Iranian Oil Corporation was Britain's single largest overseas economic investment. Threats of nationalization by the reformist regime of Iranian premier Mohammed Mossadegh led Britain to conspire with the United States, which was concerned about possible pro-Soviet sympathies on the part of Mossadegh, in the overthrow of his government. Britain, though having surrendered territorial control, sought to remain the predominant power in the increasingly important Middle East, from which 70 per cent of Western Europe's oil supplies derived. It took the lead in establishing the Baghdad Pact in 1955, modelled on the idea of NATO, comprising Britain, Iraq, Turkey, Pakistan, and Iran. Britain also retained strong influence in Jordan.

The chief opponent of British influence was the Arab nationalist Egyptian leader, Colonel Nasser. The growing confrontation between Nasser's Egypt and the former regional imperial powers, Britain and France, would result in the 1956 Suez crisis.

After Britain and France had withdrawn from the Middle East, the region continued to be the centre of a complex web of conflicts. The Egyptian monarchy had been overthrown in 1952 and Colonel Nasser became president in 1954. Nasser's government embarked on a campaign of escalating confrontation with Israel. Egypt blocked Israeli shipping from passing through the Suez Canal or out of the Gulf of

Aqaba. Nasser began to build up the Egyptian army with arms purchased from the Soviet bloc in 1955, a move which caused concern among the Western powers and which was seen as bringing the Middle East into the cold war. France had poor relations with Egypt because of its support for the insurgents in Algeria fighting for independence from French rule. Britain likewise had poor relations with Egypt, which generally opposed British influence and pro-British regimes in the region.

In accordance with a 1954 Anglo-Egyptian Treaty Britain withdrew its last forces from the Suez Canal in June 1956. This was soon followed by Nasser's decision in July to nationalize the Suez Canal, jointly owned by Britain and France, in order to raise the funds to build a vast hydroelectric complex at Aswan. This led Britain, France, and Israel to decide upon joint action against their common enemy. It was agreed that Israel would attack Egypt, moving to the canal, and that Britain and France would then demand that the belligerents each withdraw from the canal area, to ensure its protection. To enforce this an Anglo-French force would intervene to take control of the canal under the 1954 Anglo-Egyptian treaty, which allowed intervention if the security of the canal was threatened. This act of 'collusion' was meant to provide an excuse for Anglo-French intervention. Israel duly initiated the scheme by attacking Egypt at the end of October.

Israeli forces were extremely successful, reaching the Suez Canal and reopening the Gulf of Aqaba. In accordance with the collusion scheme an Anglo-French ultimatum had been given on 30 October, but it was not until 5 November that an Anglo-French force landed, by airdrop, near the canal. This was followed by an amphibious landing. Meanwhile, both the United States and the Soviet Union, in a rare act of concurrence, demanded a ceasefire through the UN on 2 November. In the face of this international, but particularly American, pressure, the British and French agreed to desist, and a ceasefire was agreed on 6 November. A United Nations emergency force was dispatched to separate the belligerents in the Sinai, and the Anglo-French force was evacuated, while Israeli forces withdrew from Egypt and the Gaza Strip.

A more rapid Anglo-French response might have won the day. The delay in landing forces allowed international opinion to mount against them. The Soviet Union took the opportunity caused by this distraction to crush the liberal Hungarian government, which was attempting to break from the Soviet bloc. In the Middle East British and French prestige were badly damaged by their humiliating withdrawal. The British prime minister, Anthony Eden, who had supported the intervention, resigned. Suez marked the end of Britain and France's role as great powers capable of acting on a par with the most powerful states of the international system. After 1956 it was clear that the international system had become a bipolar world, with the United States and the Soviet Union as the superpowers. Suez had revealed the limits of European power.

After Suez Britain went through a process of repositioning itself, which led over the next few years to the linked process of seeking membership in the EEC and in ridding itself of various bits of empire which no longer suited British interests in the wake of the larger decolonization already implemented. Britain was turning consciously from an overseas-focused to a euro-focused state. The Conservative government decided in 1959 to disengage from Africa as rapidly as possible after the next general election. In 1960 at Cape Town the British prime minister, Harold Macmillan, spoke of the 'winds of change' sweeping across Africa. By 1963 Britain had liquidated almost all of its once vast African empire. In the mid-1960s the Labour government of Prime Minister Harold Wilson confronted the reality that with the loss of empire its power had declined, both economically and militarily, and adopted a new strategic view which called for Britain to terminate its position 'east of Suez'. So as not to make some former colonies feel unduly cut adrift, the Commonwealth was given a heightened profile and its own secretariat. Simultaneously a number of small colonies were suddenly, and even unexpectedly, granted independence.

Britain's disengagement was gradual. It acted to support Malaysia, which had become independent of Britain in 1957, when Indonesia initiated a policy of harassment aimed at Malaysia. The Indonesian threat was repulsed with the assistance of 50,000 Commonwealth forces provided by Britain, Australia, and New Zealand. The confrontation dragged on into 1964, with Indonesia threatening intensification of the conflict, though meanwhile it was dissolving into economic chaos, and an abortive communist coup led to an army takeover in 1965, with Sukarno slowly being eased from power. Sukarno had claimed that the real enemy was British imperialism and neo-colonialism, which had created a puppet Malaysia. The economic and political strains of the confrontation exacerbated the situation within Indonesia and contributed to the unrest, which led to Sukarno's downfall. The attempt to repeat the success of the earlier confrontation with the Netherlands failed, owing to British firmness. As a result British prestige was enhanced by its effective support of Malaysia. Britain, as the former imperial power, also played an important part in brokering the transition to majority rule in Rhodesia–Zimbabwe, during which Britain briefly again became the governing power in order to oversee elections.

France was the most active of the European colonial powers in attempting to maintain a sphere of influence amongst its former territories. Although by the mid-1960s the French Community had lost any substantive meaning, France continued to play an active role in its former sub-Saharan empire, supporting the widely used Central African franc and maintaining a military presence which was often decisive in maintaining a regime or playing a role in a change of government.

An example of France's ongoing involvement in the region was the war between Chad and Libya. The Libyan regime of Colonel Qaddafi was intent on a claim to the mineral-rich Aozu strip in neighbouring Chad. Several Libyan attempts to seize the strip had been rebuffed by Chad with French assistance. When this occurred again in 1983, President Mitterrand of France decided on direct French intervention. A French force of about 3,000 established a no-go area, the *zone rouge*, between the warring armies. In September 1984 an agreement was reached for the withdrawal of foreign forces, but while the French withdrew, the Libyans remained. In February 1986 Libyan forces advanced, hoping that the French parliamentary elections then being held would distract French attention. French forces were rapidly deployed, with the United States providing $10 million in support. With heavy Franco-American support Chadian forces began a successful northern drive, defeating the Libyans and regaining control of the Aozu strip.

France has been reluctant to relinquish the remaining pieces of its colonial empire. It has found French Guyana a convenient launch pad for satellites, while its Pacific Ocean territories provided until 1996 a venue for the testing of French nuclear weapons. In 1985 French agents boarded and sank a Greenpeace vessel in New Zealand which had been engaged in protests against French nuclear testing, an action which led to a serious rift in relations. France pre-empted any serious attempt by New Zealand for redress by using its weight within the EC to threaten economic retaliation against New Zealand.

Various remnants of the once vast colonial empires are still controlled by European states. Britain retains a number of island possessions, primarily in the Caribbean and the Atlantic. One of these, the Falklands, was the cause of war between Argentina and Britain in 1982. Great Britain and Argentina had a long-running territorial dispute over the sovereignty of the Falkland Islands (Las Malvinas), lying 300 miles east of the Argentine coast. The military government in Argentina sought a triumph to help restore its flagging popularity, through a dramatic victory over the Falklands issue. It therefore increased pressure on Britain to withdraw from the islands. There had been indications that the British government might be prepared to make some arrangement over the islands, and it was probably believed that Britain would be unwilling, or unable, to fight a distant war over 1,800 people and 400,000 sheep. War erupted over the illegal landing of a group of Argentinian scrap-metal merchants on South Georgia, a dependency of the Falkland Islands colony, in March 1982. This was followed by a full-scale Argentine invasion of the Falklands.

The Argentinian invading force rapidly overwhelmed the garrisons on the Falklands and South Georgia, and the British governor was deported. Britain responded to the crisis by dispatching a large naval task force, which arrived in late April after an 8,000-mile journey. During this lull in the hostilities all efforts at a diplomatic solution proved unavailing. A 200-mile 'total exclusion zone' was declared by Britain around the Falklands. A controversial incident occurred with the sinking of the Argentine battlecruiser *General Belgrano* while outside the total exclusion zone. British forces soon recaptured South Georgia at the end of April, followed by a series of successful landings on the Falklands, which rapidly overwhelmed the Argentine garrison. As a result of their defeat the Argentine military-led government fell from power. The new government accepted the *de facto* end of hostilities, and Anglo-Argentine relations improved after the restoration of civilian government in Argentina in late 1983.

The growth of the EU, and the receding legacy of the colonial age, has slowly led to a reshaping of Europe's relations with the non-European world. The Lomé Conventions of 1975 and 1980, concluded between the EC and sixty African, Caribbean, and Pacific states, allowed for almost all the agricultural produce of these states to enter the EC without duty, while allowing a common duty to be levelled on goods from the EC.

Europe, which for centuries had been a place of emigration, in the post-war era became a place for immigration, with large numbers of peoples, predominantly from the former colonial world, seeking to resettle, usually in the former colonial power. Britain at first avidly recruited immigrants from its empire in the aftermath of the Second World War, when the country faced severe labour shortages. A landmark event was the arrival in June 1948 of the *Empire Windrush* from Jamaica carrying the first group of such immigrants. All Commonwealth citizens had the free right of immigration, but as numbers mounted, the British government passed in 1972 the Commonwealth Immigration Act, which for the first time sought to control numbers.

Since 1945 immigrants have relocated to Europe as a result of either economic or political problems in their home countries. In 1951 Britain had a population of 74,000 from the New Commonwealth countries; by 1981 this had risen to 2.2 million. France in 1990 had a population of 1.5 million African immigrants, and just under 0.5 million from Asia. Spain and Portugal, historically emigrant countries, also became receiving countries. Portugal after the collapse of its empire found itself with a population of 800,000 immigrants out of a population of just 10 million. Political upheavals in the former colonial world continued to have an impact long after independence. In 1972 Uganda expelled its ethnic Asian population, causing 29,000 British passport holders to move to Britain, where they went on to become one of the most economically successful groups. There also remains a notable flow of emigrants from Britain; for example during the economically troubled early 1980s more people emigrated from Britain than migrated to it, with 465,000 people moving to the Old Commonwealth countries and the United States during 1979–83.

Such population movements have helped change the cultural map of Europe, for the first time giving Western and Central Europe a noticeable Muslim population. Economic immigrants from Turkey have augmented this phenomenon. One effect of this has been to embroil Europe in affairs of the Muslim world. In 1989 the Indian-born British author Salman Rushdie was the subject of a fatwa by Iran's senior religious leader, the Ayatollah Khomeini, which called for the writer's death on account of a charge of blasphemy in his book *The Satanic Verses*. This led to a long-term breach in Anglo-Iranian relations and the brief outbreak, in support of the fatwa, of book-burning by some Muslim communities of volumes viewed as blasphemous.

Europe's interaction with the non-European world is based on a long and complex history. For the former colonial world there often remains a linguistic legacy, which remains an important link. A common language has provided access for the films and literature of the former colonial states, and in an age where broadcast media are rapidly expanding, this gives the European states a significant cultural influence. The former colonial powers remain a destination for higher education on the part of students from their former empires. The globalization of information has served to connect the former colonial world to the old imperial powers. Just as decolonization seemed to be an event that would see the separation of the European powers from the non-European world, globalization has seen them being driven together in new ways.

Globalization and internationalization

Two closely related processes have set many of the social, economic, and political contexts within which Europe's interaction with the outside world has taken place. 'Globalization' refers to the way in which much economic activity since 1945 has increasingly occurred within markets that were essentially worldwide rather than confined within national or even regional boundaries. Global markets helped to produce global actors, such as the giant transnational corporations, or media moguls like Rupert Murdoch, and also a global, mainly Western or (some would argue) American culture. 'Internationalization' refers to the way in which states have responded to globalization and other pressures by pooling their resources—economic, diplomatic, and military—in a wide range of international organizations. Both processes have profoundly affected all aspects of world politics and the global political economy.

Although there has been an intense debate over the true extent of globalization, and its impact on the nation state, some basic facts are beyond dispute: daily financial transactions around the world are well in excess of $1 trillion, the speed with which such transactions can now take place has been reduced to less than a second, improvements in productivity combined with steadily reducing trade barriers have placed a premium on concentrating various economic activities within ever vaster transnational corporations, and trade has grown steadily since 1945, both in terms of total volume and as a percentage of total world domestic product. Furthermore, a host of statistics can be provided to show Europe's (especially Western Europe's) central-ity in all these processes—and therefore its dependency upon and vulnerability to them. Banks located in Britain alone hold nearly a quarter of international loans, the EU is responsible for around 40 per cent of total trade and 20 per cent of trade outside the Union, and more than half of the world's total investment flows between the EU, on the one hand, and North America and Japan, on the other. The EU is also responsible for some 31 per cent of total world output, as against the United States' 27 per cent and Japan's 21 per cent.

Until the 1990s the Warsaw Pact countries were largely excluded from these processes since they pursued policies that fell somewhere between autarky and a division of labour amongst the members of Comecon, set up in 1949 to promote economic cooperation among them. Their experience since 1989 has been varied: most were initially seen as emerging markets offering exciting growth prospects, and some received large loans and investment. The largest loan recipient, Russia, has failed to realize its economic potential and has fallen more deeply into debt to the International Monetary Fund (IMF) and other sources. Other economies, such as those of Poland and Slov-enia, have begun to show evidence of significant and firmly founded growth.

The initial impetus to economic integration in Europe came not so much from globalization at first as from a variety of political pres-sures. These included the American insistence that Europe should provide a common response to Marshall aid, which took the form of the establishment in 1948 of the Organization of European Economic Cooperation (later Organization of Economic Cooperation and Development, including the United States and Canada). Equally a product of American pressure, the establishment a year earlier of the General Agreement on Tariffs and Trade (GATT) created the most important common forum within which trade discourse amongst the major states took place. Here too, in the face of increasing tension over trade issues with the United States, the EU partners have tended to operate as a single unit. Trade disputes reached a peak in the 1980s, with each side accusing the other of a range of restrictive practices and protectionism, especially in the areas of agriculture and governmental procurement policies. This did not prevent the Uruguay Round of trade negotiations, which commenced in 1986, from reaching agreement in 1994, including the establishment of a successor to GATT, the World Trade Organization.

GATT was one of three international economic organizations set up after the war to provide some degree of management for the global economy, the others being the IMF and the World Bank, whose original role, to channel assistance to Europe, had been superseded by a new function of providing loans for developing countries. By 1970 Japan had clearly joined the United States and Western Europe as one of the three major centres of economic power. After the collapse of the Bretton Woods system in 1971 and the first of a series of huge increases in the price of oil in 1973, these three centres added an important informal institution: the Group of Seven (G7) summit meetings. These originated in an initiative by the French president, Valéry Giscard d'Estaing, in 1975. His original idea was to hold irregular, highly informal meetings of 'those who really matter in the world'—the heads of government of the United States, Japan, Germany, Britain, Canada, France, and Italy—with the aim being to allow them to concentrate their collective wisdom on the big issues of the day, free from the constraints of armies of bureaucrats. This always somewhat romantic picture of power in the modern world foundered on the rock of the different political systems and cultures represented by the seven: other political leaders did not enjoy the seven-year period of office of the French president and were less free to focus on the big picture at the expense of short-term electoral considerations. Moreover, the European and to some extent Japanese leaders tended to have enjoyed greater experience at governmental level, often in finance offices, than their American counterparts, which made the US president reluctant to engage in high-level discussions without advisers present. This meant that the meetings became much more formal, regular, highly publicized, and well organized than in the original French conception. They also began to consider a much wider range of issues than those relating to the international economy, with the environment, terrorism, and the ongoing Balkans crisis appearing on the agenda.

When the G7 meetings began, the dominant economic orthodoxy was still a belief in the possibilities of Keynesian demand management. This led to various strategems for a coordinated approach to global economic problems, of which the most successful is often claimed to be the Bonn summit of 1978, when West Germany and Japan agreed to reflate their economies in return for an American commitment to tighten fiscal policy to counter inflation. However, the Germans came later to believe that they had been pushed into policies that exacerbated their own inflation without having any long-term impact on world economic problems: a view that fitted the neo-liberal orthodoxy of the 1980s represented by Ronald Reagan and Margaret Thatcher. Reagan also attempted to use the meetings to further his strategy of confrontation of the Soviet Union, which resulted in several serious disputes with his European partners, most notably at the 1982 Versailles summit, when Reagan wanted to pressurize the Russians by withholding agreement over the proposed trans-Siberian pipeline: a move that would have cost many European jobs. Eight years later, when the issue was what to do about a Soviet Union in the throes of collapse, the G7 were equally unable to reach agreement, with West Germany and France opting to go ahead with their bilateral aid programmes, the US calling for more security concessions, Japan for aid to be linked to progress on the disputed Kuril Islands, and Britain for more thoroughgoing restructuring. Russia is now a member of this inner circle—more because of apprehensions about the dangers of leaving Russia out in the cold than because Russia meets the basic economic criteria for membership, although Russia's presence at the 1999 G8 meeting was valuable given her links to the intransigent Yugoslav government, then undergoing a NATO aerial bombardment because of its policy of 'ethnic cleansing' in its southern province of Kosovo.

The 1991 G7 summit declaration stated that the group intended to make much greater use of the United Nations for such purposes as conflict resolution, preventive diplomacy, and cooperation in various political, economic, ecological, and humanitarian areas. This marked a turn about from the position of several G7 members in the 1970s and 1980s, which tended to regard the UN as anti-Western and ineffectual. When the UN was created in 1945, it was dominated by the

United States and its allies, with Britain and France receiving two of the five permanent places on the security council, and Latin America and Western Europe making up the majority of the general assembly. Western Europe also provided the first two secretaries-general of the UN, in Norway's Trygve Lie and Sweden's Dag Hammarskjöld—both men incurring the wrath of the Soviet Union for their alleged pro-Western bias. But by the mid-1960s the majority of UN members were from Afro-Asian states, which vigorously pushed an agenda where development issues and anti-colonialism were far higher than cold war concerns. Western support for Israel and, to a lesser extent, South Africa helped to create an atmosphere in which the United States and leading former colonial powers such as Britain often found themselves at the sharp end of impotent but irritating speeches and resolutions in the general assembly. At the same time the difficulty of securing the necessary unanimity among the permanent five on the security council prevented the UN from playing the important role in international security that had originally been envisaged. Hence the 1991 G7 statement was important in symbolizing a new Western intent to make full use of the UN. In the event the 'new world order', of which this return to the UN was seen as a significant part, proved illusory. There was a major European contribution to UN peacekeeping activities in Somalia, Rwanda, Bosnia, and elsewhere, but these produced mixed results, and when NATO decided to commence its bombardment of Yugoslavia in 1999, it refrained from seeking a UN mandate because of the probability of a Russian veto in the security council.

One important international institutional response to globalization has been for the members of the EU to seek coordinated, if not common, responses to various kinds of international challenge. In certain areas—notably negotiations over trade, agriculture, and fisheries—the EU functions virtually as a single actor; in others, such as aid to developing countries, overall EU policy is governed by instruments such as the Lomé Convention, although individual EU members differ considerably in the amount of aid they actually give. Under the Maastricht Treaty the EU committed itself to proceed towards a common foreign and security policy (CFSP). Implementing CFSP in a thoroughgoing manner has served mainly to reveal the problems with this concept, but in practice the EU has moved close to a common policy on an ad hoc basis over the last two decades in areas like the environment and human rights and also in its approach to other regional groupings.

A commitment to sustainable development was included in the Maastricht Treaty, and reaffirmed in the mandates of the new European Bank for Reconstruction and Development and the European Investment Bank. More concretely, the EU adopted a common negotiating position at the 1992 UN Conference on Environment and Development and the 1997 Kyoto Conference on Global Climate Change. However, although the first of these was successful in laying down general principles, the second revealed sharp differences between the EU and the other major participants. Kyoto was concerned primarily with establishing specific commitments to reduce the emission of greenhouse gases, for one quarter of which the United States is responsible, with the EU's share being 15 per cent. The EU's position was that all major industrialized states should reduce their emissions by 15 per cent by 2010, from a 1990 baseline. In the event only a total reduction of about 5 per cent was agreed, including an 8 per cent reduction by most European countries, 7 per cent by the United States, and 6 per cent by Japan. But other increasingly significant sources of greenhouse gases, notably China and India, were given only voluntary targets. The issue of global warming seems set to become one of the major sources of international tension over the next few decades. While Europe as a whole might well succeed in reducing its own contribution to the problem so long as Western Europe picks up the lion's share of the East European bill in this respect, coal-burning developing nations undergoing rapid industrialization are, in effect, refusing to curtail their emissions unless the huge cost ($1 trillion) of transferring to alternative technologies is met by the West. Not only is there little sign of this happening, but the United States seems intent on remaining a major offender.

Europe, which has been the location of the worst violations of human rights in history, up to and including the 1990s experience of former Yugoslavia, has, none the less, also devised the most effective and far-reaching system for the international protection of human rights in the form of the forty-member Council of Europe. In the last ten years the EU has increasingly attempted to promote 'good governance' principles such as democracy, human rights observance, and the rule of law outside Europe. This commitment was written into its

1989 Lomé IV Agreement with its associates in the developing world, and emphasized more strongly in several subsequent documents. In 1995 two important statements by the EU Commission made it clear that human rights clauses would be included in all EU agreements with third parties, with provisions for suspension of agreements in the event of human rights violations. The issue of the international protection of human rights has always been fraught with difficulties, and the EU's experience has tended to confirm this. Different cultures and religions have different approaches to human rights, states still assert the sovereign right to determine matters within their domestic jurisdiction, and security and commercial interests tend to lead states into applying human rights standards unequally. In the case of the EU, this last consideration has led to a softer line towards China than towards the EU's Lomé partners, and to ignoring mistreatment of indigenous peoples in North America and Australia. In contrast, many African countries have incurred EU sanctions of various kinds over human rights questions, although even here practice is not uniform: France was able to prevent sanctions being imposed on its former colony Cameroon.

The strengthening of various processes of regional integration worldwide in the last twenty years has been generally interpreted as a response to globalization. As the commercial and financial forces confronting states grew more powerful, so states felt the need to unite their resources both to survive and to gain the maximum benefit from globalization. States that were excluded from one regional grouping sought opportunities elsewhere: Russia entered the Asia–Pacific Economic Cooperation group in 1997, while Turkey, also excluded from the EU despite many years of seeking entry, tried to build up traditional links with Central Asia and the Middle East. This process affected not only states: business enterprises ranging from telecommunications, aerospace, and automobiles to oil, banking, and soft drinks became involved in ever larger mergers both within regions and between them. One inevitable consequence of this was that regional groupings came increasingly to deal with each other as blocs rather than on a country-to-country basis. For example, the EU and the Association of South East Asian Nations (ASEAN) reached a Cooperation Agreement in 1980, and in 1996 the EU and ten Asian states, including the seven ASEAN members, agreed to formalize and build upon their ongoing dialogue through the initiation of the

Asia–Europe Meeting. Similarly the EU and the Mercosur group of South American states (Argentina, Brazil, Paraguay, and Uruguay), with which the bulk of EU trade in the region—some $50 billion in total—is done, signed a Framework Agreement in 1995, seen as the precursor of more far-reaching linkages.

Conclusion

In 1945 Europe was still—formally—the ruler of much of the world. In reality its power had weakened both in relation to the superpowers and with regard to the task of maintaining its hold on colonies, some of which had been promised much by a Japan that had posed as the liberator from white domination during the war. The transition from imperial status took place unevenly: Britain was able to shed its colonies with comparative ease, but was slow to see the need to substitute a purely regional role for its historic world role; France played the European game exceptionally well so far as its own interests were concerned, but found it far harder to relinquish imperial grandeur. In the East Russia found itself—not for the first time—in but not of Europe. In some respects its response to this state of affairs was not entirely dissimilar to that of its West European enemies, notwithstanding ideological and other differences. For example, like Britain and France in their different ways, Moscow sought to build up a world role for itself in part to balance the power of the United States. It also tried to establish a rival European system in the East to that emerging in the West, albeit one held together essentially by force.

In the event Moscow was the biggest loser in the great power contests of the post-war era, shedding much of its own sovereign territory, losing its East European allies, and gaining little or nothing from its costly ventures outside Europe. But by the end of the 1990s some sense of a common destiny in what Gorbachev had referred to as 'our common European home' had begun to become apparent. In the broadest sense, this could be seen as a product of globalization. Germany in particular, but also other European powers, were well aware that the consequences of an economic, political, and social collapse in Russia could not be contained within Russian borders, and were prepared to grant substantial aid to help more moderate factions in Russia maintain some grip on the situation. In another context the reluctant but ultimately effective NATO response to developments in former Yugoslavia suggested that a kind of ethical globalization was influencing events, so that states—at least European states—needed to measure up to a certain minimum standard of civilized behaviour to win full acceptance from the international community. NATO, which had not fired a shot in anger during the cold war, appeared to be emerging as the instrument of this new conception of international relations (not without some unease from its new members, the Czech Republic, Poland, and Hungary, as well as from some older members, notably Greece and Italy). Moreover, although Russia frequently expressed its disquiet about these developments, it also showed a willingness to participate in the international interventions in Bosnia and Kosovo. Although it went to some lengths to distance itself from NATO (especially from any implication of NATO control over its forces) in these activities, the astonishing reality was that the United States, Russia, and the European members of NATO were pursuing a common purpose in former Yugoslavia. Like so much else in international affairs this could easily end in tears, but it is at the very least a remarkable development with potentially profound implications in the coming decades.

APPENDIX Independence or transfer of sovereignty of European colonies,
protectorates, mandates, and trusteeships since 1945

Date of independence	Place	Former colonial power
1946		
22 March	Jordan	Great Britain
17 April	Syria	France
31 August[a]	Lebanon	France
1947		
14 August	India	Great Britain
15 August	Pakistan	Great Britain
1948		
4 January	Burma	Great Britain
4 February	Ceylon (Sri Lanka)	Great Britain
14 May	Israel	Great Britain
5 June	Vietnam	France
1949		
13 July	Laos	France
8 November	Cambodia	France
27 December	Indonesia	Netherlands
1951		
2 February	Chandernagore[b]	France
1954		
21 October	Pondicherry, Yanaon, Karikal, Mahé[b]	France
1956		
1 January	Sudan	Great Britain & Egypt
2 March	Morocco	France
20 March	Tunisia	France
4 April	Spanish Morocco[c]	Spain
29 October	Tangier	International[d]
1957		
6 March	Ghana	Great Britain
31 August	Malaya	Great Britain
1958		
2 October	Guinea	France
1960		
1 January	Cameroon	France
27 April	Togo	France
20 June	Mali (Mali and Senegal)	France
26 June	Madagascar	France
26 June	British Somaliland[e]	Great Britain
30 June	Congo	Belgium
1 July	Italian Somaliland[e]	Italy
1 August	Dahomey (Benin)	France
3 August	Niger	France
5 August	Upper Volta (Burkina Faso)	France
7 August	Côte d'Ivoire	France

11 August	Chad	France
13 August	Central African Republic	France
15 August	Congo	France
16 August	Cyprus	Great Britain
17 August	Gabon	France
1 October	Nigeria	Great Britain
28 November	Mauritania	France
1961		
27 April	Sierra Leone	Great Britain
19 June	Kuwait	Great Britain
1 October	Southern Cameroons [f]	Great Britain
9 December	Tanganyika (Tanzania)	Great Britain
18/19 December	Portuguese India [g] (Goa)	Portugal
1962		
1 July	Burundi	Belgium
1 July	Rwanda	Belgium
3 July	Algeria	France
6 August	Jamaica	Great Britain
31 August	Trinidad and Tobago	Great Britain
9 October	Uganda	Great Britain
1963		
1 May	West New Guinea [h]	Netherlands
16 September	Singapore	Great Britain
16 September	Sarawak	Great Britain
16 september	North Borneo	Great Britain
10 December	Zanzibar (Tanzania)	Great Britain
12 December	Kenya	Great Britain
1964		
6 July	Malawi	Great Britain
21 September	Malta	Great Britain
24 October	Zambia	Great Britain
1965		
18 February	Gambia	Great Britain
26 July	Maldives	Great Britain
11 November	Rhodesia (Zimbabwe) [i]	Great Britain
1966		
26 May	Guyana	Great Britain
30 September	Botswana	Great Britain
4 October	Basutoland (Lesotho)	Great Britain
30 November	Barbados	Great Britain
1967		
30 November	South Yemen	Great Britain
1968		
31 January	Nauru	Great Britain
12 March	Mauritius	Great Britain
12 August	Equatorial Guinea	Spain
6th September	Swaziland	Great Britain

1969		
4 January	Ifni [c]	Spain
1970		
4 June	Tonga	Great Britain
10 October	Fiji	Great Britain
1971		
15 August	Bahrain	Great Britain
1 September	Qatar	Great Britain
1 December	Abu Dhabi	Great Britain
1 December	Ajman	Great Britain
1 December	Dubai	Great Britain
1 December	Fujaira	Great Britain
1 December	Ras Khaima	Great Britain
1 December	Sharja	Great Britain
1 December	Umm Qaiwain	Great Britain
1973		
10 July	Bahamas	Great Britain
1974		
7 February	Grenada	Great Britain
10 September	Guinea Bissau	Portugal
1975		
25 June	Mozambique	Portugal
5 July	Cape Verde	Portugal
6 July	Comoros	France
12 July	São Tomé and Principe	Portugal
11 November	Angola	Portugal
25 November	Surinam	Netherlands
7 December	East Timor [j]	Portugal
1976		
26 February	Western Sahara [k]	Spain
29 June	Seychelles	Great Britain
1977		
27 June	Djibouti	France
1978		
7 July	Solomon Islands	Great Britain
1 October	Ellice Islands (Tuvalu)	Great Britain
3 November	Dominica	Great Britain
1979		
22 February	St Lucia	Great Britain
12 July	Gilbert Islands (Kiribati)	Great Britain
27 October	St Vincent and Grenadines	Great Britain
1980		
30 July	New Hebrides (Vanuatu)	France & Great Britain
1981		
21 September	British Honduras (Belize)	Great Britain
1 November	Antigua and Barbuda	Great Britain
1983		
19 September	St Christopher and Nevis	Great Britain

1984		
1 January	Brunei	Great Britain
1997		
1 July	Hong Kong[l]	Great Britain
1999		
20 December	Macao[l]	Portugal

Notes

a Final withdrawal of French and British forces.
b To India.
c Rejoined Morocco.
d An international zone under control of Belgium, Britain, France, Italy, the Netherlands, Portugal, Spain, Sweden, and the United States. Rejoined Morocco.
e Merged to form Somalia.
f Federation formed with former French Cameroon.
g Seized by India.
h Transferred to UN, and then to Indonesia 1 May 1963.
i Rhodesia issued a Unilateral Declaration of Independence under a minority government, 11 Nov. 1965. British colonial rule was briefly re-established on 11 Dec. 1979 to oversee transition to majority rule with independence effective 18 Apr. 1980.
j Invaded by Indonesia, which officially annexed it on 13 Dec. 1975.
k Spain left without establishing any successor regime. It became a matter of dispute.
l To China.

8

Conclusion

Mary Fulbrook

The year 2000 (like the accompanying millennium celebrations) is but a figment of an artificially imposed convention for counting the passage of time. Unlike 1945 or 1989–90, it is not a key turning-point in European history. But, given the human propensity to impose periods on history, the close of the twentieth century—and with it the close of two millennia of our dating system, inspired by European Christianity but now an intellectual convention accepted across faiths, across civilizations, and indeed across the globe—is a point at which to register and take stock of the wider course of historical change.

Later twentieth-century Europe in long-term perspective

At first blush the later twentieth century appears to be a period of major European convergence and integration. More European states became, internally, more like one another in a variety of respects, including even, most remarkably, the post-communist states of Eastern Europe; and more European states became part of a widening European system, at first economic, increasingly also political, with a developing set of supranational European institutions.

This is clearly a collective transformation of major significance, and we shall reflect on it again in a moment. But it is worth first pausing to look back, however briefly and superficially, over a longer sweep. Against the long-term backdrop, it is perhaps the immediately preceding era—when the nation state was the key unit where economic, political, and cultural loyalties and policies coincided and overlapped most precisely—which stands out as particularly remarkable. What was bundled together in particular concentration within the historically constructed borders of the modern nation state, for only little over a century in some instances, is now being unbundled once again.

'Europe', we should remember, was not a new invention of the post-war era, and European history—whether participants (or indeed later historians) were aware of it or not—has long been more than the sum of its parts. There are common themes and variations stretching back over centuries, together constituting a particular form of European civilization, a particular economic, social, and political history. A widespread and well-institutionalized tendency to think, talk, and write in terms of national histories and their interactions has blinkered us to the ways in which these intertwine, and are as much formed by as together constituting some wider European history.

Patterns of cultural and intellectual development in the European arena have been supranational over centuries. The spread of Roman civilization across vast swathes of Western Europe; an ever-expanding, missionary, if internally divided Christianity, the widespread intellectual—and often also political and economic—hegemony of the churches, and the challenges of Islam; the growth of universities and new classes of intellectuals and bureaucrats; the export of European ideas (and peoples) to the rest of the world in voyages of discovery, trade, and colonization; the European Enlightenment, and attempts both to understand and to control the universe; the explosion of knowledge and communications in the industrial and information revolutions; all these features have meant that there have never been hermetically sealed national cultures, however diverse and variable the local and regional patterns in the European kaleidoscope were.

Similarly, interweaving strands of economic development, with long-distance trading, population migration, political and military competition for access to valuable resources, and the complex interactions of more advanced and less developed areas—both within the European arena, and across the globe as a whole—mean that European economic history cannot sensibly be perceived in purely national terms.

On the political front the very formation of modern states was as much a consequence of military, political, economic, and cultural interaction among smaller, pre-national units—dynastic possessions, church properties, free cities, and so on—as it was of the historically emergent concept of 'the nation' embodied in modern political and cultural nationalism. 'Nation states' themselves, which, in the later twentieth century, seemed the most natural unit of analysis—and of history writing—are but a very late product of European history, which has a broader unity long pre-dating the emergence of nation states within a particular type of European political system in the last two centuries of the second millennium.

Just to give one example from a plenitude of possibilities: the case of Germany, currently powerhouse of European integration. German unification in 1871 highlights some of the different factors involved, among which an emergent sense of national identity comes a rather long way down the list. As the unification of 'small Germany' clearly demonstrates, the borders and character of the twentieth-century nation states we take so much for granted were forged through a series of processes and events that could have had quite different historical outcomes. These included: the long-term expansion, in the context of industrialization, of economic markets (the development of the customs union or *Zollverein*); military and political competition among different possible leading forces (the long-standing rivalry between Austria and Prussia for hegemony); the exploitation of what was perceived, or could be presented, as a common threat from without (Bismarck's use of the conflict with France); as well as a desire for political unity in certain liberal and national circles, premissed also on a sense of cultural affinity among some intellectual circles, not always shared by provincial rulers— who often put up strong opposition to loss of sovereignty—or their populations, for many of whom horizons were primarily local and regional.

Viewed in long-term perspective, then, it was only for a relatively short period that the nation state was the dominant (but even then by no means the only) vessel of political and economic organization, and the peculiar focus of claims to legitimacy and loyalty. Nation states were, in short, not natural givens, but historical constructions, often with quite arbitrary lines of inclusion and exclusion created more through the realities of politics and warfare over decades than the sort of organic, inner cultural unity that is the stuff of nationalist idealism.

What is perhaps distinctive about the latter half of the twentieth century is that, for many Europeans, the existence of sovereign nation states seemed so utterly natural, so utterly taken for granted, that wider patterns of interdependence and interaction over centuries almost disappeared from their mental horizons. Yet, of course, this was against the short-term backdrop of that unusually violent conflict among nation states, beginning in the era of high nationalism in the nineteenth century and culminating in the cataclysmic catastrophe, the *Götterdämmerung*, of the Second World War. It is scarcely surprising that, against this violent background, the search for a new European order, new forms of European integration, should both take such high priority on the agenda and appear so fragile, so contrary to the 'natural order of things'.

What, cumulatively, do the major developments of the later twentieth century amount to for the character of the new Europe?

First, of course, is the dramatic relocation of Europe within the world. From being a set of mutually competitive states, some of whom at least considered themselves to be at the centre of the world (symbolized for the British as pink areas on the map, the empire on which the sun never set, its capital straddling the Greenwich meridian from whence East and West are measured), to being but a junior and divided part of a bipolar world under two superpowers; and then, after the collapse of communism, from being a divided continent to being a reconstructed but ever more integrated arena in a more open and uncertain world; this global shift can also perhaps be seen as one of the increasing economic subordination of the European arena within an ever more globalized economic system.

Along with these shifts in global location came changes in the movements of peoples and rights to citizenship. First, there was the shift from the influx of Commonwealth and other post-colonial citizens, and of cheap labour from less developed contiguous areas, to increasing closure of European borders to the outside world—and particularly closure of European Union borders to non-European citizens. Secondly, within this ever more clearly defined European arena (as far as the outside world was concerned), there was increased internal movement across ever more porous internal borders: from national borders which in some instances were fiercely guarded—not least, the Iron Curtain—to increasingly open borders and movements of peoples across and within Europe, and particularly for citizens of the European Union. Thirdly, the consequences of successive waves of population movement meant a shift from relatively homogenous 'native' populations, with sometimes only very provincial horizons (although, in the case of the elites of colonial societies, also global perspectives), to increasingly multicultural societies, many of whose members had cultural and family ties with other parts of the globe. All these shifts have been accompanied by a rethinking of collective identities, whether ethnic, cultural, regional, national, or—at arguably the most lukewarm, contested, and minority end of this spectrum—European. Looking at Europe as a whole, there has been a dissociation of citizenship entitlement from perceptions of collective identity. Moreover, while there has been a degree of integration in the sense of a common EU citizenship, access to this depends on citizenship within one of the member states—which retain an extraordinary variety of assumptions and regulations concerning who is or is not entitled to become a national citizen (thus entailing European citizenship), and what political rights this brings with it.

Within individual states some countries have experienced more dramatic changes than others; and the periodizations have been somewhat different in different areas. There are of course common caesuras, as far as overall political periodization is concerned: the immediate post-war years, the years of cold war division, the turning-point of 1989–90, are all Europe-wide. Similarly, there are broad economic phases which provide an overall framework within which different states responded to common challenges in divergent ways, depending on different social and historical backgrounds, different cultural expectations and institutional frameworks. There were also, however, key differences between certain families of states. East European states ran the full gamut of economic and social experimentation under communist regimes and were, by the close of the twentieth century, in the early years of yet further major reorientation and reconstruction on the lines of Western models. For those East European countries which had suffered from Nazi occupation, and from liberation and subsequent enforced transformation at the hands of the Red Army, 1989–90 was the key moment in which, perhaps, the century of ideological dictatorships finally came to an end. For countries in Southern Europe subjected to fascist regimes in the post-war period, this transformation occurred a couple of decades or so earlier. Post-colonial powers, and those 'inner core' states closely involved in processes of European integration, underwent different experiences and sensed different periodizations again; as did more peripheral or neutral regions, such as the Scandinavian countries, Switzerland, even post-Nazi Austria with its acquired post-war identity as 'Hitler's first victim'. In short, different areas of Europe became involved in the processes of convergence and integration at very different times, and from very different backgrounds.

Yet at the same time long secular processes of social, economic, and technological change had affected—in different ways, at different rates—all areas of Europe, producing everywhere a very different society from that of half a century before. More Europeans—whether they felt themselves to share such an identity or not—had more in common, and more chance to communicate with one another (and with the rest of the world), than ever before.

Does all this add up to anything like a process of formation, however incomplete, of a 'United States of Europe'—as some of the early exponents of a European vision would have liked, and some supporters of European integration still propose? There are, it is true, clear parallels with processes of nation state formation in nineteenth-century Europe: the economic logic of a common market over an ever wider area bringing in its wake the need for common regulatory institutions, and thence political institutions which need, increasingly, to be democratically accountable; the existence of leading forces, leading states, and those who lag or indeed actively and vociferously resist changes in the direction of integration; the elite articulation of a common identity well before any sense of this among popular perceptions on the ground, which historically have generally been formed by common institutions, practices, and mobility *after* the political and economic integration of any given state, rather than actually contributing to such integration.

There are, however, also crucial differences in world historical context, particularly with respect to the increasingly global character of both military and economic matters. What is missing, for example, in the comparison of later twentieth-century European integration with examples of nineteenth-century nation state formation is the perceived need for common defence forces against a common enemy abroad. So long as a degree of responsibility for international peace and security is maintained by supra-European organizations and frameworks—not least NATO and the United Nations—such an external threat is unlikely to provide the crucial impetus for the formation of any kind of Euro-state. The increasing globalization of the economy is of course another crucial difference in world-historical context. So, for all the parallels, European integration in the later twentieth century has not, by the close of the twentieth century, followed quite the same pattern or developed under the same conditions as did nation state formation in a previous era. Whether it will in the course of the twenty-first century is not a matter for historians to guess: the future is always open.

From the Wall to Wales—and back again

We began this volume, for purposes of the historical imagination, at Bahnhof Friedrichstrasse in Berlin. Let us take, finally, another imaginative leap: this time, not to a location like Berlin in the centre of Europe, at the very heart of the most dramatic political transformations of the later twentieth century, but rather to one of the more distant fringes. We could, for these purposes, go East—to the economic reconstruction and political turmoils of one of the post-communist states, which too exemplify some of the most dramatic developments of the century. But let us take, instead, a mental journey to an apparently altogether less exciting area of Europe. No less than post-Nazi Germany or post-communist Poland or Russia, Europe's western fringes illustrate—perhaps less dramatically, but no less powerfully—some of the underlying yet fundamental transformations in later twentieth-century Europe.

Take, for example, the case of the South Wales valleys, whose coalmines for decades powered British industrialization. In the later 1940s and 1950s inhabitants of the drab terraced houses of the Rhondda Valley, opening straight onto the pavements and lacking any indoor sanitation, lived under the shadow of dust from the coalmines, from the black coal tips and slag heaps on which children played on the slopes behind the houses, from the domestic chimneys and coal fires; and under the shadow of premature death from dust on the lungs, if miners had not previously been killed by explosions or accidents underground. Male employment rates were high, as was attendance at chapel on special occasions—and the pub on a daily basis. Educational achievement was also high—for those children lucky enough to pass the selection exam at 11, and whose families could afford for them to stay at school rather than being sent out to work at the earliest opportunity. Private ownership of cars, television sets, telephones, was virtually nil. Rationing was a distant reverberation of the war; and loss of loved ones was still acutely painful in many families. But horizons were local. This was in the main a community where— apart from those men who had served in one or both of the world wars and lived to return—experience of travel meant little more than a day out to Barry Island to eat candy floss in the funfair. A summer holiday worthy of aspiration might mean a week or so in the Welsh coastal resort of Tenby.

Leap ahead to South Wales in 1999. The closure of mines in the 1980s had left many males out of work. The tips were covered over, with grass thinly growing on the still bare hillsides; the air was cleaner, and the houses in the terraced streets boasted indoor toilets and bathrooms; the streets were colonized by dispirited teenagers in cheap sportswear, the rows of shops pock-marked by discount outlets and boarded-up stores that had closed for lack of business; though the pubs still did a good trade, the chapels were virtually empty. A few mines had been preserved and exploited for the heritage industry: visitors would be shown around a designated or reconstructed area of the pit, with the standard range of tourist trinkets, marginally localized by the imprint of a Welsh Dragon or mining museum logo, for sale at the exit.

Nearby Cardiff, capital of Wales, was booming: the development of new industries and businesses, decades of urban regeneration, pedestrianization of the city centre, improved transport links to the rest of Britain by road and rail, and finally also a degree of political devolution, had all made their mark. Dual language signs had sprouted in all public places; the Welsh language was making rapid advances among the younger generation of what had been an almost entirely English-speaking population a generation earlier. At the same time people were increasingly international in tastes, outlook, and experience: consuming Indian or Italian food, American coffee with bagels as well as traditional tea with Welsh cakes; enjoying a range of international music and entertainment through a variety of media; thinking nothing of international travel on cheap flights to faraway places.

Teenagers in Cardiff and Berlin would have far more to say to each other, far more experiences, aspirations, and interests in common—and probably, between them, far better command of at least one mutually understood language—in 1999 than they would have done at the start of our period. From Cardiff Central station to Bahnhof Friedrichstrasse, though clearly still involving a transition between cultures, would no longer amount to a journey to another planet. And what is more, the journey could be undertaken in either direction.

Further Reading

Politics

For a view on the first years of postwar reconstruction see Alan S. Milward, *The Reconstruction of Western Europe 1945–51* (London, 1984) (especially the introduction and the conclusion); see also David Ellwood, *Rebuilding Europe. Western Europe, America and Postwar Reconstruction* (Harlow, Essex, 1992).

On the welfare state in Europe see Peter Baldwin, *The Politics of Social Solidarity. Class Bases of the European Welfare State 1875–1975* (Cambridge, 1990). See also the pathbreaking *The Three Worlds of Welfare Capitalism* by Gøsta Esping-Andersen (Oxford, 1990).

For a comparative history of socialist and communist parties in Western Europe see Donald Sassoon, *One Hundred Years of Socialism. The West European Left in the Twentieth Century* (paperback edn., 1997) (most of the book is devoted to the post-1945 period). See also Fritz W. Scharpf's important *Crisis and Choice in European Social Democracy* (Ithaca and London, 1991). On the events of 1968 in Europe and the world see Carole Fink and Philipp Gassert (eds.), *1968: the World Transformed* (Cambridge, 1998).

Eastern and Central Europe

For an overview of eastern and central Europe see Ivan Berend, *Central and Eastern Europe 1944–1993*, (Cambridge, 1996); Norman Naimark and Leonid Gibianskii (eds.), *The Establishment of Communist Regimes in Eastern Europe, 1944–1949*, (Oxford, 1997). See also Z.A.B. Zeman, *The Making and Breaking of Communist Europe* (Oxford, 1991) and *Eastern Europe Since 1945* by Geoffrey Swain and Nigel Swain (Basingstoke, 1998). On economic reforms, see *Planning and Market in Soviet and East European Thought, 1960s–1992* by Jan Adam (Basingstoke, 1993).

Southern Europe

For an overview of Southern Europe see Giulio Sapelli, *Southern Europe: Politics, Society and Economics Since 1945* (Harlow, 1995). See also James Kurth and James Petras (eds.), *Mediterranean Paradoxes. The Politics and Social Structure of Southern Europe* (Providence and Oxford, 1993).

France

On France see Maurice Larkin, *France since the Popular Front. Government and People 1936–86* (Oxford, 1988), and Robert Gildea's *France Since 1945* (Oxford, 1997). For the period after the war see Richard Vinen, *Bourgeois Politics in France, 1945–1951* (Cambridge, 1995); on the Fifth Republic see Henri Mendras and Alistair Cole (eds.), *Social Change in the Fifth Republic*, (Cambridge, 1991); for the Mitterrand period see George Ross, Stanley Hoffmann and Sylvia Malzacher (eds.), *The Mitterrand Experiment* (Oxford, 1987); Patrick McCarthy (ed.), *The French Socialists in Power 1981–1986* (New York, 1987), and *The Mitterrand Years* by Mairi Maclean (Basingstoke, 1997). On the French communist party see Maurice Adereth, *The French Communist Party. A Critical History (1920–84) from Comintern to 'the colours of France'* (Manchester, 1984). On the socialists see D.S. Bell and Byron Criddle, *The French Socialist Party* (Oxford, 1988).

Italy

On Italy see Paul Ginsborg, *A History of Contemporary Italy. Society and Politics* (Harmondsworth, 1990); see also Donald Sassoon, *Contemporary Italy* (2nd edn., Harlow, 1997). On the crisis of Italy's first republic (1992–3) see Patrick McCarthy, *The Crisis of the Italian State* (New York, 1997) and Stephen Gundle and Simon Parker (eds.), *The New Italian Republic: from the Fall of the Berlin Wall to Berlusconi* (London, 1996).

Britain

On Britain see Kenneth O. Morgan, *The People's Peace: British History Since 1945*, (Oxford, 1999) and Peter Clarke, *Hope and Glory: Britain, 1900–1990* (Harmondsworth, 1997). For the period of reconstruction see Peter Hennessy, *Never Again. Britain 1945–1951* (London, 1992). On the Conservative Party see John Ramsden's numerous monographs, for an overview see his *An Appetite for Power: a History of the Conservative Party since 1830* (London, 1998). On the Labour Party see Eric Shaw, *The Labour Party since 1945: Old Labour: New Labour* (Oxford, 1996); see also the polemical essay by Gregory Elliott, *Labourism and the English Genius. The Strange Death of Labour England?* (London, 1993).

Germany

On Germany (East and West), see Mary Fulbrook, *The Divided Nation: Germany 1918–1990* (London, 1991); also her *Interpretations of the Two Germanies, 1945–1990* (rev. edn., Basingstoke, 2000), with overview of debates and guide to further reading. On West Germany, A. J. Nicholls, *The*

Bonn Republic: West German Democracy 1945–1990 (London, 1997), and Peter Pulzer, *German Politics 1945–1995* (Oxford, 1995); also the volumes edited by Gordon Smith et al, *Developments in West German Politics* (Basingstoke, 1989), and *Developments in German Politics* (2 vols., Basingstoke, 1992 and 1996). On relations between the two Germanies, see A. J. McAdams, *Germany Divided* (Princeton N.J., 1993).

Spain

On Franco's Spain see Raymond Carr and Juan Pablo Fusi, *Spain: Dictatorship to Democracy* (London, 1979); Paul Preston, (ed.), *Spain in Crisis. The Evolution and Decline of the Franco Régime* (Sussex, 1976). See also Preston's book on the transition to democracy, see his *The Triumph of Democracy in Spain* (London, 1987). On post-Franco's Spain see *The Return of Civil Society* by Victor M. Perez-Diaz (Cambridge Mass., 1998). On the socialist party see Richard Gillespie, *The Spanish Socialist Party: a History of Factionalism* (Oxford, 1989).

Sweden

On Sweden see Henry Milner, *Sweden: Social Democracy in Practice* (Oxford, 1989). Francis Castles, *The Social Democratic Image of Society: A Study of the Achievements and Origins of Scandinavian Social Democracy in Comparative Perspective* (London, 1978). See also Klaus Misgeld et al. (eds.), *Creating Social Democracy: a Century of the Social Democratic Labor Party in Sweden* (Pennsylvania, 1992) and Jan-Erik Lane (ed.), *Understanding the Swedish Model* (London, 1991).

Greece

On Greece see Richard Clogg, *Parties and Elections in Greece. The Search for Legitimacy* (London, 1987) and edited by the same author see both *Greece, 1981–89. The Populist Decade* (New York, 1993) and *Greece in the 1980s* (Basingstoke, 1983).

Portugal

On Portugal see Tom Gallagher, *Portugal. A Twentieth-century Interpretation* (Manchester, 1983); on the revolution of 1974 and its aftermath see Hugo Gil Ferreira and Michael W. Marshall, *Portugal's Revolution: Ten Years on* (Cambridge, 1986). See also Lawrence S. Graham and Harry M. Makler (eds.), *Contemporary Portugal. The Revolution and its Antecedents* (Austin Texas, 1979).

The Netherlands

On the politics of the Netherlands see Ken Gladdish, *Governing from the Centre. Politics and Policy-Making in the Netherlands* (London, 1991).

Austria

On Austria see Barbara Jelavich, *Modern Austria. Empire and Republic 1815–1986* (Cambridge, 1986).

Finland

On Finland see David G. Kirby, *Finland in the Twentieth Century* (London, 1979).

USSR

On the USSR see John Keep, *Last of the Empires: a History of the Soviet Union 1945–1991* (Oxford, 1996). On Soviet relations with the rest of Europe see Francesca Gori and Silvio Pons (eds.), *The Soviet Union and Europe in the Cold War*, 1943–53 (Basingstoke, 1996). On the break-up of the USSR see R.W. Davies's *Soviet History in the Yeltsin Era* (Basingstoke, 1996) and his *Soviet History in the Gorbachev Revolution* (Basingstoke, 1989). See also *The Gorbachev Factor* by Archie Brown (Oxford, 1997), Robert V. Daniels, *The End of the Communist Revolution* (London, 1993) and *Rebirth of a Nation* by John Lloyd (London, 1998).

Hungary Poland, Czechoslavakia

On the 1956 crisis in Hungary see this collection by Hungarian historians: Gyorgy Litvan, Janos M. Bak and Lyman H. Legters (eds.), *The Hungarian Revolution of 1956* (Harlow, 1996). On subsequent developments see Andrew Felkay, *Hungary and the USSR, 1956–1988: Kadar's Political Leadership* (New York, 1989). On the break-up of communism in Hungary see Rudolf L. Tökés, *Hungary's Negotiated Revolution. Economic Reform, Social Change and Political Succession* (Cambridge, 1996), on Poland see Kazimier Z. Poznanski, *Poland's Protracted Transition* (Cambridge, 1997), on Czechoslovakia see Carol Skalnik Leff, *The Czech and Slovak Republics* (Boulder, 1996).

Yugoslavia, Albania, Romania

On the disintegration and crisis of Yugoslavia see *Balkan Tragedy: Chaos and Dissolution After the Cold War* by Susan L. Woodward (Washington, 1994), and *The Fall of Yugoslavia* by Misha Glenny (Harmondsworth, 1996). See also the collection *Burn this House: the Making and Unmaking of Yugoslavia* edited by Jasminka Udovicki and James Ridgeway (Durham, 1997). Though not short (over 500 pages) see also *Kosovo: a Short History* by Noel Malcolm (Basingstoke, 1998). On Albania see Miranda Vickers, *The Albanians: a Modern History* (London, 1995). On Romania see Stephen Fischer-Galati, *Twentieth Century Rumania* (New York, 1991) and Gilberg Trond, *Nationalism and Communism in Romania: the Rise and Fall of Ceausescu's Personal Dictatorship* (Boulder, 1990).

Social History

A social history of the whole of Europe since 1945 has not yet been written. For Western Europe since the 1880s, see G. Ambrosius and W.H. Hubbard, *Social and Economic History of 20th Century Europe* (Cambridge, 1989); Antony Sutcliffe, *An Economic and Social History of Western Europe since 1945* (London, 1996); and H. Kaelble, *A Social History of Western Europe, 1880–1980* (Dublin, 1990). Foreign language reference books on the social history of Western Europe are published in French by two French groups of historians for the period up to 1970: E. Bussière, P. Griset, C. Bouneau and J.-P. Williot, *Industrialisation et sociétés en Europe occidentale 1880–1970* (Paris, 1998); and P. Saly, M. Margairaz, M. Pigenet and J.-L. Robert, *Industrialisation et sociétés. Europe occidentale 1880–1970* (Paris, 1998), and in German, see Stefan Hradil and Stefan Immerfall, Hg., *Die westeuropäischen Gesellschaften im Vergleich* (Opladen, 1997). For Europe as a whole, and again published in German, see Wolfram Fischer, (ed.), *Handbuch der europäischen Wirtschafts- und Sozialgeschichte, Bd. 6: Europäische Wirtschafts- und Sozialgeschichte vom Ersten Weltkrieg bis zur Gegenwart* (Stuttgart, 1987). For a social history of the world including Europe during the short twentieth century (between 1914 and 1989/91), see Eric Hobsbawm, *Age of Extremes* (London, 1994). The book which comes closest to being a manual on the social history of Europe as a whole from 1945 to the present day is Swedish sociologist Göran Therborn, *European Modernity and Beyond. The Trajectory of European Societies 1945–2000* (London, 1995), which contains many valuable statistical data and is organised according to sociological concepts and theories.

Economic History

Three overviews of Europe's growth in the second half of the 20th century, written from very different perspectives, are Angus Maddison, *Monitoring the World Economy* (OECD, 1995), Philip Armstrong, Andrew Glyn and John Harrison, *Capitalism Since World War II: The Making and Breakup of the Great Boom* (London, 1984), and N.F.R. Crafts and Gianni Toniolo (eds.), *Economic Growth in Europe since 1945* (Cambridge, 1996). The postwar recovery, and especially the role of the Marshall Plan, are the subject of a large literature and intense controversy; for contending views, see Alan Milward, *The Reconstruction of Western Europe 1945–1951* (London, 1984) and Helge Berger and Albrecht Ritschl, 'Germany and the Political Economy of the Marshall Plan: A Re-Revisionist View,' in Barry Eichengreen (ed.), *Europe's Postwar Recovery* (Cambridge, 1995) pp. 199–245. Early efforts at European integration are the subject of Milward, *The European Rescue of the Nation State* (London, 1992), Jacob J. Kaplan and Gunther Schleiminger, *The European Payments Union: Financial Diplomacy in the 1950s* (Oxford, 1989), and John Gillingham, *Coal, Steel and the Rebirth of Europe* (Cambridge, 1992). On the role of the postwar social compact and corporatist institutions, see Colin Crouch, 'Conditions for Trade Union Wage Restraint,' in Leon Lindberg and Charles Maier (eds.), *The Politics of Inflation and Economic Stagnation* (Washington, 1984), pp. 105–139, and Peter Katzenstein, *Corporatism and Change* (Cornell, 1984). Britain's economic decline is traced by N.F.R. Crafts, 'Forging Ahead and Falling Behind: The Rise and Relative Decline of the First Industrial Nation,' *Journal of Economic Perspectives* 12 (Spring 1998), pp. 193–210. Mounting difficulties elsewhere are the subject of Andrea Boltho (ed.), *The European Economy: Growth and Crisis* (Oxford, 1982). On the persistence of European unemployment and its disagnosis in terms of structural rigidities, see Michael Bruno and Jeffrey D. Sachs, *The Economics of Worldwide Stagflation* (Harvard, 1985). On the integrationist response, in the monetary domain in particular, see Francesco Giavazzi and Alberto Giovannini, *Limiting Exchange Rate Flexibility: The European Monetary System* (Massachusetts, 1989) and Daniel Gross and Niels Thygesen, *European Monetary Integration* (2nd edn., Harlow, Essex, 1998). The now classic treatment of the economics of German unification is Gerlinde Sinn and Hans-Werner Sinn, *Jumpstart: The Economic Unification of Germany* (Massachusetts, 1992). A survey of developments in Eastern Europe in the first postwar decades is Derek H. Aldcroft and Steven Morewood, *Economic Change in Eastern Europe Since 1918* (London, 1995). On the collapse of planning and the difficulties of the transition to the market, see Anders Asland, Peter Boone, and Simon Johnson, 'How to Stabilize: Lessons from Post-Communist Countries,' *Brookings Papers on Economic Activity* 1 (1996), pp. 217–314.

Culture

There is as yet no comprehensive cultural history of 20th century Europe. The reader might want to refer to traditional histories of literature, music or the arts all of which follow a different aim than the one presented in this chapter. Michael Archer, *Art since 1960* (London, 1997) is an extremely well written outline of the arts during the last decades of the century. John Bale, *Sports, Space and the City* (London and New York, 1993) offers a sociological and anthropological interpretation of recent developments in European football and provides many useful references for further reading. David Bathrick, *The Powers of Speech. The Politics of Culture in the GDR* (Lincoln and London, 1995) is an excellent and most challenging investigation into the position of intellectuals in the GDR. James Brown, *A History of Western Education* (vol. 3, London, 1981); only the last chapter is concerned with our period; the reader might want to refer to the annual UNESCO reports for detailed information. Georges Duby and Michelle Perrot (eds.), *A History of Women* (London, 1994); the last of the five volumes, edited by Françoise Thébaudet, gives a very detailed overview on the social history of women in the twentieth century, the development of the women's movement and of feminist thought. Ronald Fraser, *1968: A Student Generation in Revolt* (London, 1988) is a fine example of oral history on the ideas and memories of the student revolt. Simon Frith, 'Music and Identity', in Stuart Hall and Paul du Gay (eds.), *Questions of Cultural Identity* (London, 1996), 108–127, analyses the social function of music in the formation of generational and ethnic identities. See also his book *The Sociology of Rock* (London, 1978). See also Ernst H. Gombrich, *The Story of Art* (1950; London, 1972). Stuart Hall and Paul du Gay (eds.), *Questions of Cultural Identity* (London, 1996) is a rich collection of essays reaching from music to tourism and an interesting introduction to the topic of cultural studies. Eric Hobsbawm, *Age of Extremes. The Short Twentieth Century. 1914–1991* (1994; London, 1995) gives an excellent overview of social and cultural transformation and places Europe within the broader context. Richard Hoggart, *The Uses of Literacy* (1957; Harmondsworth, 1965), is a classic on the popular reception of magazines, mass literature and films. See also Reinhard Kannonier, *Bruchlinien in der Geschichte der modernen Kunstmusik* (Wien, 1987) and Kaspar Maase, *Grenzenloses Vergnügen. Der Aufstieg der Massenkultur 1850–1970* (Frankfurt, 1997). Nicholas Rzhevsky (ed.), *Cambridge Companion to Modern Russian Culture* (London, 1998) is a useful introduction to modern developments in the arts, music, and literature and explains important socio-cultural concepts of Russian thought. See also Kay Richardson and Ulrike H. Meinhof, *Worlds in common? Television discourse in a changing Europe* (London and New York, 1999). Preben Sepstrup, *Transnationalisation of TV in Western Europe* (London, Paris and

Rome, 1990); Alessandro Silj et al., *East of Dallas. The European Challenge to American Television* (London, 1988) and Pierre Sorlin, *European Cinemas. European Societies* (London, 1991) which is particularly useful for the first decades of post-war cinema in Western Europe.

Relations within Europe

General histories include J.M. Roberts, *History of Europe* (London, 1996) and David Reynolds, *One World Divisible: A Global History since 1945* (London, 2000).

On the cold war, see John L. Gaddis, *We Now Know: Rethinking Cold War History* (Oxford, 1997) and Mel Leffler, *A Preponderance of Power: National Security, the Truman Administration, and the Cold War* (Stanford, 1992). The cold war's European dimension is emphasized in David Reynolds (ed.), *The Origins of the Cold War in Europe: International Perspectives* (New Haven, 1994) and Charles Maier (ed.), *The Cold War in Europe: Era of a Divided Continent* (3rd edn., Princeton, 1996); see also Dana H. Allin, *Cold War Illusions: America, Europe and Soviet Power, 1969–89* (Basingstoke, 1995), Geir Lundestad, *'Empire' by Integration: The United States and European Integration, 1945–1997* (Oxford, 1998), and Francis H. Heller and John R. Gillingham (eds), *The United States and the Integration of Europe: Legacies of the Postwar Era* (Basingstoke, 1992).

The early transatlantic security relationship is still best explored in Lawrence S. Kaplan, *The United States and NATO: The Formative Years* (Lexington, KY, 1984) and Olav Riste (ed.), *Western Security: The Formative Years: European and Atlantic Defence, 1947–1953* (Oslo, 1985). For the later developments see William C. Cromwell, *The United States and the European Pillar: The Strained Alliance* (Basingstoke, 1992). The Soviet Union's activities are explored in Odd Arne Westad, Sven Holtsmark and Iver B. Neumann (eds), *The Soviet Union in Eastern Europe, 1945–89* (Basingstoke, 1994), George Schöpflin, *Politics in Eastern Europe, 1945–1992* (Oxford, 1993), G. and N. Swain, *Eastern Europe since 1945* (Basingstoke, 1993). Still very informative is Adam B. Ulam, *Expansion and Coexistence: Soviet Foreign Policy, 1917–73* (New York, 1974) and its sequel *Dangerous Relations: The Soviet Union in World Politics, 1970–82* (Oxford, 1983). On early Soviet policy, based on newly available Soviet archival material, see Vladislav Zubok and Constantine Pleshakov, *Inside the Kremlin's Cold War: From Stalin to Khrushchev* (Cambridge, Mass., 1996). The crucial German question, which dominated many aspects of the cold war in Europe, has resulted in a wealth of books and articles. See for example Wolfram Hanrieder, *Germany, America, Europe: Forty Years of German Foreign Policy* (New Haven, 1989), Hannes Adomeit, *Imperial Overstretch: Germany in Soviet Policy from Stalin to Gorbachev* (Baden-Baden, 1998), William R. Smyser, *From Yalta to Berlin: The Cold War*

Struggle over Germany (Basingstoke, 1999), and Peter Alter, *The German Question and Europe: A History* (London, 2000).

On European integration, see Peter M.R. Stirk, *A History of European Integration since 1914* (London, 1996), J. Robert Wegs, *Europe since 1945: A Concise History* (4th edn., Basingstoke, 1996), and Derek W. Urwin, *Western Europe since 1945* (new edn., London, 1997). On the institutions and policies of the European Union, see Neill Nugent, *The Government and Politics of the EU* (4th edn., 1999), Desmond Dinan, *Ever Closer Union: An Introduction to the EU* (2nd edn., Basingstoke, 1999), and William Nicoll and Trevor Salmon, *Understanding the New European Union* (Hemel Hempstead, 1999). The European core countries are covered by M. Donald Hancock et al. (eds), *Politics in Western Europe: An Introduction to the Politics of the UK, France, Germany, Italy, Sweden and the EU* (2nd edn., Chatham, NJ, 1998) and Jurg Steiner, *European Democracies* (4th edn., New York, 1997). On individual countries in relation to Europe, see Jean Lacouture, *De Gaulle: The Ruler, 1945–1970* (New York, 1993), E.A. Kolodziej, *French International Policy under De Gaulle and Pompidou* (Ithaca, 1971), Robert O. Paxton and Nicholas Wahl (eds), *De Gaulle and the United States: A Centennial Reappraisal* (Providence and Oxford, 1994), Hain Simonian, *The Privileged Partnership: Franco-German Relations in the European Community* (Oxford, 1985), Klaus Larres (ed. with E. Meehan), *Uneasy Allies: British-German Relations and European Integration since 1945* (Oxford, 2000), Geoffrey Pridham (ed.), *The New Mediterranean Democracies: Regime Transition in Spain, Greece and Portugal* (London, 1984), Allan Williams (ed.), *Southern Europe Transformed: Political and Social Change in Greece, Italy, Portugal and Spain* (London, 1984), G. Sapelli, *Southern Europe since 1945* (London, 1995), and K. Lavdas and J. Magone, *Politics and Governance in Southern Europe: the political systems of Italy, Greece, Spain and Portugal* (Boulder, 1997). For northern Europe see for example the still valuable T. Miljan, *The Reluctant Europeans* (London, 1977) and N. Elder et al, *The Consensual Democracies?* (rev. edn., Oxford, 1988).

On the Marshall Plan, see John Gimbel, *The Origins of the Marshall Plan* (Stanford, 1976), Alan Milward, *The Reconstruction of Western Europe, 1945–51* (Berkeley, Ca., 1984), Michael J. Hogan, *The Marshall Plan: America, Britain and the Reconstruction of Western Europe 1947–1952* (Cambridge, 1987), John Killick, *The United States and European Reconstruction, 1945–1960* (Edinburgh, 1997). The impact of the Suez crisis is analysed in William Roger Louis and Roger Owen (eds), *Suez 1956: the Crisis and its Consequences* (Oxford, 1989), Anthony Gorst and Lewis Johnman (eds), *The Suez Crisis* (London, 1997). For the Berlin/Cuba crises, see John C. Ausland, *Kennedy, Khrushchev, and the Berlin-Cuba Crisis, 1961–64* (Oslo, 1996), and John P.S. Gearson, *Harold Macmillan and the Berlin Wall Crisis, 1958–62: The Limits of Interest and Force* (Basingstoke, 1998). West German Ostpolitik under Chancellor

Brandt is well-analysed in William E. Grifftith, *The Ostpolitik of the Federal Republic of Germany* (Cambridge, MA, 1978), Roger Tilford (ed.), *The Ostpolitik and political change in Germany* (Farborough, Hants, 1975), Lawrence L. Whetten, *Germany's Ostpolitik: Relations between the Federal Republic and the Warsaw Pact Countries* (London, 1971), and in Helga Haftendorn's important book *Security and Détente: Conflicting Priorities in German Foreign Policy* (New York, 1985). Students will find rich information in Timothy Garton Ash, *In Europe's Name: Germany and the divided continent* (London, 1993) which is however somewhat confusingly structured. For the East German perspective, see A. James McAdams, *East Germany and Détente: Building Authority after the Wall* (Cambridge, 1985). On East-West détente in general, see John van Oudenaren, *Détente in Europe: the Soviet Union and the West since 1953* (Durham, NC, and London, 1991), Kenneth Dyson (ed.), *European détente: a case study of the politics of East-West relations* (London, 1986), and Richard W. Stevenson, *The Rise and Fall of Détente: Relaxations of Tension in US-Soviet Relations, 1953–1984* (Basingstoke, 1985). The standard work on East-West détente is Raymond L. Garthoff, *Détente and Confrontation: American-Soviet relations from Nixon to Reagan* (2nd edn., Washington DC, 1994).

The complex economic and political crises of the 1970s which led to severe strains in European-American relations are analysed in Rainer Hellmann, *Gold, the Dollar, and the European Currency Systems* (New York, 1979), Thomas L. Ilgen, *Autonomy and Independence: US-Western European Monetary and Trade Relations, 1958–84* (Totowa, NJ, 1985); see also Loukas Tsoukalis (ed.), *Europe, America and the World Economy* (Oxford, 1985), Harold James, *International monetary Co-operation since Bretton Woods* (Oxford, 1996), and Derek H. Aldcroft, *The European Economy, 1914–70* (London, 1978). Security related crisis situations of the 1970s are traced in Sherri Wasserman, *The Neutron Bomb Controversy: A Study in Alliance Politics* (New York, 1983), Anthony J. Blinken, *Ally versus ally: America, Europe, and the Siberian pipeline crisis* (New York, 1987), Bruce W. Jentleson, *Pipeline Politics: the complex political economy of East-West energy trade* (Ithaca, N.Y., 1986), Jonathan Haslam, *The Soviet Union and the Politics of Nuclear Weapons in Europe, 1969–87: The Problem of the SS-20* (Basingstoke, 1989).

The end of the cold war is explored in Michael R. Beschloss and Strobe Talbott, *At the Highest Levels: The Inside Story of the End of the Cold War* (Boston and London, 1993), Don Oberdorfer, *From the Cold War to a New Era: The United States and the Soviet Union 1983–1991* (rev. edn., Baltimore, 1998), Philip Zelikow and Condoleeza Rice, *Germany Unified and Europe Transformed. A Study in Statecraft* (Cambridge, Mass., 1995), Robert L. Hutchings, *American Policy and the End of the Cold War: An Insider's Account of US Policy in Europe, 1989–1992* (Baltimore, 1997), Davis S. Mason,

Revolution in East-Central Europe: the rise and fall of Communism and the Cold War (Boulder, 1992), Michael Hogan (ed.), *The End of the Cold War: its meaning and implications* (Cambridge, 1992).

On post-1990 developments, see for example Leslie Holmes, *Post-Communism: An Introduction* (Cambridge, 1997), Michael Cox, Ken Booth and Tim Dunne (eds), *The Interregnum: Controversies in World Politics, 1989–1999* (Cambridge, 2000), John W. Holmes, *The United States and Europe after the Cold War: a new alliance?* (Columbia, SC, 1997), and David C. Gompert and F. Stephen Larrabee (eds), *America and Europe: A Partnership for a New Era* (Cambridge, 1999). On post-cold war security relations, see William Park and G. Wyn Rees (eds), *Rethinking Security in post-Cold War Europe* (Harlow, 1998), Willem F. van Eekelen, *Debating European Security, 1948–1998* (The Hague, 1998), Simon Duke, *The Elusive Quest for European security: from EDC to CFSP* (Basingstoke, 1999), James Sperling and Emil Kirchner (eds), *Recasting the European Order: Security Architectures and Economic Co-operation* (Manchester, 1997), and Beatrice Heuser, *NATO, Britain, France, and the FRG: nuclear strategies and forces for Europe, 1949–2000* (Basingstoke, 1997). The reform process of the European Union in the 1990s is analysed in P. Lynch, N. Neuwahl, W. Rees (eds), *Reforming the European Union from Maastricht to Amsterdam* (London, 2000) and Karlheinz Neunreither and Antje Wiener (eds), *European Integration after Amsterdam* (Oxford, 2000). On the crises of the post-cold war 'new world order' see Lawrence Freedman and Efraim Karsh, *The Gulf Conflict, 1990–91: diplomacy and war in the new world order* (2nd edn., London, 1994), R.D. Kaplan, *Balkan Ghosts: A Journey Through History* (New York, 1993), Misha Glenny's books *The Balkans, 1804–1999: Nationalism, War and the Great Powers* (London, 1999), *The Rebirth of History: Eastern Europe in the Age* of Democracy (new edn., Harmondsworth, 1993), and *The Fall of Yugoslavia: the third Balkan War* (3rd edn., London, 1996), and the two books by Noel Malcolm, *Bosnia: a short history* (Basingstoke, 1994) and *Kosovo: a short history* (New York, 1998).

Interaction with the Non-European World

On decolonization in Asia see Robin Jeffrey, (ed.), *Asia the Winning of Independence* (Houndmills, 1981) which covers the Philippines, Indonesia, Vietnam, and Malaya; the most comprehensive account on British decolonization is John Darwin, *Britain and Decolonisation: the Retreat from Empire in the Post-war World* (Houndmills, 1988); likewise on France there is Raymond Betts, *France and Decolonisation, 1900–1960* (Houndmills, 1991) and Anthony Clayton, *The Wars of French Decolonization* (London, 1994). A useful comparative study is M. Kahler, *Decolonization in Britain and France: The Domestic Consequences of International Relations* (Princeton, 1984); on the Portuguese experience there is M. Newitt, *Portugal in Africa* (London, 1981), and Norrie MacQueen, *The Decolonization of Portuguese Africa* (London, 1997); the end of Spain's African empire is covered by Tony Hodges, *Western Sahara: the Roots of a Desert War* (Westport, Conn., 1984). The vast and always controversial topic of the origins of the cold war is undergoing reconsideration in the light of newly available Soviet documents. John Lewis Gaddis, *We Now Know: Rethinking Cold War History* (Oxford, 1997) is a sometimes controversial contribution from a respected cold war historian. Also useful is Vojtech Mastny, *The Cold War and Soviet Insecurity: the Stalin Years* (Oxford, 1996). Globalisation has provoked thousands of books and articles, of which Kenichi Ohmae's *The Borderless World* (London, 1990) is a leading protagonist, while a more sceptical view of the phenomenon is to be found in Paul Hirst and Grahame Thompson, *Globalisation in Question* (Cambridge, 1996). The best studies of the Group of Seven are Robert D. Putnam and Nicholas Bayne, *Hanging Together: Cooperation and Conflict in the Seven-Power Summits* (Cambridge, Mass., 1987) and C. Fred Bergsten and C. Randall Henning, *Global Economic Leadership and the Group of Seven* (Washington D.C., 1996). Two excellent books on Sino-Soviet relations that make use of recently available documents are Odd Arne Westad (ed.), *Brothers in Arms: the Rise and Fall of the Sino-Soviet Alliance 1945–63* (Washington D.C. 1998) and Michael Sheng *Battling Western Imperialism: Mao, Stalin and the US* (Princeton, 1997).

Chronology

1944   Elections in France. Women vote for the first time
Bretton Woods conference

1945   Defeat of Nazi Germany. End of Second World War
In Britain Labour Party wins elections
Federal People's Republic of Yugoslavia proclaimed
Deaths of Béla Bartók and Anton Webern

1945–7   Nationalizations in Britain, Austria, and France

1946–9   Civil war in Greece

1946   De Gaulle resigns. Constitution of the Fourth Republic
Republic proclaimed in Italy. Women vote for first time
Elections in Belgium. Women vote for first time
National Health Service established in Britain

1947   British rule in India ends. India and Pakistan established
Truman Doctrine and Marshall Plan
Communists forced out of government in France, Italy, and
Belgium
Adorno and Horkheimer publish *Dialektik der Aufklärung*

1947–8   Communist takeover in Czechoslovakia, Poland, Hungary,
Romania, Bulgaria, Albania (1945)

1948   New Italian constitution. Christian Democratic victory at
election
Tito breaks with Stalin
Berlin airlift
Bertolt Brecht returns to Berlin (East)

1949   Berlin airlift ends

Foundation of the Federal Republic of Germany (West Germany) under conservative coalition government (Konrad Adenauer)

Foundation of the German Democratic Republic (East Germany)

North Atlantic Treaty Organization (NATO) created

Dutch rule in Dutch East Indies ends. Indonesia established

George Orwell publishes *Nineteen Eighty-Four*

1950   Schuman Plan
Korean war begins
Sino-Soviet Alliance Treaty

1951   Conservative Party wins election in Britain
Treaty of Paris for a common market in steel and coal

1952   European Coal and Steel Community (ECSC) established

1953   Death of Stalin
Korean war ends
Uprising in East Germany
Khrushchev comes to power in Soviet Union

1954   French forces surrender to Vietminh at Dien Bien Phu

1955   Relations improve between Tito and Stalin's successors
West Germany joins NATO
Warsaw Pact created

1956   Khrushchev's de-Stalinization speech at Twentieth Congress of the Communist Party of the Soviet Union (CPSU)
Workers unrest in Poland
Hungarian anti-communist revolution. Soviet intervention
Britain and France invade Egypt: The Suez crisis

1957   British rule ends in Gold Coast. Ghana established
Treaty of Rome: European Economic Community (EEC) established
Soviet Union launches sputnik into space

1958   De Gaulle returns to power in France. The Fifth Republic
Nobel prize for Boris Pasternak
Karlheinz Stockhausen, *Gruppen für drei Orchester*

1959   European Free Trade Association (EFTA) established

1960   First Beatles concerts

1961   Albania breaks relations with USSR
Berlin Wall built
First publication in French of Franz Fanon, *The Wretched of the Earth*, with preface by Jean-Paul Sartre

1962   Cuban missile crisis

1963   De Gaulle vetoes British membership of EEC
Franco-German Treaty
Presidential system (direct election) introduced in France
In Italy socialists and Christian democrats form new centre-left coalition
West German chancellor Konrad Adenauer retires after fourteen years in power
Test Ban Treaty

1964   Khrushchev forced to resign. Succeeded by Brezhnev
After thirteen years in opposition Labour returns to power in Britain, with Harold Wilson as prime minister

1965   De Gaulle wins presidential election against François Mitterrand (candidate of the left)

1966   Grand coalition between CDU and SPD in Germany following seventeen years of conservative government
De Gaulle announces French withdrawal from NATO

1967   Military takeover in Greece

1968   Prague Spring, Soviet intervention in Czechoslovakia, May events in France, student unrest in Italy and Germany

Britain introduces restrictions on immigration from people of Asian ancestry

1969   Massive strikes in Italy (the 'hot autumn'). Terrorist offensive begins
De Gaulle resigns and is succeeded by Georges Pompidou in France
SPD–FDP coalition under Willy Brandt in West Germany
Sino-Soviet border conflict

1970   Edward Heath's Conservatives return to power in Britain
Divorce introduced in Italy
Nobel prize for Aleksandr Solzhenitsyn
Last LP of the Beatles (*Let it Be*)

1971   Walter Ulbricht replaced by Erich Honecker in East Germany
Death of Igor Stravinsky
Dmitri Shostakovich completes his last symphony

1972   Basic Treaty between East and West Germany
Strategic Arms Limitation Treaty

1973   Britain, Ireland, and Denmark join EEC
Oil crisis

1974   Giscard d'Estaing elected president of France
Return of democracy in Greece
Left-wing military takeover in Portugal
Labour wins elections in Britain
Helmut Schmidt takes over from Willy Brandt as West German chancellor
Italian referendum to abolish divorce lost

1975   First free elections in Portugal
Death of Franco. Beginning of Spanish transition to democracy
Helsinki Final Agreement on security and human rights
First Group of Seven meeting

1976   Working-class unrest in Poland
            Italian communists make electoral gains

1977   First free elections in Spain
            Brezhnev becomes president of USSR

1978   In Italy the DC leader, Aldo Moro, is kidnapped and killed by
            Red Brigade terrorists

1979   Margaret Thatcher's Conservatives win election in Britain
            Workers' unrest in Poland. Rise of trade union Solidarność
            (Solidarity)
            First direct elections to European parliament
            Soviet army invades Afghanistan

1980   Military coup in Poland
            Death of Tito
            Death of Jean-Paul Sartre

1981   Greece joins EEC
            Mitterrand wins presidential elections, dissolves parliament.
            Socialists and communists form first left government of the
            5th Republic in France
            PASOK (socialists) wins elections in Greece
            Martial law in Poland

1982   Spanish Socialist Party wins election in Spain
            CDU–FDP coalition under Helmut Kohl takes power in West
            Germany
            Falklands War between Britain and Argentina
            Death of Brezhnev. Replaced by Andropov

1983   First performance of Olivier Messiaen's *Saint François
            d'Assise*

1984   Death of Andropov. Replaced by Chernenko

1985   Death of Chernenko. Mikhail Gorbachev becomes leader of
            the USSR. Doctrines of glasnost and perestroika introduce
            reforms

1986   Spain and Portugal join EEC

Chernobyl nuclear accident

French parliamentary elections: victory of Gaullists and allies. 'Cohabitation' with Mitterrand

Simone de Beauvoir dies in Paris

1988   Free elections in the USSR

USSR withdraws forces from Afghanistan

Mitterrand re-elected president of France. Socialists return to power.

1989   First free elections in Poland, massive Solidarność gains

Unrest in GDR. Krenz briefly replaces Honecker

Fall of the Berlin Wall

1989–91   End of communism in Eastern Europe

1990   Break-up of Czechoslovakia

First free elections in Hungary, Bulgaria, Romania, Czech Republic, and Slovakia

Unification of Germany (East Germany reconstitutes its *Länder*, which join the FRG). Kohl re-elected chancellor of united Germany

Margaret Thatcher forced to resign. John Major elected leader of British Conservative Party

Former Pink Floyd member, Roger Waters, for $7.5 performs the rock opera *The Wall* in Berlin, watched on television by 1 billion people

1991   Maastricht Treaty

Italian Communist Party becomes Democratic Party of the Left

Gulf War

Dissolution of the Warsaw Pact

Attempted coup in the USSR. Gorbachev resigns. Yeltsin announces withdrawal of Russian federation from the USSR. Commonwealth of Independent States replaces USSR

1991–3   Slovenia, Croatia, Bosnia, and Macedonia leave the Yugoslav Federation. Only Serbia and Montenegro remain

1992   British Conservatives' fourth consecutive election victory

1992–3   Corruption scandals in Italy. Christian Democracy dissolved. Socialist Party fragments. Rise of the Northern League

1993   European Community becomes European Union (EU) Gaullists win general election

1994   In Italy media tycoon Silvio Berlusconi becomes prime minister in coalition with former neo-fascist party In Norway electorate votes against joining EU in referendum Gallimard publishes Albert Camus, *Le Premier Homme*

1995   Austria, Finland, and Sweden join EU Jacques Chirac elected president of France

1996   In Italy centre-left coalition wins election

1997   British Labour Party under Tony Blair wins election French socialists under Lionel Jospin win election

1998   Massimo D'Alema, a former communist, becomes prime minister of Italy Defeat of Helmut Kohl. Social-democratic and green coalition under Gerhard Schröder in Germany

1999   Introduction of the euro NATO admits Poland, Hungary, Czech Republic Kosovo War President Yeltsin of Russia resigns on New Year's Eve

2000   Millennium celebrations across Europe and the world

Maps

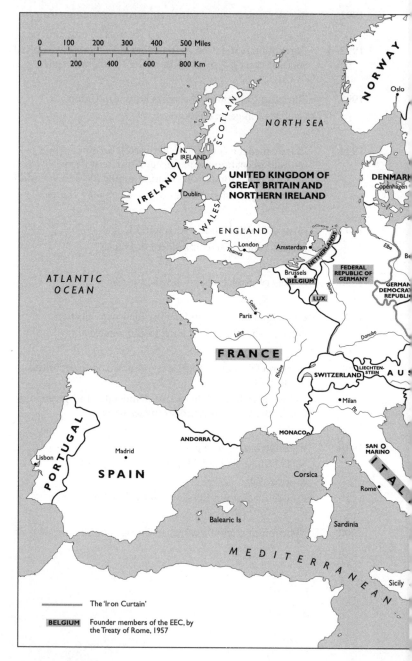

Map 1: Europe after 1949

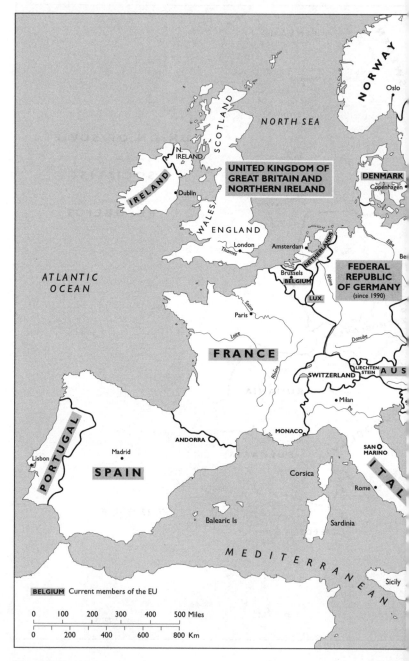

Map 2: Europe in 2000

Index